ALLEN GIN[...]

Selected Poems
1947–1995

'No suffering, no cause of suffering, no
nirvana, no path; no wisdom, also no attainment
because no non-attainment.'
Prajnaparamita Sutra

PENGUIN BOOKS

PENGUIN CLASSICS

Published by the Penguin Group
Penguin Books Ltd, 80 Strand, London WC2R 0RL, England
Penguin Group (USA) Inc., 375 Hudson Street, New York, New York 10014, USA
Penguin Group (Canada), 90 Eglinton Avenue East, Suite 700, Toronto, Ontario, Canada M4P 2Y3
(a division of Pearson Penguin Canada Inc.)
Penguin Ireland, 25 St Stephen's Green, Dublin 2, Ireland (a division of Penguin Books Ltd)
Penguin Group (Australia), 250 Camberwell Road, Camberwell, Victoria 3124, Australia
(a division of Pearson Australia Group Pty Ltd)
Penguin Books India Pvt Ltd, 11 Community Centre, Panchsheel Park, New Delhi – 110 017, India
Penguin Group (NZ), 67 Apollo Drive, Rosedale, North Shore 0632, New Zealand
(a division of Pearson New Zealand Ltd)
Penguin Books (South Africa) (Pty) Ltd, 24 Sturdee Avenue,
Rosebank, Johannesburg 2196, South Africa

Penguin Books Ltd, Registered Offices: 80 Strand, London WC2R 0RL, England

www.penguin.com

First published in the USA by HarperCollins 1996
Published in Penguin Books 1997
Reprinted in Penguin Classics 2001
013

Printed in England by Clays Ltd, St Ives plc

ISBN: 978-0-141-18476-0

www.greenpenguin.co.uk

ALWAYS LEARNING   **PEARSON**

To Gregorio Nunzio Corso
Wisdom Maestro
American Genius of Antique & Modern Idiom
Father Poet of Concision

CONTENTS

VII. KING OF MAY: AMERICA TO EUROPE (1963-1965)

VIII. THE FALL OF AMERICA (1965-1971)

IX. MIND BREATHS ALL OVER THE PLACE (1972-1977)

XII. COSMOPOLITAN GREETINGS (1986–1992)

XIII. NEW POEMS (1992–   )

ACKNOWLEDGMENTS

Author wishes to thank friends who've collaborated to initiate, type, track, edit, critique and illustrate *Selected Poems 1947–1995*.

Tony Lacey at Penguin Viking originally requested *Selected Poems*. Fritz Arnold, Michael Krüger, Luca Formenton, Christian & Dominique Bourgois, Yves LePellec, Istvan Eörsi, Eric Thÿgesen, Andrew Wylie & Sarah Chalfant encouraged its completion.

Bob Rosenthal, Bill Morgan, Althea Crawford, Kevin Glassco and indefatigable Peter Hale assembled typescript and images.

Dr. Gordon Ball, Istvan Eörsi, David Greenberg, Eliot Katz, Bill Morgan and Ben Schafer actively advised selection.

Terry Karten, Kera Bolonik and Alma Orenstein at HarperCollins were patient with hesitations and delays.

Sid Kaplan and Brian Graham did elegant printmaking.

Steven Taylor completed all music notation anew.

Robert LaVigne's familiar art is included. Elements of Harry Smith's original cover design have been adapted for new format.

George Condo labored many months with painstaking generosity on front-cover portrait.

Robert Frank amicably picked up a still camera for back-cover photograph of author.

ALLEN GINSBERG
May 31, 1996

All poems (including those originally printed in Lawrence Fer-linghetti's City Lights Pocket Poets series) were taken from the more extensive Harper & Row and HarperCollins *Collected Poems 1947–1980*, *White Shroud: Poems 1980–1985*, and *Cosmopolitan Greetings: Poems 1986–1992*.

The bulk of songs, first time integrated here with other Poetries, come only from the out-of-print *First Blues: Rags, Ballads & Harmonium Songs 1971–1974*, Full Court Press, 1975.

New poems, written since 1992, were printed in *City Lights Journal*, *Harvard Magazine*, *The Nation* and *Newsday*.

APOLOGIA OF SELECTION

I've consulted fellow verse-men familiar with my poetry to help select poems most vividly remembered. Each made checklists from various books including *First Blues, Collected Poems 1947–1980, White Shroud, & Cosmopolitan Greetings.* I sifted these, tabulated favorites, added choice pivotal scribings, & included recent uncollected works. Methods of poetry composition in this late XX Century era have emphasized spontaneity & mind process. This volume summarizes what I deem most honest, most penetrant of my writing.

Selected Poems 1948–1995 isolates & points attention to work less known, more subtle, rhetorically wild, beyond "Beat Generation" literary stereotypes. I'm pleased with the progression of political, devotional & sexual themes displayed, spiritual paths outlined with candor, varieties of verse explored in open "projective" modes & rhymed lyric stanzas.

A few early writings included are exemplary of style or theme as "Paterson" (1949) & "In Back of the Real" (1954). Major poems from the lyric "Howl" (1956) thru narrative "Kaddish" (1957) have their own charisma, & need no explanation for inclusion.

"Magic Psalm" (1960) seems a senseless appeal to Transcendency but gorgeous as surreal rhetoric & stentor breath. As in Hart Crane's "Atlantis," devotion is its own answer, its own grounding—a psychedelic invocation of an Impossible Absolute.

Kerouac liked "T.V. Baby" (1961) for its manic language-crossreference, puns, mental static, amphetaminesque mind-confusion aptly expressed, humor buoying an hyperbolic extravaganza of thought. Paranoia in chains!

The mind-switch goes back to fact-grounded sketches in India. Thirst-for-eternity-psychobabble resolves in the East with "The Change" (1963) a new beginning, affective, political, individual, non-theist. "Today" (1964) through "King of May" and "Who Be Kind To" (1965) mark reclamation of emotion, with silver lining of messianic hint.

Thereafter a return to America to confront the nation at war. I wanted realistic poetry, grounded in common ideal emotions of democracy's citizens, to make bardic prophecy & help end war by affecting the Nation's consciousness, and invoke an awakening new age in America—If not then, in Spirit, in Future Spirit, a "Found Generation" as Jack Kerouac once prophesied. I imagined a force field of language counter to the hypnotic force-field control apparatus of media Government secret police & military with their Dollar billions of inertia, disinformation, brainwash, mass hallucination. Notable that war chief Robert McNamara U.S. Secretary of Defense came 30 years later to conclusions parallel to "Wichita Vortex Sutra" (1966).

By "Wales Visitation" (1967) synchronization of Eternal apparition & realistic detail, (byproduct of combination psychedelic substance & natural meditation practice on breath) was possible, a primary successful union of these legendary but supposedly irreconcilable modes.

Feedback of poet Bob Dylan's influence begins 1971, sparked by the minstrel's advice to imitate any song form noticed. I'm pleased with this intergenerational exchange of influence which confirms old traditions of artistic & spiritual transmission. "September on Jessore Road" written for Dylan, combines naturalistic detail with Blakean rhymes ("Can I see anothers' woe?"). "Jimmy Berman Rag" was unrevised improvisation on guitar chords Dylan strummed in NY's Record Plant studio. "Road to Suva" is traditional chanty song form, filled with minute particulars as might've been noticed by Objectivist poets W. C. Williams, Charles Reznikoff & Carl Rakosi. Throughout that year I imitated lyric rhymed stanzas appropriate to stringed instrument & returns of tune, published with limited circulation as Full Court Press *First Blues* (1972). Here these songs are integrated with other poetries first time, though they were favorites to intersperse with spoken poetry for several decades' public readings.

Following the path of musical vocalization, "Ayers Rock" is performed with Australian Aborigine song sticks given me by Pitjenjara tribe song-men with whom I collaborated during Adelaide Poetry Festival 1972—same technique as "Put Down Yr. Cigarette Rag" begun that year & polished up in the '90's.

Songs & poems soon bend towards another influence, Eastern Thought: Suffering, transitoriness, anatma (no permanent self-hood), and transformation of passion into humor, waste to treasure, meditative Dharma themes. "Profane" lyric spontaneity of "Beat" and older Bohemian aesthetics was reinforced by Tibetan Lama's encouragement & sitting practice. Folk song & Buddhist open heart come to balance in "Father Death Blues" (1975) which for accuracy of emotion & simplicity of means weighs equal in strength to earlier energies & long verse pyrotechnics.

"Contest of Bards" (1977) is an idiosyncratic baroque erotic narrative, by-product of several weeks' uninterrupted reading of Blake's complete poetical works. Several purple passages therefrom were too exquisite to exclude from this summary volume.

In "White Shroud" (1983) the Naturalistic or Objectivist texture is wrapped arround a dream narrative in which few distortions or magnifications indicate "Dream" till the end—a happy mixture of magical phantasy with grounded detail: "Eternity is in love with the productions of time," or "Only thru time is time conquered." That is, "No ideas but in things." A dream of WCW (in China! 1984) follows with consistent advice, "Take your/chances/on/your accuracy."

In *Cosmopolitan Greetings* meditation experience progresses with one-line pith instructions, energetic sound poems composed of political and health adjurations, & verses questioning the solidity of fix'd identity, proposing mutability & inherent emptiness (Sunyata) nature of selfhood. Recordings of rich day-dream activity develop as conscious magic, equally available & prominent as night-dream data. The paradox of form & emptiness co-emergent in ordinary mind ("Negative Capability") provides access to quotidian visionary poetry, see "After Lalon" & "Charnel Ground."

The original task was to "widen the area of consciousness," make pragmatic examination of the texture of consciousness, even somewhat transform consciousness. In the last decade elements of meditative and poetic practice appear to merge. That's the inner structure or progression of this book.

ALLEN GINSBERG
January 9, 1996

I
EMPTY MIRROR: GATES OF WRATH
(1947–1952)

'To find the Western path
Right thro' the Gates of Wrath
I urge my way;
Sweet Mercy leads me on:
With soft Repentant moan
I see the break of day.'

'Thus is the heaven a vortex pass'd already, and the earth
A vortex not yet pass'd by the traveller thro' Eternity.'

'The yearning infinite recoils,
For terrible is earth!'

To HERBERT E. HUNCKE
for his *Confessions*

In Society

I walked into the cocktail party
room and found three or four queers
talking together in queertalk.
I tried to be friendly but heard
myself talking to one in hiptalk.
"I'm glad to see you," he said, and
looked away. "Hmn," I mused. The room
was small and had a double-decker
bed in it, and cooking apparatus:
icebox, cabinet, toasters, stove;
the hosts seemed to live with room
enough only for cooking and sleeping.
My remark on this score was under-
stood but not appreciated. I was
offered refreshments, which I accepted.
I ate a sandwich of pure meat; an
enormous sandwich of human flesh,
I noticed, while I was chewing on it,
it also included a dirty asshole.

More company came, including a
fluffy female who looked like
a princess. She glared at me and
said immediately: "I don't like you,"
turned her head away, and refused
to be introduced. I said, "What!"
in outrage. "Why you shit-faced fool!"
This got everybody's attention.
"Why you narcissistic bitch! How
can you decide when you don't even
know me," I continued in a violent
and messianic voice, inspired at
last, dominating the whole room

Dream New York–Denver, Spring 1947

The Bricklayer's Lunch Hour

Two bricklayers are setting the walls
of a cellar in a new dug out patch
of dirt behind an old house of wood
with brown gables grown over with ivy
on a shady street in Denver. It is noon
and one of them wanders off. The young
subordinate bricklayer sits idly for
a few minutes after eating a sandwich
and throwing away the paper bag. He
has on dungarees and is bare above
the waist; he has yellow hair and wears
a smudged but still bright red cap
on his head. He sits idly on top
of the wall on a ladder that is leaned
up between his spread thighs, his head
bent down, gazing uninterestedly at
the paper bag on the grass. He draws
his hand across his breast, and then
slowly rubs his knuckles across the
side of his chin, and rocks to and fro
on the wall. A small cat walks to him
along the top of the wall. He picks
it up, takes off his cap, and puts it
over the kitten's body for a moment.
Meanwhile it is darkening as if to rain
and the wind on top of the trees in the
street comes through almost harshly.

Denver, Summer 1947

The Trembling of the Veil

Today out of the window
the trees seemed like live
organisms on the moon.

Each bough extended upward
covered at the north end
with leaves, like a green

hairy protuberance. I saw
the scarlet-and-pink shoot-tips
of budding leaves wave

delicately in the sunlight,
blown by the breeze,
all the arms of the trees
bending and straining downward

at once when the wind
pushed them.

Paterson, August 1948

A Western Ballad

When I died, love, when I died
my heart was broken in your care;
I never suffered love so fair
as now I suffer and abide
when I died, love, when I died.

When I died, love, when I died
I wearied in an endless maze
that men have walked for centuries,
as endless as the gate was wide
when I died, love, when I died.

When I died, love, when I died
there was a war in the upper air:
all that happens, happens there;
there was an angel at my side
when I died, love, when I died.

Paterson, August 1948

Pull My Daisy

Pull my daisy
tip my cup
all my doors are open
Cut my thoughts
for coconuts
all my eggs are broken
Jack my Arden
gate my shades
woe my road is spoken
Silk my garden
rose my days
now my prayers awaken

Bone my shadow
dove my dream
start my halo bleeding
Milk my mind &
make me cream
drink me when you're ready
Hop my heart on
harp my height
seraphs hold me steady
Hip my angel
hype my light
lay it on the needy

Heal the raindrop
sow the eye
bust my dust again
Woe the worm
work the wise
dig my spade the same
Stop the hoax
what's the hex
where's the wake
how's the hicks
take my golden beam

Rob my locker
lick my rocks
leap my cock in school
Rack my lacks
lark my looks
jump right up my hole
Whore my door
beat my boor
eat my snake of fool
Craze my hair
bare my poor
asshole shorn of wool

Say my oops
ope my shell
bite my naked nut
Roll my bones
ring my bell
call my worm to sup
Pope my parts
pop my pot
raise my daisy up
Poke my pap
pit my plum
let my gap be shut

Allen Ginsberg, Jack Kerouac & Neal Cassady
New York, Spring–Fall 1949

The Shrouded Stranger

Bare skin is my wrinkled sack
When hot Apollo humps my back
When Jack Frost grabs me in these rags
I wrap my legs with burlap bags

My flesh is cinder my face is snow
I walk the railroad to and fro
When city streets are black and dead
The railroad embankment is my bed

I sup my soup from old tin cans
And take my sweets from little hands
In Tiger Alley near the jail
I steal away from the garbage pail

In darkest night where none can see
Down in the bowels of the factory
I sneak barefoot upon stone
Come and hear the old man groan

I hide and wait like a naked child
Under the bridge my heart goes wild
I scream at a fire on the river bank
I give my body to an old gas tank

I dream that I have burning hair
Boiled arms that claw the air
The torso of an iron king
And on my back a broken wing

Who'll go out whoring into the night
On the eyeless road in the skinny moonlight
Maid or dowd or athlete proud
May wanton with me in the shroud

Who'll come lie down in the dark with me
Belly to belly and knee to knee
Who'll look into my hooded eye
Who'll lie down under my darkened thigh?

New York, 1949–1951

Tonite all is well . . . What a
terrible future. I am twenty-three,
year of the iron birthday,
gate of darkness. I am ill,
I have become physically and
spiritually impotent in my madness this month.
I suddenly realized that my head
is severed from my body;
I realized it a few nights ago
by myself,
lying sleepless on the couch.

Paterson, Summer 1949

Fyodor

The death's head of realism
and superhuman iron mask
that gapes out of *The Possessed*,
sometimes: Dostoievski.
My original version of D.
before I read him, as the dark
haunted-house man, wild, agèd,
spectral Russian. I call him
Dusty now but he is
Dostoyevsky. What premonitions
I had as a child.

Paterson, June 1949

Metaphysics

This is the one and only
firmament; therefore
it is the absolute world.
There is no other world.
The circle is complete.
I am living in Eternity.
The ways of this world
are the ways of Heaven.

New York, Mid-1949

Paterson

What do I want in these rooms papered with visions of money?

How much can I make by cutting my hair? If I put new heels on my shoes,

bathe my body reeking of masturbation and sweat, layer upon layer of excrement

dried in employment bureaus, magazine hallways, statistical cubicles, factory stairways,

cloakrooms of the smiling gods of psychiatry;

if in antechambers I face the presumption of department store supervisory employees,

old clerks in their asylums of fat, the slobs and dumbbells of the ego with money and power

to hire and fire and make and break and fart and justify their reality of wrath

and rumor of wrath to wrath-weary man,

what war I enter and for what a prize! the dead prick of commonplace obsession,

harridan vision of electricity at night and daylight misery of thumb-sucking rage.

I would rather go mad, gone down the dark road to Mexico, heroin dripping in my veins,

eyes and ears full of marijuana,

eating the god Peyote on the floor of a mudhut on the border

or laying in a hotel room over the body of some suffering man or woman;

rather jar my body down the road, crying by a diner in the Western sun;

rather crawl on my naked belly over the tincans of Cincinnati;

rather drag a rotten railroad tie to a Golgotha in the Rockies;

rather, crowned with thorns in Galveston, nailed hand and foot in Los Angeles, raised up to die in Denver,

pierced in the side in Chicago, perished and tombed in New Orleans and resurrected in 1958 somewhere on Garret Mountain,

come down roaring in a blaze of hot cars and garbage,

streetcorner Evangel in front of City Hall, surrounded by statues of agonized lions,

with a mouthful of shit, and the hair rising on my scalp,

screaming and dancing in praise of Eternity annihilating the sidewalk, annihilating reality,

screaming and dancing against the orchestra in the destructible ballroom of the world,

blood streaming from my belly and shoulders
flooding the city with its hideous ecstasy, rolling over the pavements and
    highways
by the bayoux and forests and derricks leaving my flesh and my bones
    hanging on the trees.

New York, November 1949

The Archetype Poem

Joe Blow has decided
he will no longer
        be a fairy.
He involves himself
in various snatches
        and then hits
a nut named Mary.

He gets in bed with her
        and performs
as what in his mind
would be his usual
        okay job,
which should be solid
        as a rock
        but isn't.

What goes wrong here?
        he says
to himself. I want
        to take her
but she doesn't want
        to take me.

I thought I was
        giving her * * *
and she was giving
        me a man's
position in the world.

Now suddenly she lays
        down the law.
I'm very tired, she says,
        please go.

Is this it? he thinks.
        I didn't want it
to come to that but

I've got to get out
          of this situation.

          So the question
resolves itself: do
          you settle for her
or go? I wouldn't
          give you a nickel,
you aren't much of a doll
          anyway. And he

picks up his pride
and puts on his pants
          —glad enough
to have pants to wear—
          and goes.

Why is it that versions
          of this lack
of communication are
          universal?

New York, Late 1950

Marijuana Notation

How sick I am!
       that thought
always comes to me
       with horror.
Is it this strange
       for everybody?
But such fugitive feelings
have always been
       my métier.

Baudelaire—yet he had
great joyful moments
       staring into space,
looking into the
       middle distance,
contemplating his image
       in Eternity.
They were his moments
       of identity.
It is solitude that
produces these thoughts.

       It is December
almost, they are singing
       Christmas carols
in front of the department
stores down the block on
       Fourteenth Street.

New York, November 1951

A Crazy Spiritual

A faithful youth
with artificial legs
drove his jalopy
through the towns of Texas.

He got sent out
of the Free Hospital
of Galveston, madtown
on the Gulf of Mexico

after he recovered.
They gave him a car
and a black mongrel;
name was Weakness.

He was a thin kid
with golden hair
and a frail body
on wire thighs,

who never traveled
and drove northward
timid on the highway
going about twenty.

I hitched a hike
and showed him the road.
I got off at Small Town
and stole his dog.

He tried to drive away,
but lost control,
rode on the pavement
near a garage,

and smashed his doors
and fenders on trees

and parked cars,
and came to a halt.

The Marshal came,
stopping everything
pulled him out
of the wreck cursing.

I watched it all
from the lunch cart,
holding the dog
with a frayed rope.

"I'm on my own
from the crazyhouse.
Has anybody
seen my Weakness?"

What are they saying?
"Call up the FBI.
Crazy, ha? What
is he a fairy?

He must do funny
things with women,
we bet he * * *
them in the * * *."

Poor child meanwhile
collapsed on the ground
with innocent expression
is trying to get up.

Along came a Justice
of the Supreme Court,
barreling through town
in a blue limousine.

He stopped by the crowd
to find out the story,
got out on his pegleg
with an angry smile.

"Don't you see
he has no legs?
That's you fools
what crazy means."

He picked the boy
up off the ground.
The dog ran to them
from the lunch cart.

He put them both in
the back seat of his car
and stood in the square
hymning at the crowd:

"Rock rock rock
for the tension
of the people
of this country

rock rock rock
for the craziness
of the people
of America

tension is a rock
and god will
rock our rock

craziness is a rock
and god will
rock our rock

Lord we shall all
be sweet again."

He showed his wooden leg
to the boy, saying:
"I promise to drive you
home through America."

Paterson, April 1952

II
THE GREEN
AUTOMOBILE
(1953–1954)

The Green Automobile

If I had a Green Automobile
        I'd go find my old companion
        in his house on the Western ocean.
                Ha! Ha! Ha! Ha! Ha!

I'd honk my horn at his manly gate,
        inside his wife and three
        children sprawl naked
                on the living room floor.

He'd come running out
        to my car full of heroic beer
        and jump screaming at the wheel
                for he is the greater driver.

We'd pilgrimage to the highest mount
        of our earlier Rocky Mountain visions
        laughing in each other's arms,
                delight surpassing the highest Rockies,

and after old agony, drunk with new years,
        bounding toward the snowy horizon
        blasting the dashboard with original bop
                hot rod on the mountain

we'd batter up the cloudy highway
        where angels of anxiety
        careen through the trees
                and scream out of the engine.

We'd burn all night on the jackpine peak
        seen from Denver in the summer dark,
        forestlike unnatural radiance
                illuminating the mountaintop:

childhood youthtime age & eternity
        would open like sweet trees
        in the nights of another spring
                and dumbfound us with love,

for we can see together
           the beauty of souls
           hidden like diamonds
                      in the clock of the world,

like Chinese magicians can
           confound the immortals
           with our intellectuality
                      hidden in the mist,

in the Green Automobile
           which I have invented
           imagined and visioned
                      on the roads of the world

more real than the engine
           on a track in the desert
           purer than Greyhound and
                      swifter than physical jetplane. .

Denver! Denver! we'll return
           roaring across the City & County Building lawn
           which catches the pure emerald flame
                      streaming in the wake of our auto.

This time we'll buy up the city!
           I cashed a great check in my skull bank
           to found a miraculous college of the body
                      up on the bus terminal roof.

But first we'll drive the stations of downtown,
           poolhall flophouse jazzjoint jail
           whorehouse down Folsom
                      to the darkest alleys of Larimer

paying respects to Denver's father
           lost on the railroad tracks,
           stupor of wine and silence
                      hallowing the slum of his decades,

salute him and his saintly suitcase
           of dark muscatel, drink

and smash the sweet bottles
            on Diesels in allegiance.

Then we go driving drunk on boulevards
            where armies march and still parade
            staggering under the invisible
                    banner of Reality—

hurtling through the street
            in the auto of our fate
            we share an archangelic cigarette
                    and tell each other's fortunes:

fames of supernatural illumination,
            bleak rainy gaps of time,
            great art learned in desolation
                    and we beat apart after six decades . . .

and on an asphalt crossroad,
            deal with each other in princely
            gentleness once more, recalling
                    famous dead talks of other cities.

The windshield's full of tears,
            rain wets our naked breasts,
            we kneel together in the shade
                    amid the traffic of night in paradise

and now renew the solitary vow
            we made each other take
            in Texas, once:
                    I can't inscribe here. . . .

                    • • • • • •
                    • • • • • •

How many Saturday nights will be
            made drunken by this legend?
            How will young Denver come to mourn
                    her forgotten sexual angel?

How many boys will strike the black piano
            in imitation of the excess of a native saint?

Or girls fall wanton under his spectre in the high
        schools of melancholy night?

While all the time in Eternity
        in the wan light of this poem's radio
        we'll sit behind forgotten shades
            hearkening the lost jazz of all Saturdays.

Neal, we'll be real heroes now
        in a war between our cocks and time:
        let's be the angels of the world's desire
            and take the world to bed with us before we die.

Sleeping alone, or with companion,
        girl or fairy sheep or dream,
        I'll fail of lacklove, you, satiety:
            all men fall, our fathers fell before,

but resurrecting that lost flesh
        is but a moment's work of mind:
        an ageless monument to love
            in the imagination:

memorial built out of our own bodies
        consumed by the invisible poem—
        We'll shudder in Denver and endure
            though blood and wrinkles blind our eyes.

So this Green Automobile:
        I give you in flight
        a present, a present
            from my imagination.

We will go riding
        over the Rockies,
        we'll go on riding
            all night long until dawn,

then back to your railroad, the SP
        your house and your children
        and broken leg destiny
            you'll ride down the plains

in the morning: and back
          to my visions, my office
          and eastern apartment
                    I'll return to New York.

New York, May 22–25, 1953

Green Valentine Blues

The Green Automobile

tine, my green va - len - tine,

How did I use my green va - len - tine?

I went in the forest to look for a sign
Fortune to tell and thought to refine;
My green valentine, my green valentine,
What do I know of my green valentine?

I found a strange wild leaf on a vine
Shaped like a heart and as green as was mine,
My green valentine, my green valentine,
How did I use my green valentine?

Bodies I've known and visions I've seen,
Leaves that I gathered as I gather this green
Valentine, valentine, valentine, valentine;
Thus did I use my green valentine.

Madhouse and jailhouses where I shined
Empty apartment beds where I pined,
O desolate rooms! My green valentine,
Where is the heart in which you were outlined?

Souls and nights and dollars and wine,
Old love and remembrance—I resign
All cities, all jazz, all echoes of Time,
But what shall I do with my green valentine?

Much have I seen, and much am I blind,
But none other than I has a leaf of this kind.
Where shall I send you, to what knowing mind,
My green valentine, my green valentine?

Yesterday's love, tomorrow's more fine?
All tonight's sadness in your design.
What does this mean, my green valentine?
Regret, O regret, my green valentine.

Chiapas, 1954

Green Valentine Blues   29

Siesta in Xbalba

and
Return to the States

For Karena Shields

I

. . . —One could pass valuable months
and years perhaps a lifetime
doing nothing but lying in a hammock
reading prose with the white doves
                    copulating underneath
and monkeys barking in the interior
                    of the mountain
and I have succumbed to this
                    temptation— . . .

Dreaming back I saw
an eternal kodachrome
souvenir of a gathering
of souls at a party,
crowded in an oval flash:
cigarettes, suggestions,
laughter in drunkenness,
broken sweet conversation,
acquaintance in the halls,
faces posed together,
stylized gestures,
odd familiar visages
and singular recognitions
that registered indifferent
greeting across time:
Anson reading Horace
with a rolling head,
white-handed Hohnsbean
camping gravely
with an absent glance,
bald Kingsland drinking
out of a huge glass,

Dusty in a party dress,
Durgin in white shoes
gesturing from a chair,
Keck in a corner waiting
for subterranean music,
Helen Parker lifting
her hands in surprise:
all posturing in one frame,
superficially gay
or tragic as may be,
illumined with the fatal
character and intelligent
actions of their lives . . .

As I leaned against a tree
          inside the forest
expiring of self-begotten love,
I looked up at the stars absently,
          as if looking for
something else in the blue night
          through the boughs,
and for a moment saw myself
          leaning against a tree . . .

. . . back there the noise of a great party
          in the apartments of New York,
half-created paintings on the walls, fame,
          cocksucking and tears,
money and arguments of great affairs,
          the culture of my generation . . .

One might sit in this Chiapas
recording the apparitions in the field
          visible from a hammock
looking out across the shadow of the pasture
in all the semblance of Eternity

          palms with lethargic feelers
rattling in presage of rain,
          shifting their fronds

in the direction of the balmy wind,
                monstrous animals
sprayed up out of the ground
                settling and unsettling
as in water . . .
                and later in the night
a moment of premonition
when the plenilunar cloudfilled sky
                is still and small . . .

                High dim stone portals,
entablatures of illegible scripture,
bas-reliefs of unknown perceptions:
                and now the flicker of my lamp
and smell of kerosene on dust-
                strewn floor where ant wends
its nightly ritual way toward great faces
                worn down by rain.

In front of me a deathshead
                half a thousand years old
—and have seen cocks a thousand
old grown over with moss and batshit
                stuck out of the wall
in a dripping vaulted house of rock—
                but deathshead's here
on portal still and thinks its way
                through centuries the thought
of the same night in which I sit
                in skully meditation
—sat in many times before by
                artisan other than me
until his image of ghostly change
                appeared unalterable—
but now his fine thought's vaguer
                than my dream of him:
and only the crude skull figurement's
                gaunt insensible glare is left
with broken plumes of sensation,

headdresses of indecipherable intellect
                scattered in the madness of oblivion
to holes and notes of elemental stone,
blind face of animal transcendency
                over the sacred ruin of the world
dissolving into the sunless wall of a blackened room
                on a time-rude pyramid rebuilt
                in the bleak flat night of Yucatán
where I come with my own mad mind to study
                alien hieroglyphs of Eternity.

My hat woven of henequen
                on the stone floor
as a leaf on the waters,
                as perishable;
my candle wavers continuously
                and will go out.

Pale Uxmal,
                unhistoric, like a dream,
Tulum shimmering on the coast in ruins;
Chichén Itzá naked
                constructed on a plain;
Palenque, broken chapels in the green
                basement of a mount;
lone Kabah by the highway;
                Piedras Negras buried again
by dark archaeologists;
                Yaxchilan
resurrected in the wild,
and all the limbo of Xbalba still unknown—
                floors under roofcomb of branch,
foundation to ornament
                tumbled to the flowers,
pyramids and stairways
                raced with vine,
limestone corbels
                down in the river of trees,

pillars and corridors
           sunken under the flood of years . . .

Yet these ruins so much
           woke me to nostalgia
for the classic stations
           of the earth,
the ancient continent
           I have not seen
and the few years
           of memory left
before the ultimate night
           of war—

As if these ruins were not enough,
           as if man could go
no further before heaven
           till he exhausted
the physical round
           of his own mortality
in the obscure cities
           hidden in the aging world

. . . the few actual
           ecstatic conscious souls
certain to be found,
           familiars . . .
returning after years
           to my own scene
transfigured:
           to hurry change
to hurry the years
           bring me to my fate.

So I dream nightly of an embarkation,
           captains, captains,
iron passageways, cabin lights;
           Brooklyn across the waters,
the great dull boat, visitors, farewells,
           the blurred vast sea—
one trip a lifetime's loss or gain:

as Europe is my own imagination
                    —many shall see her,
           many shall not—
though it's only the old familiar world
and not some abstract mystical dream.

And in a moment of previsioning sleep
                    I see that continent in rain,
black streets, old night, a
                    fading monument . . .

And a long journey unaccomplished
                    yet, on antique seas
rolling in gray barren dunes under
                    the world's waste of light
toward ports of childish geography
                    the rusty ship will
harbor in . . .

What nights might I not see
                    penniless among the Arab
mysteries of dirty towns around
                    the casbahs of the docks?
Clay paths, mud walls,
                    the smell of green cigarettes,
creosote and rank salt water—
                    dark structures overhead,
shapes of machinery and facade
                    of hull: and a bar lamp
burning in the wooden shack
                    across from the dim
mountain of sulphur on the pier.

                    Toward what city
will I travel? What wild houses
                    do I go to occupy?
What vagrant rooms and streets
                    and lights in the long night
urge my expectation? What genius
                    of sensation in ancient

halls? what jazz beyond jazz
            in future blue saloons?
what love in the cafés of God?

I thought, five years ago
            sitting in my apartment,
my eyes were opened for an hour
            seeing in dreadful ecstasy
the motionless buildings
            of New York rotting
under the tides of Heaven.

There is a god
dying in America

already created
in the imagination of men
made palpable
for adoration:
there is an inner
anterior image
of divinity
beckoning me out
to pilgrimage.

O future, unimaginable God.

                              Finca Tacalapan de San
                                 Leandro, Palenque,
                              Chiapas, Mexico 1954–
                                 San Francisco 1955

II
. . . What solitude I've
            finally inherited.

            Afterward fifteen hours
on rubbled single lane,
            broken bus rocking along
the maws and continental crags
            of mountain afternoon,

the distant valleys fading,
                    regnant peaks beyond
to days on the Pacific
                    where I bathed—

then riding, fitful,
                    gazing, sleeping
through the desert
                    beside a wetback
sad-faced old-man-
                    youth, exhausted
to Mexicali

                    to stand
near one night's dark shack
                    on the garbage cliffs
of bordertown overhanging
                    the tin house poor

man's village below,
                    a last night's
timewracked brooding
                    and farewell,
the end of a trip.

—Returning
                    armed with New Testament,
critic of horse and mule,
                    tanned and bearded
satisfying Whitman, concerned
                    with a few Traditions,
metrical, mystical, manly
. . . and certain characteristic flaws

                    —enough!

The nation over the border
grinds its arms and dreams
                    of war: I see
the fiery blue clash
                    of metal wheels

clanking in the industries
             of night, and
detonation of infernal bombs

             . . . and the silent downtown
of the States
             in watery dusk submersion.

Guanajuato–Los Angeles, 1954

Song

The weight of the world
   is love.
Under the burden
   of solitude,
under the burden
   of dissatisfaction

   the weight,
the weight we carry
   is love.

Who can deny?
   In dreams
it touches
   the body,
in thought
   constructs
a miracle,
   in imagination
anguishes
   till born
in human—

looks out of the heart
   burning with purity—
for the burden of life
   is love,

but we carry the weight
   wearily,
and so must rest
in the arms of love
   at last,
must rest in the arms
   of love.

No rest
   without love,
no sleep
   without dreams

of love—
        be mad or chill
obsessed with angels
        or machines,
the final wish
        is love
—cannot be bitter,
        cannot deny,
cannot withhold
        if denied:

the weight is too heavy

        —must give
for no return
        as thought
is given
        in solitude
in all the excellence
        of its excess.

The warm bodies
        shine together
in the darkness,
        the hand moves
to the center
        of the flesh,
the skin trembles
        in happiness
and the soul comes
        joyful to the eye—

yes, yes,
        that's what
I wanted,
        I always wanted,
I always wanted,
        to return
to my body
        where I was born.

San Jose, 1954

In back of the real

railroad yard in San Jose
    I wandered desolate
in front of a tank factory
    and sat on a bench
near the switchman's shack.

A flower lay on the hay on
    the asphalt highway
—the dread hay flower
    I thought—It had a
brittle black stem and
    corolla of yellowish dirty
spikes like Jesus' inchlong
    crown, and a soiled
dry center cotton tuft
    like a used shaving brush
that's been lying under
    the garage for a year.

Yellow, yellow flower, and
    flower of industry,
tough spiky ugly flower,
    flower nonetheless,
with the form of the great yellow
    Rose in your brain!
This is the flower of the World.

San Jose, 1954

On Burroughs' Work

The method must be purest meat
    and no symbolic dressing,
actual visions & actual prisons
    as seen then and now.

Prisons and visions presented
    with rare descriptions
corresponding exactly to those
    of Alcatraz and Rose.

A naked lunch is natural to us,
    we eat reality sandwiches.
But allegories are so much lettuce.
    Don't hide the madness.

San Jose, 1954

Love Poem on Theme by Whitman

I'll go into the bedroom silently and lie down between the bridegroom and
      the bride,
those bodies fallen from heaven stretched out waiting naked and restless,
arms resting over their eyes in the darkness,
bury my face in their shoulders and breasts, breathing their skin,
and stroke and kiss neck and mouth and make back be open and known,
legs raised up crook'd to receive, cock in the darkness driven tormented
      and attacking
roused up from hole to itching head,
bodies locked shuddering naked, hot hips and buttocks screwed into each
      other
and eyes, eyes glinting and charming, widening into looks and abandon,
and moans of movement, voices, hands in air, hands between thighs,
hands in moisture on softened hips, throbbing contraction of bellies
till the white come flow in the swirling sheets,
and the bride cry for forgiveness, and the groom be covered with tears of
      passion and compassion,
and I rise up from the bed replenished with last intimate gestures and kisses
      of farewell—
all before the mind wakes, behind shades and closed doors in a darkened
      house
where the inhabitants roam unsatisfied in the night,
nude ghosts seeking each other out in the silence.

San Jose, 1954

Drawing by Robert LaVigne, San Francisco, 1954

III
HOWL, BEFORE & AFTER: SAN FRANCISCO BAY AREA
(1955–1956)

'Unscrew the locks from the doors!
Unscrew the doors themselves from their jambs!'

To

JACK KEROUAC, new Buddha of American prose, who spit forth intelligence into eleven books written in half the number of years (1951–1956)—*On the Road, Visions of Neal, Dr Sax, Springtime Mary, The Subterraneans, San Francisco Blues, Some of the Dharma, Book of Dreams, Wake Up, Mexico City Blues,* and *Visions of Gerard*—creating a spontaneous bop prosody and original classic literature. Several phrases and the title of *Howl* are taken from him.

WILLIAM SEWARD BURROUGHS, author of *Naked Lunch*, an endless novel which will drive everybody mad.

NEAL CASSADY, author of *The First Third*, an autobiography (1949) which enlightened Buddha.

All these books are published in Heaven.

Malest Cornifici Tuo Catullo

I'm happy, Kerouac, your madman Allen's
finally made it: discovered a new young cat,
and my imagination of an eternal boy
walks on the streets of San Francisco,
handsome, and meets me in cafeterias
and loves me. Ah don't think I'm sickening.
You're angry at me. For all of my lovers?
It's hard to eat shit, without having visions;
when they have eyes for me it's like Heaven.

San Francisco, 1955

Dream Record: June 8, 1955

A drunken night in my house with a
boy, San Francisco: I lay asleep:
darkness:

        I went back to Mexico City
and saw Joan Burroughs leaning
forward in a garden chair, arms
on her knees. She studied me with
clear eyes and downcast smile, her
face restored to a fine beauty
tequila and salt had made strange
before the bullet in her brow.

We talked of the life since then.
Well, what's Burroughs doing now?
Bill on earth, he's in North Africa.
Oh, and Kerouac? Jack still jumps
with the same beat genius as before,
notebooks filled with Buddha.
I hope he makes it, she laughed.
Is Huncke still in the can? No,
last time I saw him on Times Square.
And how is Kenney? Married, drunk
and golden in the East. You? New
loves in the West—

        Then I knew
she was a dream: and questioned her
—Joan, what kind of knowledge have
the dead? can you still love
your mortal acquaintances?
What do you remember of us?

        She
faded in front of me— The next instant
I saw her rain-stained tombstone
rear an illegible epitaph
under the gnarled branch of a small
tree in the wild grass
of an unvisited garden in Mexico.

Howl

For Carl Solomon

I

I saw the best minds of my generation destroyed by madness, starving
hysterical naked,

dragging themselves through the negro streets at dawn looking for an
angry fix,

angelheaded hipsters burning for the ancient heavenly connection to the
starry dynamo in the machinery of night,

who poverty and tatters and hollow-eyed and high sat up smoking in the
supernatural darkness of cold-water flats floating across the tops of
cities contemplating jazz,

who bared their brains to Heaven under the El and saw Mohammedan
angels staggering on tenement roofs illuminated,

who passed through universities with radiant cool eyes hallucinating Ar-
kansas and Blake-light tragedy among the scholars of war,

who were expelled from the academies for crazy & publishing obscene
odes on the windows of the skull,

who cowered in unshaven rooms in underwear, burning their money in
wastebaskets and listening to the Terror through the wall,

who got busted in their pubic beards returning through Laredo with a belt
of marijuana for New York,

who ate fire in paint hotels or drank turpentine in Paradise Alley, death, or
purgatoried their torsos night after night

with dreams, with drugs, with waking nightmares, alcohol and cock and
endless balls,

incomparable blind streets of shuddering cloud and lightning in the mind
leaping toward poles of Canada & Paterson, illuminating all the
motionless world of Time between,

Peyote solidities of halls, backyard green tree cemetery dawns, wine
drunkenness over the rooftops, storefront boroughs of teahead
joyride neon blinking traffic light, sun and moon and tree vibra-
tions in the roaring winter dusks of Brooklyn, ashcan rantings and
kind king light of mind,

who chained themselves to subways for the endless ride from Battery to
holy Bronx on benzedrine until the noise of wheels and children
brought them down shuddering mouth-wracked and battered
bleak of brain all drained of brilliance in the drear light of Zoo,

who sank all night in submarine light of Bickford's floated out and sat
    through the stale beer afternoon in desolate Fugazzi's, listening to
    the crack of doom on the hydrogen jukebox,
who talked continuously seventy hours from park to pad to bar to Bellevue
    to museum to the Brooklyn Bridge,
a lost battalion of platonic conversationalists jumping down the stoops off
    fire escapes off windowsills off Empire State out of the moon,
yacketayakking screaming vomiting whispering facts and memories and anec-
    dotes and eyeball kicks and shocks of hospitals and jails and wars,
whole intellects disgorged in total recall for seven days and nights with
    brilliant eyes, meat for the Synagogue cast on the pavement,
who vanished into nowhere Zen New Jersey leaving a trail of ambiguous
    picture postcards of Atlantic City Hall,
suffering Eastern sweats and Tangerian bone-grindings and migraines of
    China under junk-withdrawal in Newark's bleak furnished room,
who wandered around and around at midnight in the railroad yard won-
    dering where to go, and went, leaving no broken hearts,
who lit cigarettes in boxcars boxcars boxcars racketing through snow
    toward lonesome farms in grandfather night,
who studied Plotinus Poe St. John of the Cross telepathy and bop kabbalah
    because the cosmos instinctively vibrated at their feet in Kansas,
who loned it through the streets of Idaho seeking visionary indian angels
    who were visionary indian angels,
who thought they were only mad when Baltimore gleamed in supernatural
    ecstasy,
who jumped in limousines with the Chinaman of Oklahoma on the im-
    pulse of winter midnight streetlight smalltown rain,
who lounged hungry and lonesome through Houston seeking jazz or sex or
    soup, and followed the brilliant Spaniard to converse about Amer-
    ica and Eternity, a hopeless task, and so took ship to Africa,
who disappeared into the volcanoes of Mexico leaving behind nothing but
    the shadow of dungarees and the lava and ash of poetry scattered in
    fireplace Chicago,
who reappeared on the West Coast investigating the FBI in beards and
    shorts with big pacifist eyes sexy in their dark skin passing out
    incomprehensible leaflets,
who burned cigarette holes in their arms protesting the narcotic tobacco
    haze of Capitalism,
who distributed Supercommunist pamphlets in Union Square weeping
    and undressing while the sirens of Los Alamos wailed them down,
    and wailed down Wall, and the Staten Island ferry also wailed,
who broke down crying in white gymnasiums naked and trembling before
    the machinery of other skeletons,

who bit detectives in the neck and shrieked with delight in policecars for
    committing no crime but their own wild cooking pederasty and
    intoxication,
who howled on their knees in the subway and were dragged off the roof
    waving genitals and manuscripts,
who let themselves be fucked in the ass by saintly motorcyclists, and
    screamed with joy,
who blew and were blown by those human seraphim, the sailors, caresses of
    Atlantic and Caribbean love,
who balled in the morning in the evenings in rosegardens and the grass of
    public parks and cemeteries scattering their semen freely to
    whomever come who may,
who hiccuped endlessly trying to giggle but wound up with a sob behind a
    partition in a Turkish Bath when the blond & naked angel came to
    pierce them with a sword,
who lost their loveboys to the three old shrews of fate the one eyed shrew
    of the heterosexual dollar the one eyed shrew that winks out of the
    womb and the one eyed shrew that does nothing but sit on her ass
    and snip the intellectual golden threads of the craftsman's loom,
who copulated ecstatic and insatiate with a bottle of beer a sweetheart a pack-
    age of cigarettes a candle and fell off the bed, and continued along the
    floor and down the hall and ended fainting on the wall with a vision of
    ultimate cunt and come eluding the last gyzym of consciousness,
who sweetened the snatches of a million girls trembling in the sunset, and
    were red eyed in the morning but prepared to sweeten the snatch
    of the sunrise, flashing buttocks under barns and naked in the lake,
who went out whoring through Colorado in myriad stolen night-cars,
    N.C., secret hero of these poems, cocksman and Adonis of
    Denver—joy to the memory of his innumerable lays of girls in
    empty lots & diner backyards, moviehouses' rickety rows, on
    mountaintops in caves or with gaunt waitresses in familiar road-
    side lonely petticoat upliftings & especially secret gas-station so-
    lipsisms of johns, & hometown alleys too,
who faded out in vast sordid movies, were shifted in dreams, woke on a
    sudden Manhattan, and picked themselves up out of basements
    hung-over with heartless Tokay and horrors of Third Avenue iron
    dreams & stumbled to unemployment offices,
who walked all night with their shoes full of blood on the snowbank docks
    waiting for a door in the East River to open to a room full of
    steam-heat and opium,
who created great suicidal dramas on the apartment cliff-banks of the
    Hudson under the wartime blue floodlight of the moon & their
    heads shall be crowned with laurel in oblivion,

who ate the lamb stew of the imagination or digested the crab at the muddy bottom of the rivers of Bowery,

who wept at the romance of the streets with their pushcarts full of onions and bad music,

who sat in boxes breathing in the darkness under the bridge, and rose up to build harpsichords in their lofts,

who coughed on the sixth floor of Harlem crowned with flame under the tubercular sky surrounded by orange crates of theology,

who scribbled all night rocking and rolling over lofty incantations which in the yellow morning were stanzas of gibberish,

who cooked rotten animals lung heart feet tail borsht & tortillas dreaming of the pure vegetable kingdom,

who plunged themselves under meat trucks looking for an egg,

who threw their watches off the roof to cast their ballot for Eternity outside of Time, & alarm clocks fell on their heads every day for the next decade,

who cut their wrists three times successively unsuccessfully, gave up and were forced to open antique stores where they thought they were growing old and cried,

who were burned alive in their innocent flannel suits on Madison Avenue amid blasts of leaden verse & the tanked-up clatter of the iron regiments of fashion & the nitroglycerine shrieks of the fairies of advertising & the mustard gas of sinister intelligent editors, or were run down by the drunken taxicabs of Absolute Reality,

who jumped off the Brooklyn Bridge this actually happened and walked away unknown and forgotten into the ghostly daze of Chinatown soup alleyways & firetrucks, not even one free beer,

who sang out of their windows in despair, fell out of the subway window, jumped in the filthy Passaic, leaped on negroes, cried all over the street, danced on broken wineglasses barefoot smashed phonograph records of nostalgic European 1930s German jazz finished the whiskey and threw up groaning into the bloody toilet, moans in their ears and the blast of colossal steamwhistles,

who barreled down the highways of the past journeying to each other's hotrod-Golgotha jail-solitude watch or Birmingham jazz incarnation,

who drove crosscountry seventytwo hours to find out if I had a vision or you had a vision or he had a vision to find out Eternity,

who journeyed to Denver, who died in Denver, who came back to Denver & waited in vain, who watched over Denver & brooded & loned in Denver and finally went away to find out the Time, & now Denver is lonesome for her heroes, who fell on their knees in hopeless cathedrals praying for each other's salvation and light and breasts, until the soul illuminated its hair for a second,

who crashed through their minds in jail waiting for impossible criminals with golden heads and the charm of reality in their hearts who sang sweet blues to Alcatraz,

who retired to Mexico to cultivate a habit, or Rocky Mount to tender Buddha or Tangiers to boys or Southern Pacific to the black locomotive or Harvard to Narcissus to Woodlawn to the daisy-chain or grave,

who demanded sanity trials accusing the radio of hypnotism & were left with their insanity & their hands & a hung jury,

who threw potato salad at CCNY lecturers on Dadaism and subsequently presented themselves on the granite steps of the madhouse with shaven heads and harlequin speech of suicide, demanding instantaneous lobotomy,

and who were given instead the concrete void of insulin Metrazol electricity hydrotherapy psychotherapy occupational therapy pingpong & amnesia,

who in humorless protest overturned only one symbolic pingpong table, resting briefly in catatonia,

returning years later truly bald except for a wig of blood, and tears and fingers, to the visible madman doom of the wards of the madtowns of the East,

Pilgrim State's Rockland's and Greystone's foetid halls, bickering with the echoes of the soul, rocking and rolling in the midnight solitude-bench dolmen-realms of love, dream of life a nightmare, bodies turned to stone as heavy as the moon,

with mother finally ******, and the last fantastic book flung out of the tenement window, and the last door closed at 4 A.M. and the last telephone slammed at the wall in reply and the last furnished room emptied down to the last piece of mental furniture, a yellow paper rose twisted on a wire hanger in the closet, and even that imaginary, nothing but a hopeful little bit of hallucination—

ah, Carl, while you are not safe I am not safe, and now you're really in the total animal soup of time—

and who therefore ran through the icy streets obsessed with a sudden flash of the alchemy of the use of the ellipsis catalogue a variable measure and the vibrating plane,

who dreamt and made incarnate gaps in Time & Space through images juxtaposed, and trapped the archangel of the soul between 2 visual images and joined the elemental verbs and set the noun and dash

of consciousness together jumping with sensation of Pater Om-
nipotens Aeterna Deus
to recreate the syntax and measure of poor human prose and stand before
you speechless and intelligent and shaking with shame, rejected
yet confessing out the soul to conform to the rhythm of thought in
his naked and endless head,
the madman bum and angel beat in Time, unknown, yet putting down here
what might be left to say in time come after death,
and rose reincarnate in the ghostly clothes of jazz in the goldhorn shadow
of the band and blew the suffering of America's naked mind for
love into an eli eli lamma lamma sabacthani saxophone cry that
shivered the cities down to the last radio
with the absolute heart of the poem of life butchered out of their own
bodies good to eat a thousand years.

II

What sphinx of cement and aluminum bashed open their skulls and ate up
their brains and imagination?
Moloch! Solitude! Filth! Ugliness! Ashcans and unobtainable dollars!
Children screaming under the stairways! Boys sobbing in armies!
Old men weeping in the parks!
Moloch! Moloch! Nightmare of Moloch! Moloch the loveless! Mental
Moloch! Moloch the heavy judger of men!
Moloch the incomprehensible prison! Moloch the crossbone soulless jail-
house and Congress of sorrows! Moloch whose buildings are
judgment! Moloch the vast stone of war! Moloch the stunned
governments!
Moloch whose mind is pure machinery! Moloch whose blood is running
money! Moloch whose fingers are ten armies! Moloch whose
breast is a cannibal dynamo! Moloch whose ear is a smoking tomb!
Moloch whose eyes are a thousand blind windows! Moloch whose sky-
scrapers stand in the long streets like endless Jehovahs! Moloch
whose factories dream and croak in the fog! Moloch whose smoke-
stacks and antennae crown the cities!
Moloch whose love is endless oil and stone! Moloch whose soul is electric-
ity and banks! Moloch whose poverty is the specter of genius!
Moloch whose fate is a cloud of sexless hydrogen! Moloch whose
name is the Mind!
Moloch in whom I sit lonely! Moloch in whom I dream Angels! Crazy in
Moloch! Cocksucker in Moloch! Lacklove and manless in Mo-
loch!

Moloch who entered my soul early! Moloch in whom I am a consciousness without a body! Moloch who frightened me out of my natural ecstasy! Moloch whom I abandon! Wake up in Moloch! Light streaming out of the sky!

Moloch! Moloch! Robot apartments! invisible suburbs! skeleton treasuries! blind capitals! demonic industries! spectral nations! invincible madhouses! granite cocks! monstrous bombs!

They broke their backs lifting Moloch to Heaven! Pavements, trees, radios, tons! lifting the city to Heaven which exists and is everywhere about us!

Visions! omens! hallucinations! miracles! ecstasies! gone down the American river!

Dreams! adorations! illuminations! religions! the whole boatload of sensitive bullshit!

Breakthroughs! over the river! flips and crucifixions! gone down the flood! Highs! Epiphanies! Despairs! Ten years' animal screams and suicides! Minds! New loves! Mad generation! down on the rocks of Time!

Real holy laughter in the river! They saw it all! the wild eyes! the holy yells! They bade farewell! They jumped off the roof! to solitude! waving! carrying flowers! Down to the river! into the street!

III

Carl Solomon! I'm with you in Rockland
    where you're madder than I am
I'm with you in Rockland
    where you must feel very strange
I'm with you in Rockland
    where you imitate the shade of my mother
I'm with you in Rockland
    where you've murdered your twelve secretaries
I'm with you in Rockland
    where you laugh at this invisible humor
I'm with you in Rockland
    where we are great writers on the same dreadful typewriter
I'm with you in Rockland
    where your condition has become serious and is reported on the radio
I'm with you in Rockland
    where the faculties of the skull no longer admit the worms of the senses

I'm with you in Rockland
> where you drink the tea of the breasts of the spinsters of Utica

I'm with you in Rockland
> where you pun on the bodies of your nurses the harpies of the Bronx

I'm with you in Rockland
> where you scream in a straightjacket that you're losing the game of the actual pingpong of the abyss

I'm with you in Rockland
> where you bang on the catatonic piano the soul is innocent and immortal it should never die ungodly in an armed madhouse

I'm with you in Rockland
> where fifty more shocks will never return your soul to its body again from its pilgrimage to a cross in the void

I'm with you in Rockland
> where you accuse your doctors of insanity and plot the Hebrew socialist revolution against the fascist national Golgotha

I'm with you in Rockland
> where you will split the heavens of Long Island and resurrect your living human Jesus from the superhuman tomb

I'm with you in Rockland
> where there are twentyfive thousand mad comrades all together singing the final stanzas of the Internationale

I'm with you in Rockland
> where we hug and kiss the United States under our bedsheets the United States that coughs all night and won't let us sleep

I'm with you in Rockland
> where we wake up electrified out of the coma by our own souls' airplanes roaring over the roof they've come to drop angelic bombs the hospital illuminates itself   imaginary walls collapse   O skinny legions run outside   O starry-spangled shock of mercy the eternal war is here   O victory forget your underwear we're free

I'm with you in Rockland
> in my dreams you walk dripping from a sea-journey on the highway across America in tears to the door of my cottage in the Western night

San Francisco, 1955–1956

Footnote to Howl

Holy! Holy! Holy! Holy! Holy! Holy! Holy! Holy! Holy! Holy! Holy!
   Holy! Holy! Holy! Holy!
The world is holy! The soul is holy! The skin is holy! The nose is holy! The
   tongue and cock and hand and asshole holy!
Everything is holy! everybody's holy! everywhere is holy! everyday is in
   eternity! Everyman's an angel!
The bum's as holy as the seraphim! the madman is holy as you my soul are
   holy!
The typewriter is holy the poem is holy the voice is holy the hearers are
   holy the ecstasy is holy!
Holy Peter holy Allen holy Solomon holy Lucien holy Kerouac holy
   Huncke holy Burroughs holy Cassady holy the unknown bug-
   gered and suffering beggars holy the hideous human angels!
Holy my mother in the insane asylum! Holy the cocks of the grandfathers
   of Kansas!
Holy the groaning saxophone! Holy the bop apocalypse! Holy the jazz-
   bands marijuana hipsters peace peyote pipes & drums!
Holy the solitudes of skyscrapers and pavements! Holy the cafeterias filled
   with the millions! Holy the mysterious rivers of tears under the
   streets!
Holy the lone juggernaut! Holy the vast lamb of the middleclass! Holy the
   crazy shepherds of rebellion! Who digs Los Angeles IS Los An-
   geles!
Holy New York Holy San Francisco Holy Peoria & Seattle Holy Paris
   Holy Tangiers Holy Moscow Holy Istanbul!
Holy time in eternity holy eternity in time holy the clocks in space holy the
   fourth dimension holy the fifth International holy the Angel in
   Moloch!
Holy the sea holy the desert holy the railroad holy the locomotive holy the
   visions holy the hallucinations holy the miracles holy the eyeball
   holy the abyss!
Holy forgiveness! mercy! charity! faith! Holy! Ours! bodies! suffering!
   magnanimity!
Holy the supernatural extra brilliant intelligent kindness of the soul!

Berkeley, 1955

A Strange New Cottage in Berkeley

All afternoon cutting bramble blackberries off a tottering brown fence

under a low branch with its rotten old apricots miscellaneous under the leaves,

fixing the drip in the intricate gut machinery of a new toilet;

found a good coffeepot in the vines by the porch, rolled a big tire out of the scarlet bushes, hid my marijuana;

wet the flowers, playing the sunlit water each to each, returning for godly extra drops for the stringbeans and daisies;

three times walked round the grass and sighed absently:

my reward, when the garden fed me its plums from the form of a small tree in the corner,

an angel thoughtful of my stomach, and my dry and lovelorn tongue.

1955

Block print by Robert LaVigne

A Supermarket in California

What thoughts I have of you tonight, Walt Whitman, for I walked down the sidestreets under the trees with a headache self-conscious looking at the full moon.

In my hungry fatigue, and shopping for images, I went into the neon fruit supermarket, dreaming of your enumerations!

What peaches and what penumbras! Whole families shopping at night! Aisles full of husbands! Wives in the avocados, babies in the tomatoes!—and you, García Lorca, what were you doing down by the watermelons?

I saw you, Walt Whitman, childless, lonely old grubber, poking among the meats in the refrigerator and eyeing the grocery boys.

I heard you asking questions of each: Who killed the pork chops? What price bananas? Are you my Angel?

I wandered in and out of the brilliant stacks of cans following you, and followed in my imagination by the store detective.

We strode down the open corridors together in our solitary fancy tasting artichokes, possessing every frozen delicacy, and never passing the cashier.

Where are we going, Walt Whitman? The doors close in an hour. Which way does your beard point tonight?

(I touch your book and dream of our odyssey in the supermarket and feel absurd.)

Will we walk all night through solitary streets? The trees add shade to shade, lights out in the houses, we'll both be lonely.

Will we stroll dreaming of the lost America of love past blue automobiles in driveways, home to our silent cottage?

Ah, dear father, graybeard, lonely old courage-teacher, what America did you have when Charon quit poling his ferry and you got out on a smoking bank and stood watching the boat disappear on the black waters of Lethe?

Berkeley, 1955

Sunflower Sutra

I walked on the banks of the tincan banana dock and sat down under the
huge shade of a Southern Pacific locomotive to look at the sunset
over the box house hills and cry.

Jack Kerouac sat beside me on a busted rusty iron pole, companion, we
thought the same thoughts of the soul, bleak and blue and sad-
eyed, surrounded by the gnarled steel roots of trees of machinery.

The oily water on the river mirrored the red sky, sun sank on top of final
Frisco peaks, no fish in that stream, no hermit in those mounts,
just ourselves rheumy-eyed and hung-over like old bums on the
riverbank, tired and wily.

Look at the Sunflower, he said, there was a dead gray shadow against the
sky, big as a man, sitting dry on top of a pile of ancient sawdust—

—I rushed up enchanted—it was my first sunflower, memories of Blake—
my visions—Harlem

and Hells of the Eastern rivers, bridges clanking Joes Greasy Sandwiches,
dead baby carriages, black treadless tires forgotten and unre-
treaded, the poem of the riverbank, condoms & pots, steel knives,
nothing stainless, only the dank muck and the razor-sharp artifacts
passing into the past—

and the gray Sunflower poised against the sunset, crackly bleak and dusty
with the smut and smog and smoke of olden locomotives in its
eye—

corolla of bleary spikes pushed down and broken like a battered crown,
seeds fallen out of its face, soon-to-be-toothless mouth of sunny
air, sunrays obliterated on its hairy head like a dried wire spider-
web,

leaves stuck out like arms out of the stem, gestures from the sawdust root,
broke pieces of plaster fallen out of the black twigs, a dead fly in its
ear,

Unholy battered old thing you were, my sunflower O my soul, I loved you
then!

The grime was no man's grime but death and human locomotives,

all that dress of dust, that veil of darkened railroad skin, that smog of cheek,
that eyelid of black mis'ry, that sooty hand or phallus or pro-
tuberance of artificial worse-than-dirt—industrial—modern—all
that civilization spotting your crazy golden crown—

and those blear thoughts of death and dusty loveless eyes and ends and
withered roots below, in the home-pile of sand and sawdust, rub-

ber dollar bills, skin of machinery, the guts and innards of the weeping coughing car, the empty lonely tincans with their rusty tongues alack, what more could I name, the smoked ashes of some cock cigar, the cunts of wheelbarrows and the milky breasts of cars, wornout asses out of chairs & sphincters of dynamos—all these entangled in your mummied roots—and you there standing before me in the sunset, all your glory in your form!

A perfect beauty of a sunflower! a perfect excellent lovely sunflower existence! a sweet natural eye to the new hip moon, woke up alive and excited grasping in the sunset shadow sunrise golden monthly breeze!

How many flies buzzed round you innocent of your grime, while you cursed the heavens of the railroad and your flower soul?

Poor dead flower? when did you forget you were a flower? when did you look at your skin and decide you were an impotent dirty old locomotive? the ghost of a locomotive? the specter and shade of a once powerful mad American locomotive?

You were never no locomotive, Sunflower, you were a sunflower!

And you Locomotive, you are a locomotive, forget me not!

So I grabbed up the skeleton thick sunflower and stuck it at my side like a scepter,

and deliver my sermon to my soul, and Jack's soul too, and anyone who'll listen,

—We're not our skin of grime, we're not dread bleak dusty imageless locomotives, we're golden sunflowers inside, blessed by our own seed & hairy naked accomplishment-bodies growing into mad black formal sunflowers in the sunset, spied on by our own eyes under the shadow of the mad locomotive riverbank sunset Frisco hilly tincan evening sitdown vision.

Berkeley, 1955

America

America I've given you all and now I'm nothing.
America two dollars and twentyseven cents January 17, 1956.
I can't stand my own mind.
America when will we end the human war?
Go fuck yourself with your atom bomb.
I don't feel good don't bother me.
I won't write my poem till I'm in my right mind.
America when will you be angelic?
When will you take off your clothes?
When will you look at yourself through the grave?
When will you be worthy of your million Trotskyites?
America why are your libraries full of tears?
America when will you send your eggs to India?
I'm sick of your insane demands.
When can I go into the supermarket and buy what I need with my good
      looks?
America after all it is you and I who are perfect not the next world.
Your machinery is too much for me.
You made me want to be a saint.
There must be some other way to settle this argument.
Burroughs is in Tangiers I don't think he'll come back it's sinister.
Are you being sinister or is this some form of practical joke?
I'm trying to come to the point.
I refuse to give up my obsession.
America stop pushing I know what I'm doing.
America the plum blossoms are falling.
I haven't read the newspapers for months, everyday somebody goes on trial
      for murder.
America I feel sentimental about the Wobblies.
America I used to be a communist when I was a kid I'm not sorry.
I smoke marijuana every chance I get.
I sit in my house for days on end and stare at the roses in the closet.
When I go to Chinatown I get drunk and never get laid.
My mind is made up there's going to be trouble.
You should have seen me reading Marx.
My psychoanalyst thinks I'm perfectly right.
I won't say the Lord's Prayer.
I have mystical visions and cosmic vibrations.

America I still haven't told you what you did to Uncle Max after he came
    over from Russia.
I'm addressing you.
Are you going to let your emotional life be run by Time Magazine?
I'm obsessed by Time Magazine.
I read it every week.
Its cover stares at me every time I slink past the corner candystore.
I read it in the basement of the Berkeley Public Library.
It's always telling me about responsibility. Businessmen are serious.
    Movie producers are serious. Everybody's serious but me.
It occurs to me that I am America.
I am talking to myself again.

Asia is rising against me.
I haven't got a chinaman's chance.
I'd better consider my national resources.
My national resources consist of two joints of marijuana millions of geni-
    tals an unpublishable private literature that jetplanes 1400 miles an
    hour and twentyfive-thousand mental institutions.
I say nothing about my prisons nor the millions of underprivileged who
    live in my flowerpots under the light of five hundred suns.
I have abolished the whorehouses of France, Tangiers is the next to go.
My ambition is to be President despite the fact that I'm a Catholic.

America how can I write a holy litany in your silly mood?
I will continue like Henry Ford my strophes are as individual as his
    automobiles more so they're all different sexes.
America I will sell you strophes $2500 apiece $500 down on your old
    strophe
America free Tom Mooney
America save the Spanish Loyalists
America Sacco & Vanzetti must not die
America I am the Scottsboro boys.
America when I was seven momma took me to Communist Cell meetings
    they sold us garbanzos a handful per ticket a ticket costs a nickel
    and the speeches were free everybody was angelic and sentimental
    about the workers it was all so sincere you have no idea what a
    good thing the party was in 1835 Scott Nearing was a grand old
    man a real mensch Mother Bloor the Silk-strikers' Ewig-
    Weibliche made me cry I once saw the Yiddish orator Israel Amter
    plain. Everybody must have been a spy.
America you don't really want to go to war.

America it's them bad Russians.

Them Russians them Russians and them Chinamen. And them Russians.

The Russia wants to eat us alive. The Russia's power mad. She wants to take our cars from out our garages.

Her wants to grab Chicago. Her needs a Red *Reader's Digest*. Her wants our auto plants in Siberia. Him big bureaucracy running our fillingstations.

That no good. Ugh. Him make Indians learn read. Him need big black niggers. Hah. Her make us all work sixteen hours a day. Help.

America this is quite serious.

America this is the impression I get from looking in the television set.

America is this correct?

I'd better get right down to the job.

It's true I don't want to join the Army or turn lathes in precision parts factories, I'm nearsighted and psychopathic anyway.

America I'm putting my queer shoulder to the wheel.

Berkeley, January 17, 1956

Many Loves

"Resolved to sing no songs henceforth but those of manly attachment"

—WALT WHITMAN

Neal Cassady was my animal: he brought me to my knees
and taught me the love of his cock and the secrets of his mind
And we met and conversed, went walking in the evening by the park
Up to Harlem, recollecting Denver, and Dan Budd, a hero
And we made shift to sack out in Harlem, after a long evening,
Jack and host in a large double bed, I volunteered for the cot, and Neal
Volunteered for the cot with me, we stripped and lay down.
I wore my underwear, my shorts, and he his briefs—
lights out on the narrow bed I turned to my side, with my back to his Irish
      boy's torso,
and huddled and balanced on the edge, and kept distance—
and hung my head over and kept my arm over the side, withdrawn
And he seeing my fear stretched out his arm, and put it around my breast
Saying "Draw near me" and gathered me in upon him:
I lay there trembling, and felt his great arm like a king's
And his breasts, his heart slow thudding against my back,
and his middle torso, narrow and made of iron, soft at my back,
his fiery firm belly warming me while I trembled—
His belly of fists and starvation, his belly a thousand girls kissed in Colo-
      rado
his belly of rocks thrown over Denver roofs, prowess of jumping and fists,
      his stomach of solitudes,
His belly of burning iron and jails affectionate to my side:
I began to tremble, he pulled me in closer with his arm, and hugged me
      long and close
my soul melted, secrecy departed, I became
Thenceforth open to his nature as a flower in the shining sun.
And below his belly, in white underwear, tight between my buttocks,
His own loins against me soft, nestling in comradeship, put forth & pressed
      into me, open to my awareness,
slowly began to grow, signal me further and deeper affection, sexual ten-
      derness.
So gentle the man, so sweet the moment, so kind the thighs that nuzzled
      against me smooth-skinned powerful, warm by my legs
That my body shudders and trembles with happiness, remembering—
His hand opened up on my belly, his palms and fingers flat against my skin

I fell to him, and turned, shifting, put my face on his arm resting,
my chest against his, he helped me to turn, and held me closer
his arm at my back beneath my head, and arm at my buttocks tender
holding me in,
our bellies together nestling, loins touched together, pressing and knowl-
edgeable each other's hardness, and mine stuck out of my under-
wear.
Then I pressed in closer and drew my leg up between his, and he lay half on
me with his thighs and bedded me down close, caressing
and moved together pressing his cock to my thigh and mine to his
slowly, and slowly began a love match that continues in my imagination to
this day a full decade.
Thus I met Neal & thus we felt each other's flesh and owned each other
bodies and souls.
So then as I lay on his breast with my arms clasped around his neck and his
cheek against mine,
I put my hand down to feel his great back for the first time, jaws and
pectorals of steel at my fingers,
closer and stiller, down the silken iron back to his waist, the whole of his
torso now open
my hand at his waist trembling, waited delaying and under the elastic of his
briefs,
I first touched the smooth mount of his rock buttocks, silken in power,
rounded in animal fucking and bodily nights over nurses and
schoolgirls,
O ass of long solitudes in stolen cars, and solitudes on curbs, musing fist in
cheek,
Ass of a thousand farewells, ass of youth, youth's lovers,
Ass of a thousand lonely craps in gas stations ass of great painful secrecies
of the years
O ass of mystery and night! ass of gymnasiums and muscular pants
ass of high schools and masturbation ass of lone delight, ass of mankind, so
beautiful and hollow, dowry of Mind and Angels,
Ass of hero, Neal Cassady, I had at my hand: my fingers traced the curve to
the bottom of his thighs.
I raised my thighs and stripped down my shorts to my knees, and bent to
push them off
and he raised me up from his chest, and pulled down his pants the same,
humble and meek and obedient to his mood our silence,
and naked at long last with angel & greek & athlete & hero and brother
and boy of my dreams
I lay with my hair intermixed with his, he asking me "What shall we do
now?"

—And confessed, years later, he thinking I was not a queer at first to please
       me & serve me, to blow me and make me come, maybe or if I were
       queer, that's what I'd likely want of a dumb bastard like him.
But I made my first mistake, and made him then and there my master, and
       bowed my head, and holding his buttock
Took up his hard-on and held it, feeling it throb and pressing my own at his
       knee & breathing showed him I needed him, cock, for my dreams
       of insatiety & lone love.

—And I lie here naked in the dark, dreaming

Arctic, August 10, 1956

IV

REALITY SANDWICHES:
EUROPE!
EUROPE!

(1957–1959)

'Scribbled secret notebooks, and wild typewritten pages, for yr own joy'

To
the Pure Imaginary
POET
Gregory Corso

Death to Van Gogh's Ear!

Poet is Priest
Money has reckoned the soul of America
Congress broken thru to the precipice of Eternity
the President built a War machine which will vomit and rear up Russia out
      of Kansas
The American Century betrayed by a mad Senate which no longer sleeps
      with its wife
Franco has murdered Lorca the fairy son of Whitman
just as Mayakovsky committed suicide to avoid Russia
Hart Crane distinguished Platonist committed suicide to cave in the wrong
      America
just as millions of tons of human wheat were burned in secret caverns
      under the White House
while India starved and screamed and ate mad dogs full of rain
and mountains of eggs were reduced to white powder in the halls of
      Congress
no godfearing man will walk there again because of the stink of the rotten
      eggs of America
and the Indians of Chiapas continue to gnaw their vitaminless tortillas
aborigines of Australia perhaps gibber in the eggless wilderness
and I rarely have an egg for breakfast tho my work requires infinite eggs to
      come to birth in Eternity
eggs should be eaten or given to their mothers
and the grief of the countless chickens of America is expressed in the
      screaming of her comedians over the radio
Detroit has built a million automobiles of rubber trees and phantoms
but I walk, I walk, and the Orient walks with me, and all Africa walks
and sooner or later North America will walk
Einstein alive was mocked for his heavenly politics
Bertrand Russell driven from New York for getting laid
immortal Chaplin driven from our shores with the rose in his teeth
a secret conspiracy by Catholic Church in the lavatories of Congress has
      denied contraceptives to the unceasing masses of India.
Nobody publishes a word that is not the cowardly robot ravings of a
      depraved mentality
The day of the publication of the true literature of the American body will
      be day of Revolution
the revolution of the sexy lamb

the only bloodless revolution that gives away corn
poor Genet will illuminate the harvesters of Ohio
Marijuana is a benevolent narcotic but J. Edgar Hoover prefers his deathly
    scotch
And the heroin of Lao-Tze & the Sixth Patriarch is punished by the
    electric chair
but the poor sick junkies have nowhere to lay their heads
fiends in our government have invented a cold-turkey cure for addiction as
    obsolete as the Defense Early Warning Radar System.
I am the defense early warning radar system
I see nothing but bombs
I am not interested in preventing Asia from being Asia
and the governments of Russia and Asia will rise and fall but Asia and
    Russia will not fall
the government of America also will fall but how can America fall
I doubt if anyone will ever fall anymore except governments
fortunately all the governments will fall
the only ones which won't fall are the good ones
and the good ones don't yet exist
But they have to begin existing they exist in my poems
they exist in the death of the Russian and American governments
they exist in the death of Hart Crane & Mayakovsky
Now is the time for prophecy without death as a consequence
the universe will ultimately disappear
Hollywood will rot on the windmills of Eternity
Hollywood whose movies stick in the throat of God
Yes Hollywood will get what it deserves
Time
Seepage of nerve-gas over the radio
History will make this poem prophetic and its awful silliness a hideous
    spiritual music
I have the moan of doves and the feather of ecstasy
Man cannot long endure the hunger of the cannibal abstract
War is abstract
the world will be destroyed
but I will die only for poetry, that will save the world
Monument to Sacco & Vanzetti not yet financed to ennoble Boston
Vachel Lindsay Secretary of the Interior
Poe Secretary of Imagination
Pound Secty. Economics
and Kra belongs to Kra, and Pukti to Pukti
crossfertilization of Blok and Artaud

Van Gogh's Ear on the currency
no more propaganda for monsters
and poets should stay out of politics or become monsters
I have become monsterous with politics
the Russian poet undoubtedly monsterous in his secret notebook
Tibet should be left alone
These are obvious prophecies
America will be destroyed
Russian poets will struggle with Russia
Whitman warned against this "fabled Damned of nations"
Where was Theodore Roosevelt when he sent out ultimatums from his
    castle in Camden
Where was the House of Representatives when Crane read aloud from his
    prophetic books
What was Wall Street scheming when Lindsay announced the doom of
    Money
Were they listening to my ravings in the locker rooms of Bickfords Em-
    ployment Offices?
Did they bend their ears to the moans of my soul when I struggled with
    market research statistics in the Forum at Rome?
No they were fighting in fiery offices, on carpets of heartfailure, screaming
    and bargaining with Destiny
fighting the Skeleton with sabers, muskets, buck teeth, indigestion, bombs
    of larceny, whoredom, rockets, pederasty,
back to the wall to build up their wives and apartments, lawns, suburbs,
    fairydoms,
Puerto Ricans crowded for massacre on 114th St. for the sake of an
    imitation Chinese-Moderne refrigerator
Elephants of mercy murdered for the sake of an Elizabethan birdcage
millions of agitated fanatics in the bughouse for the sake of the screaming
    soprano of industry
Money-chant of soapers—toothpaste apes in television sets—deodorizers
    on hypnotic chairs—
petroleum mongers in Texas—jet plane streaks among the clouds—
sky writers liars in the face of Divinity—fanged butchers of hats and shoes,
    all Owners! Owners! Owners! with obsession on property and
    vanishing Selfhood!
and their long editorials on the fence of the screaming negro attacked by
    ants crawled out of the front page!
Machinery of a mass electrical dream! A war-creating Whore of Babylon
    bellowing over Capitols and Academies!

Money! Money! Money! shrieking mad celestial money of illusion! Money
      made of nothing, starvation, suicide! Money of failure! Money of
      death!
Money against Eternity! and eternity's strong mills grind out vast paper of
      Illusion!

Paris, December 1957

The Lion for Real

"Soyez muette pour moi, Idole contemplative . . ."

I came home and found a lion in my living room
Rushed out on the fire escape screaming Lion! Lion!
Two stenographers pulled their brunette hair and banged the window shut
I hurried home to Paterson and stayed two days.

Called up my old Reichian analyst
who'd kicked me out of therapy for smoking marijuana
'It's happened' I panted 'There's a Lion in my room'
'I'm afraid any discussion would have no value' he hung up.

I went to my old boyfriend we got drunk with his girlfriend
I kissed him and announced I had a lion with a mad gleam in my eye
We wound up fighting on the floor I bit his eyebrow & he kicked me out
I ended masturbating in his jeep parked in the street moaning 'Lion.'

Found Joey my novelist friend and roared at him 'Lion!'
He looked at me interested and read me his spontaneous ignu high poetries
I listened for lions all I heard was Elephant Tiglon Hippogriff Unicorn
     Ants
But figured he really understood me when we made it in Ignaz Wisdom's
     bathroom.

But next day he sent me a leaf from his Smoky Mountain retreat
'I love you little Bo-Bo with your delicate golden lions
But there being no Self and No Bars therefore the Zoo of your dear Father
     hath no Lion
You said your mother was mad don't expect me to produce the Monster for
     your Bridegroom.'

Confused dazed and exalted bethought me of real lion starved in his stink
     in Harlem
Opened the door the room was filled with the bomb blast of his anger
He roaring hungrily at the plaster walls but nobody could hear him outside
     thru the window
My eye caught the edge of the red neighbor apartment building standing in
     deafening stillness

We gazed at each other his implacable yellow eye in the red halo of fur
Waxed rheumy on my own but he stopped roaring and bared a fang
 greeting.
I turned my back and cooked broccoli for supper on an iron gas stove
boilt water and took a hot bath in the old tub under the sink board.

He didn't eat me, tho I regretted him starving in my presence.
Next week he wasted away a sick rug full of bones wheaten hair falling out
enraged and reddening eye as he lay aching huge hairy head on his paws
by the egg-crate bookcase filled up with thin volumes of Plato, & Buddha.

Sat by his side every night averting my eyes from his hungry motheaten
 face
stopped eating myself he got weaker and roared at night while I had
 nightmares
Eaten by lion in bookstore on Cosmic Campus, a lion myself starved by
 Professor Kandisky, dying in a lion's flophouse circus,
I woke up mornings the lion still added dying on the floor—'Terrible
 Presence!' I cried 'Eat me or die!'

It got up that afternoon—walked to the door with its paw on the wall to
 steady its trembling body
Let out a soul-rending creak from the bottomless roof of his mouth
thundering from my floor to heaven heavier than a volcano at night in
 Mexico
Pushed the door open and said in a gravelly voice "Not this time Baby—
 but I will be back again."

Lion that eats my mind now for a decade knowing only your hunger
Not the bliss of your satisfaction O roar of the Universe how am I chosen
In this life I have heard your promise I am ready to die I have served
Your starved and ancient Presence O Lord I wait in my room at your
 Mercy.

Paris, March 1958

The Names

Time comes spirit weakens and goes blank apartments shuffled through
   and forgotten
The dead in their cenotaphs locomotive high schools & African cities small
   town motorcycle graves
O America what saints given vision are shrouded in junk their elegy a
   nameless hoodlum elegance leaning against death's military garage
Huncke who first saw the sun revolve in Chicago survived into middle-age
   Times Square
Thief stole hearts of wildcat tractor boys arrived to morphine brilliance
   Bickford table midnight neon to take a fall
arrested 41 times late 40s his acned skin & black Spanish hair grown coy
   and old and lip bitten in Rikers Island Jail
as bestial newsprint photograph we shared once busted, me scared of black
   eye cops of Manhattan
you blissful nothing to lose digging the live detectives perhaps even offer-
   ing God a cigarette
I'll answer for you Huncke I never could before—admiring your natural
   tact and charm and irony—now sad Sing Sing
whatever inept Queens burglary you goofed again let God judge his sacred
   case
rather than mustached Time Judge steal a dirty photograph of your soul—
   I knew you when—
& you loved me better than my lawyer who wanted a frightened rat for
   official thousand buck mousetrap, no doubt, no doubt—
Shine in Cell free behind bars Immortal soul why not
Hell the machine can't sentence anyone except itself, have I to do that?
It gives jail I give you poem, bars last twenty years rust in a hundred
my handwork remains when prisons fall because the hand is compassion

Brilliant bitter Morphy stalking Los Angeles after his ghost boy
haunting basements in Denver with his Montmartre black beard
Charming ladies' man for gigolo purpose I heard, great cat for Shake-
   spearean sex
first poet suicide I knew we sat on park benches I watched him despair his
   forehead star
my elder asked serious advice, gentle man! international queer pride hum-
   bled to pre-death cigarette gun fright
His love a young blond demon of broken army, his nemesis his own mad
   cock for the kids sardonic ass

his dream mouthful of white prick trembling in his head—woke a bullet in
his side days later in Passaic
last moments gasping stricken blood under stars coughing intestines &
lighted highway cars flowing past his eyes into the dark.

Joe Army's beauty forgotten that night, pain cops nightmare, drunken
AWOL through Detroit
phonecalls angels backrooms & courtsmartial lawyers trains a kaleido-
scope of instant change,
shrinkage of soul, bearded dead dreams, all Balzac read in jail,
late disappearance from the city hides metamorphosis to humancy loath-
ing that deathscene.

Phil Black hung in Tombs, horsefaced junky, dreamy strange murderer,
forgotten pistol three buck holdup, stoolpigeon suicide I save him
from the grave

Iroquois his indian head red cock intelligence buried in miserous solitaire
politics
his narcissistic blond haired hooknosed pride, I made him once he groaned
and came
Later stranger chill made me tremble, I loved him hopeless years,
he's hid in Seattle consumed by lesbian hypochondrias' stealthy commu-
nion, green bullfighters envy age,
unless I save him from the grave, but he won't talk no more
much less fall in my arms or any mental bed forgiveness before we climb
Olympics death

Carl returning to bughouse monkishness & drear stinky soupdish his
fatness fright & suffering mind insult a repetitious void
"I have done my best to make saintliness as uninteresting as possible"
and has succeeded, when did I last write or receive ambiguous message
joky hangdog prophetic Jew

Joan in dreams bent forward smiling asks news of the living
as in life the same sad tolerance, no skullbone judge of drunks
asking whereabouts sending regards from Mexican paradise garden where
life & death are one
as if a postcard from eternity sent with human hand, wish I could see you
now, it's happening as should
whatever we really need, we ought get, don't blame yourself—a photo-
graph on reverse

the rare tomb smile where trees grow crooked energy above grass—
yet died early-old teeth gone, tequila bottle in hand, an infantile paralysis
limp, lacklove, the worst—
I dreamed such vision of her secret in my frisco bed, heart can live the rest
by my, or her, best desire—love

Bill King black haired sorry drunken wop lawyer, woke up trembling in
Connecticut DT's among cows
Him there to recover I guess, but made his way back to New York shudder-
ing to fuck stiff *Time* girls,
Death charm in person, sexual childlike radiant pain
See his face in old photographs & bandaged naked wrist leaning melan-
choly contemplating the camera
awkward face now calm, kind to me in cafeteria one sober morn looking for
jobs at breakfast,
but mostly smiled at roof edge midnight, all 1920s elegance reincarnate in
black vomit bestriven suit
& screechy records *Mahagonny* airplane crash, lushed young man of 1940s
hated his fairy woe, came on Lizzie's belly or Ansen's sock in
desperate orgies of music canopener
God but I loved his murdered face when he talked with a mouthful of rain
in 14th St subway—
where he fell skull broken underground last, head crushed by the radiant
wheel on iron track at Astor Place
Farewell dear Bill that's done, you're gone, we all go into the ancient void
drunkard mouth
you made it too soon, here was more to say, & more to drink, but now too
late to sit and talk
all night toward the eternity you sought so well so fearlessly in so much
alcoholic pain with so much fire behind eyes with such
sweet manner in your heart that never won a happy fate thru what bleak
years you saw your red skull burning deathshead in the U.S. sun

Mix living dead, Neal Cassady, old hero of travel love alyosha idiot seek-
train poems, what crown you wear at last
what fameless reward for patience & pain, what golden whore come secret
from the clouds, what has god bidden for your coffin and heart
someday,
what will give back your famous arm, your happy catholic boy eye, orphan
torso shining in poolhall & library, intimate spermworks with old
girls downtown rockabelly energy,
what Paradise built high enough to hold your desire, deep enough to

encompass your cock kindnesses, soft for your children to pray, 10
foot iron wheels you fell under?
what American heaven receive you? Christ allow sufferings then will he
allow you His opening tinbarrel Iowa light as Jerusalem?
O Neal that life end we together on knees know harvest of prayers to-
gether,
Paradise autos ascend to the moon no illusion, short time earth life Bibles
bear our eyes, make it dear baby
Stay with me Angel now in Shroud of railroad lost bet racetrack broke leg
oblivion
till I get the shining Word or you the cockless cock to lay in my ass hope
mental radiance—
It's all lost we fall without glory to empty tomb comedown to nothing but
evil thinkless worm, but we know better
merely by old heart hope, or merely Desire, or merely the love whisper
breathed in your ear on lawns of long gone by Denver,
merely by the night you leaned on my body & held me for All & called me
to Adore what I wondered at as child age ten I
wandered by hopeless green hedges, when you sat under alley balcony
garbagestair, ache in our breasts for Futurity
meeting Love for Love, so wept as child now man I weep for true end,
Save from the grave! O Neal I love you I bring this Lamb into the middle
of the world happily—O tenderness—to see you again—O
tenderness—to recognize you in the middle of Time.

Paris, Spring 1958

Message

Since we had changed
rogered spun worked
wept and pissed together
I wake up in the morning
with a dream in my eyes
but you are gone in NY
remembering me Good
I love you I love you
& your brothers are crazy
I accept their drunk cases
It's too long that I have been alone
it's too long that I've sat up in bed
without anyone to touch on the knee, man
or woman I don't care what anymore, I
want love I was born for I want you with me now
Ocean liners boiling over the Atlantic
Delicate steelwork of unfinished skyscrapers
Back end of the dirigible roaring over Lakehurst
Six women dancing together on a red stage naked
The leaves are green on all the trees in Paris now
I will be home in two months and look you in the eyes

Paris, May 1958

To Lindsay

Vachel, the stars are out
dusk has fallen on the Colorado road
a car crawls slowly across the plain
in the dim light the radio blares its jazz
the heartbroken salesman lights another cigarette
In another city 27 years ago
I see your shadow on the wall
you're sitting in your suspenders on the bed
the shadow hand lifts up a Lysol bottle to your head
your shade falls over on the floor

Paris, May 1958

To Aunt Rose

Aunt Rose—now—might I see you
with your thin face and buck tooth smile and pain
              of rheumatism—and a long black heavy shoe
              for your bony left leg
limping down the long hall in Newark on the running carpet
              past the black grand piano
              in the day room
                        where the parties were
              and I sang Spanish loyalist songs
              in a high squeaky voice
                        (hysterical) the committee listening
              while you limped around the room
              collected the money—
Aunt Honey, Uncle Sam, a stranger with a cloth arm
              in his pocket
                        and huge young bald head
                        of Abraham Lincoln Brigade

—your long sad face
              your tears of sexual frustration
                        (what smothered sobs and bony hips
                        under the pillows of Osborne Terrace)
—the time I stood on the toilet seat naked
              and you powdered my thighs with calamine
              against the poison ivy—my tender
                        and shamed first black curled hairs
what were you thinking in secret heart then
              knowing me a man already—
and I an ignorant girl of family silence on the thin pedestal
              of my legs in the bathroom—Museum of Newark.

              Aunt Rose
Hitler is dead, Hitler is in Eternity; Hitler is with
              Tamburlane and Emily Brontë

Though I see you walking still, a ghost on Osborne Terrace
              down the long dark hall to the front door
              limping a little with a pinched smile

in what must have been a silken
flower dress
welcoming my father, the Poet, on his visit to Newark
—see you arriving in the living room
dancing on your crippled leg
and clapping hands his book
had been accepted by Liveright

Hitler is dead and Liveright's gone out of business
The Attic of the Past and *Everlasting Minute* are out of print
Uncle Harry sold his last silk stocking
Claire quit interpretive dancing school
Buba sits a wrinkled monument in Old
Ladies Home blinking at new babies

last time I saw you was the hospital
pale skull protruding under ashen skin
blue veined unconscious girl
in an oxygen tent
the war in Spain has ended long ago
Aunt Rose

Paris, June 1958

My Sad Self

To Frank O'Hara

Sometimes when my eyes are red
I go up on top of the RCA Building
    and gaze at my world, Manhattan—
        my buildings, streets I've done feats in,
          lofts, beds, coldwater flats
—on Fifth Ave below which I also bear in mind,
    its ant cars, little yellow taxis, men
      walking the size of specks of wool—
    Panorama of the bridges, sunrise over Brooklyn machine,
      sun go down over New Jersey where I was born
        & Paterson where I played with ants—
my later loves on 15th Street,
    my greater loves of Lower East Side,
      my once fabulous amours in the Bronx
          faraway—
paths crossing in these hidden streets,
    my history summed up, my absences
      and ecstasies in Harlem—
—sun shining down on all I own
    in one eyeblink to the horizon
      in my last eternity—
          matter is water.

Sad,
    I take the elevator and go
      down, pondering,
and walk on the pavements staring into all man's
          plateglass, faces,
    questioning after who loves,
and stop, bemused
    in front of an automobile shopwindow
standing lost in calm thought,
    traffic moving up & down 5th Avenue blocks behind me
    waiting for a moment when . . .

Time to go home & cook supper & listen to
    the romantic war news on the radio
      . . . all movement stops

& I walk in the timeless sadness of existence,
     tenderness flowing thru the buildings,
          my fingertips touching reality's face,
     my own face streaked with tears in the mirror
of some window—at dusk—
                         where I have no desire—
     for bonbons—or to own the dresses or Japanese
          lampshades of intellection—

Confused by the spectacle around me,
     Man struggling up the street
          with packages, newspapers,
                              ties, beautiful suits
          toward his desire
     Man, woman, streaming over the pavements
          red lights clocking hurried watches &
               movements at the curb—

And all these streets leading
     so crosswise, honking, lengthily,
          by avenues
     stalked by high buildings or crusted into slums
          thru such halting traffic
                         screaming cars and engines
so painfully to this
     countryside, this graveyard
          this stillness
                         on deathbed or mountain
     once seen
               never regained or desired
                    in the mind to come
where all Manhattan that I've seen must disappear.

New York, October 1958

Ignu

On top of that if you know me I pronounce you an ignu
Ignu knows nothing of the world
a great ignoramus in factories though he may own or inspire them or even
     be production manager
Ignu has knowledge of the angel indeed ignu is angel in comical form
W. C. Fields Harpo Marx ignus Whitman an ignu
Rimbaud a natural ignu in his boy pants
The ignu may be queer though like not kind ignu blows archangels for the
     strange thrill
a gnostic women love him Christ overflowed with trembling semen for
     many a dead aunt
He's a great cocksman most beautiful girls are worshipped by ignu
Hollywood dolls or lone Marys of Idaho long-legged publicity women and
     secret housewives
have known ignu in another lifetime and remember their lover
Husbands also are secretly tender to ignu their buddy
oldtime friendship can do anything cuckold bugger drunk trembling and
     happy
Ignu lives only once and eternally and knows it
he sleeps in everybody's bed everyone's lonesome for ignu ignu knew
     solitude early
So ignu's a primitive of cock and mind
equally the ignu has written liverish tomes personal metaphysics abstract
images that scratch the moon 'lightningflash-flintspark' naked lunch fried
     shoes adios king
The shadow of the angel is waving in the opposite direction
dawn of intelligence turns the telephones into strange animals
he attacks the rose garden with his mystical shears snip snip snip
Ignu has painted Park Avenue with his own long melancholy
and ignu giggles in a hard chair over tea in Paris bald in his decaying room
     a black hotel
Ignu with his wild mop walks by Colosseum weeping
he plucks a clover from Keats' grave & Shelley's a blade of grass
knew Coleridge they had slow hung-up talks at midnight over mahogany
     tables in London
sidestreet rooms in wintertime rain outside fog the cabman blows his hand
Charles Dickens is born ignu hears the wail of the babe
Ignu goofs nights under bridges and laughs at battleships

ignu is a battleship without guns in the North Sea lost O the flowerness of
    the moment
he knows geography he was there before he'll get out and die already
reborn a bearded humming Jew of Arabian mournful jokes
man with a star on his forehead and halo over his cranium
listening to music musing happy at the fall of a leaf the moonlight of
    immortality in his hair
table-hopping most elegant comrade of all most delicate mannered in the
    Sufi court
he wasn't even there at all
wearing zodiacal blue sleeves and the long peaked conehat of a magician
harkening to the silence of a well at midnight under a red star
in the lobby of Rockefeller Center attentive courteous bare-eyed enthusi-
    astic with or without pants
he listens to jazz as if he were a negro afflicted with jewish melancholy and
    white divinity
Ignu's a natural you can see it when he pays the cabfare abstracted
pulling off the money from an impossible saintly roll
or counting his disappearing pennies to give to the strange busdriver
    whom he admires
Ignu has sought you out he's the seeker of God
and God breaks down the world for him every ten years
he sees lightning flash in empty daylight when the sky is blue
he hears Blake's disembodied Voice recite the Sunflower in a room in
    Harlem
No woe on him surrounded by 700 thousand mad scholars moths fly out of
    his sleeve
He wants to die give up go mad break through into Eternity
live on and teach an aged saint or break down to an eyebrow clown
All ignus know each other in a moment's talk and measure each other up at
    once
as lifetime friends romantic winks and giggles across continents
sad moment paying the cab goodbye and speeding away uptown
One or two grim ignus in the pack
one laughing monk in dungarees
one delighted by cracking his eggs in an egg cup
one chews gum to music all night long rock and roll
one anthropologist cuckoo in the Petén rainforest
one sits in jail all year and bets karmaic racetrack
one chases girls down East Broadway into the horror movie
one pulls out withered grapes and rotten onions from his pants
one has a nannygoat under his bed to amuse visitors plasters the wall with
    his crap

collects scorpions whiskies skies etc. would steal the moon if he could
        find it
That would set fire to America but none of these make ignu
it's the soul that makes the style the tender firecracker of his thought
the amity of letters from strange cities to old friends
and the new radiance of morning on a foreign bed
A comedy of personal being his grubby divinity
Eliot probably an ignu one of the few who's funny when he eats
Williams of Paterson a dying American ignu
Burroughs a purest ignu his haircut is a cream his left finger
pinkie chopped off for early ignu reasons metaphysical spells love spells
        with psychoanalysts
his very junkhood an accomplishment beyond a million dollars
Céline himself an old ignu over prose
I saw him in Paris dirty old gentleman of ratty talk
with longhaired cough three wormy sweaters round his neck
brown mould under historic fingernails
pure genius his giving morphine all night to 1400 passengers on a sinking
        ship
'because they were all getting emotional'
Who's amazing you is ignu communicate with me
by mail post telegraph phone street accusation or scratching at my window
and send me a true sign I'll reply special delivery
DEATH IS A LETTER THAT WAS NEVER SENT
Knowledge born of stamps words coins pricks jails seasons sweet ambition
        laughing gas
history with a gold halo photographs of the sea painting a celestial din in
        the bright window
one eye in a black cloud
and the lone vulture on a sand plain seen from the window of a Turkish bus
It must be a trick.   Two diamonds in the hand one Poetry one Charity
proves we have dreamed   and the long sword of intelligence
over which I constantly stumble like my pants at the age six—embarrassed.

New York, November 1958

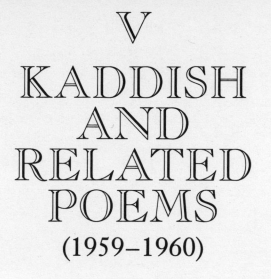

V

KADDISH
AND
RELATED
POEMS
(1959–1960)

'—Die,
If thou wouldst be with that which thou dost seek!'

To PETER ORLOVSKY
in
Paradise
'Taste my mouth in your ear'

Kaddish

For Naomi Ginsberg, 1894–1956

I

Strange now to think of you, gone without corsets & eyes, while I walk on
the sunny pavement of Greenwich Village.

downtown Manhattan, clear winter noon, and I've been up all night,
talking, talking, reading the Kaddish aloud, listening to Ray
Charles blues shout blind on the phonograph

the rhythm the rhythm—and your memory in my head three years after—
And read Adonais' last triumphant stanzas aloud—wept, realizing
how we suffer—

And how Death is that remedy all singers dream of, sing, remember,
prophesy as in the Hebrew Anthem, or the Buddhist Book of
Answers—and my own imagination of a withered leaf—at
dawn—

Dreaming back thru life, Your time—and mine accelerating toward Apoc-
alypse,

the final moment—the flower burning in the Day—and what comes after,

looking back on the mind itself that saw an American city

a flash away, and the great dream of Me or China, or you and a phantom
Russia, or a crumpled bed that never existed—

like a poem in the dark—escaped back to Oblivion—

No more to say, and nothing to weep for but the Beings in the Dream,
trapped in its disappearance,

sighing, screaming with it, buying and selling pieces of phantom, worship-
ping each other,

worshipping the God included in it all—longing or inevitability?—while it
lasts, a Vision—anything more?

It leaps about me, as I go out and walk the street, look back over my
shoulder, Seventh Avenue, the battlements of window office build-
ings shouldering each other high, under a cloud, tall as the sky an
instant—and the sky above—an old blue place.

or down the Avenue to the south, to—as I walk toward the Lower East
Side—where you walked 50 years ago, little girl—from Russia,
eating the first poisonous tomatoes of America—frightened on
the dock—

then struggling in the crowds of Orchard Street toward what?—toward
Newark—

toward candy store, first home-made sodas of the century, hand-churned
ice cream in backroom on musty brownfloor boards—
Toward education marriage nervous breakdown, operation, teaching
school, and learning to be mad, in a dream—what is this life?
Toward the Key in the window—and the great Key lays its head of light on
top of Manhattan, and over the floor, and lays down on the
sidewalk—in a single vast beam, moving, as I walk down First
toward the Yiddish Theater—and the place of poverty
you knew, and I know, but without caring now—Strange to have moved
thru Paterson, and the West, and Europe and here again,
with the cries of Spaniards now in the doorstoops doors and dark boys on
the street, fire escapes old as you
—Tho you're not old now, that's left here with me—
Myself, anyhow, maybe as old as the universe—and I guess that dies with
us—enough to cancel all that comes—What came is gone forever
every time—
That's good! That leaves it open for no regret—no fear radiators, lacklove,
torture even toothache in the end—
Though while it comes it is a lion that eats the soul—and the lamb, the
soul, in us, alas, offering itself in sacrifice to change's fierce
hunger—hair and teeth—and the roar of bonepain, skull bare,
break rib, rot-skin, braintricked Implacability.
Ai! ai! we do worse! We are in a fix! And you're out, Death let you out,
Death had the Mercy, you're done with your century, done with
God, done with the path thru it—Done with yourself at last—
Pure—Back to the Babe dark before your Father, before us all—
before the world—
There, rest. No more suffering for you. I know where you've gone, it's
good.
No more flowers in the summer fields of New York, no joy now, no more
fear of Louis,
and no more of his sweetness and glasses, his high school decades, debts,
loves, frightened telephone calls, conception beds, relatives,
hands—
No more of sister Elanor,—she gone before you—we kept it secret—you
killed her—or she killed herself to bear with you—an arthritic
heart—But Death's killed you both—No matter—
Nor your memory of your mother, 1915 tears in silent movies weeks and
weeks—forgetting, aggrieve watching Marie Dressler address hu-
manity, Chaplin dance in youth,
or Boris Godunov, Chaliapin's at the Met, halling his voice of a weeping
Czar—by standing room with Elanor & Max—watching also the
Capitalists take seats in Orchestra, white furs, diamonds,

with the YPSL's hitch-hiking thru Pennsylvania, in black baggy gym skirts
pants, photograph of 4 girls holding each other round the waste,
and laughing eye, too coy, virginal solitude of 1920

all girls grown old, or dead, now, and that long hair in the grave—lucky to
have husbands later—

You made it—I came too—Eugene my brother before (still grieving now
and will gream on to his last stiff hand, as he goes thru his cancer—
or kill—later perhaps—soon he will think—)

And it's the last moment I remember, which I see them all, thru myself,
now—tho not you

I didn't foresee what you felt—what more hideous gape of bad mouth
came first—to you—and were you prepared?

To go where? In that Dark—that—in that God? a radiance? A Lord in the
Void? Like an eye in the black cloud in a dream? Adonoi at last,
with you?

Beyond my remembrance! Incapable to guess! Not merely the yellow skull
in the grave, or a box of worm dust, and a stained ribbon—Deaths-
head with Halo? can you believe it?

Is it only the sun that shines once for the mind, only the flash of existence,
than none ever was?

Nothing beyond what we have—what you had—that so pitiful—yet Tri-
umph,

to have been here, and changed, like a tree, broken, or flower—fed to the
ground—but mad, with its petals, colored, thinking Great Uni-
verse, shaken, cut in the head, leaf stript, hid in an egg crate hospital,
cloth wrapped, sore—freaked in the moon brain, Naughtless.

No flower like that flower, which knew itself in the garden, and fought the
knife—lost

Cut down by an idiot Snowman's icy—even in the Spring—strange ghost
thought—some Death—Sharp icicle in his hand—crowned with
old roses—a dog for his eyes—cock of a sweatshop—heart of
electric irons.

All the accumulations of life, that wear us out—clocks, bodies, conscious-
ness, shoes, breasts—begotten sons—your Communism—
'Paranoia' into hospitals.

You once kicked Elanor in the leg, she died of heart failure later. You of
stroke. Asleep? within a year, the two of you, sisters in death. Is
Elanor happy?

Max grieves alive in an office on Lower Broadway, lone large mustache
over midnight Accountings, not sure. His life passes—as he sees—
and what does he doubt now? Still dream of making money, or that
might have made money, hired nurse, had children, found even
your Immortality, Naomi?

I'll see him soon. Now I've got to cut through—to talk to you—as I didn't
    when you had a mouth.
Forever. And we're bound for that, Forever—like Emily Dickinson's
    horses—headed to the End.
They know the way—These Steeds—run faster than we think—it's our
    own life they cross—and take with them.

Magnificent, mourned no more, marred of heart, mind behind,
married dreamed, mortal changed—Ass and face done with murder.
    In the world, given, flower maddened, made no Utopia, shut under
pine, almed in Earth, balmed in Lone, Jehovah, accept.
    Nameless, One Faced, Forever beyond me, beginningless, endless,
Father in death. Tho I am not there for this Prophecy, I am unmarried, I'm
hymnless, I'm Heavenless, headless in blisshood I would still adore
    Thee, Heaven, after Death, only One blessed in Nothingness, not
light or darkness, Dayless Eternity—
    Take this, this Psalm, from me, burst from my hand in a day, some
of my Time, now given to Nothing—to praise Thee—But Death
    This is the end, the redemption from Wilderness, way for the
Wonderer, House sought for All, black handkerchief washed clean by
weeping—page beyond Psalm—Last change of mine and Naomi—to
God's perfect Darkness—Death, stay thy phantoms!

II

    Over and over—refrain—of the Hospitals—still haven't written
your history—leave it abstract—a few images
    run thru the mind—like the saxophone chorus of houses and
years—remembrance of electrical shocks.
    By long nites as a child in Paterson apartment, watching over your
nervousness—you were fat—your next move—
    By that afternoon I stayed home from school to take care of you—
once and for all—when I vowed forever that once man disagreed with my
opinion of the cosmos, I was lost—
    By my later burden—vow to illuminate mankind—this is release of
particulars—(mad as you)—(sanity a trick of agreement)—
    But you stared out the window on the Broadway Church corner,
and spied a mystical assassin from Newark,
    So phoned the Doctor—'OK go way for a rest'—so I put on my
coat and walked you downstreet—On the way a grammarschool boy
screamed, unaccountably—'Where you goin Lady to Death'? I
shuddered—

and you covered your nose with motheaten fur collar, gas mask against poison sneaked into downtown atmosphere, sprayed by Grandma—

And was the driver of the cheesebox Public Service bus a member of the gang? You shuddered at his face, I could hardly get you on—to New York, very Times Square, to grab another Greyhound—

where we hung around 2 hours fighting invisible bugs and jewish sickness—breeze poisoned by Roosevelt—

out to get you—and me tagging along, hoping it would end in a quiet room in a Victorian house by a lake.

Ride 3 hours thru tunnels past all American industry, Bayonne preparing for World War II, tanks, gas fields, soda factories, diners, locomotive roundhouse fortress—into piney woods New Jersey Indians—calm towns—long roads thru sandy tree fields—

Bridges by deerless creeks, old wampum loading the streambed—down there a tomahawk or Pocahontas bone—and a million old ladies voting for Roosevelt in brown small houses, roads off the Madness highway—

perhaps a hawk in a tree, or a hermit looking for an owl-filled branch—

All the time arguing—afraid of strangers in the forward double seat, snoring regardless—what busride they snore on now?

'Allen, you don't understand—it's—ever since those 3 big sticks up my back—they did something to me in Hospital, they poisoned me, they want to see me dead—3 big sticks, 3 big sticks—

'The Bitch! Old Grandma! Last week I saw her, dressed in pants like an old man, with a sack on her back, climbing up the brick side of the apartment

'On the fire escape, with poison germs, to throw on me—at night—maybe Louis is helping her—he's under her power—

'I'm your mother, take me to Lakewood' (near where Graf Zeppelin had crashed before, all Hitler in Explosion) 'where I can hide.'

We got there—Dr. Whatzis rest home—she hid behind a closet—demanded a blood transfusion.

We were kicked out—tramping with Valise to unknown shady lawn houses—dusk, pine trees after dark—long dead street filled with crickets and poison ivy—

I shut her up by now—big house REST HOME ROOMS—gave the landlady her money for the week—carried up the iron valise—sat on bed waiting to escape—

Neat room in attic with friendly bedcover—lace curtains—spinning wheel rug—Stained wallpaper old as Naomi. We were home.

I left on the next bus to New York—laid my head back in the last seat, depressed—the worst yet to come?—abandoning her, rode in torpor—I was only 12.

Would she hide in her room and come out cheerful for breakfast? Or lock her door and stare thru the window for sidestreet spies? Listen at keyholes for Hitlerian invisible gas? Dream in a chair—or mock me, by—in front of a mirror, alone?

12 riding the bus at nite thru New Jersey, have left Naomi to Parcae in Lakewood's haunted house—left to my own fate bus—sunk in a seat—all violins broken—my heart sore in my ribs—mind was empty—Would she were safe in her coffin—

Or back at Normal School in Newark, studying up on America in a black skirt—winter on the street without lunch—a penny a pickle—home at night to take care of Elanor in the bedroom—

First nervous breakdown was 1919—she stayed home from school and lay in a dark room for three weeks—something bad—never said what—every noise hurt—dreams of the creaks of Wall Street—

Before the gray Depression—went upstate New York—recovered—Lou took photo of her sitting crossleg on the grass—her long hair wound with flowers—smiling—playing lullabies on mandolin—poison ivy smoke in left-wing summer camps and me in infancy saw trees—

or back teaching school, laughing with idiots, the backward classes—her Russian specialty—morons with dreamy lips, great eyes, thin feet & sicky fingers, swaybacked, rachitic—

great heads pendulous over Alice in Wonderland, a blackboard full of C A T.

Naomi reading patiently, story out of a Communist fairy book—Tale of the Sudden Sweetness of the Dictator—Forgiveness of Warlocks—Armies Kissing—

Deathsheads Around the Green Table—The King & the Workers—Paterson Press printed them up in the '30s till she went mad, or they folded, both.

O Paterson! I got home late that nite. Louis was worried. How could I be so—didn't I think? I shouldn't have left her. Mad in Lakewood. Call the Doctor. Phone the home in the pines. Too late.

Went to bed exhausted, wanting to leave the world (probably that year newly in love with R—— my high school mind hero, jewish boy who came a doctor later—then silent neat kid—

I later laying down life for him, moved to Manhattan—followed him to college—Prayed on ferry to help mankind if admitted—vowed, the day I journeyed to Entrance Exam—

by being honest revolutionary labor lawyer—would train for that—inspired by Sacco Vanzetti, Norman Thomas, Debs, Altgeld, Sandburg, Poe—Little Blue Books. I wanted to be President, or Senator.

ignorant woe—later dreams of kneeling by R's shocked knees declaring my love of 1941—What sweetness he'd have shown me, tho, that I'd wished him & despaired—first love—a crush—

Later a mortal avalanche, whole mountains of homosexuality, Matterhorns of cock, Grand Canyons of asshole—weight on my melancholy head—

meanwhile I walked on Broadway imagining Infinity like a rubber ball without space beyond—what's outside?—coming home to Graham Avenue still melancholy passing the lone green hedges across the street, dreaming after the movies—)

The telephone rang at 2 A.M.—Emergency—she'd gone mad— Naomi hiding under the bed screaming bugs of Mussolini—Help! Louis! Buba! Fascists! Death!—the landlady frightened—old fag attendant screaming back at her—

Terror, that woke the neighbors—old ladies on the second floor recovering from menopause—all those rags between thighs, clean sheets, sorry over lost babies—husbands ashen—children sneering at Yale, or putting oil in hair at CCNY—or trembling in Montclair State Teachers College like Eugene—

Her big leg crouched to her breast, hand outstretched Keep Away, wool dress on her thighs, fur coat dragged under the bed—she barricaded herself under bedspring with suitcases.

Louis in pajamas listening to phone, frightened—do now?—Who could know?—my fault, delivering her to solitude?—sitting in the dark room on the sofa, trembling, to figure out—

He took the morning train to Lakewood, Naomi still under bed— thought he brought poison Cops—Naomi screaming—Louis what happened to your heart then? Have you been killed by Naomi's ecstasy?

Dragged her out, around the corner, a cab, forced her in with valise, but the driver left them off at drugstore. Bus stop, two hours' wait.

I lay in bed nervous in the 4-room apartment, the big bed in living room, next to Louis' desk—shaking—he came home that nite, late, told me what happened.

Naomi at the prescription counter defending herself from the enemy—racks of children's books, douche bags, aspirins, pots, blood— 'Don't come near me—murderers! Keep away! Promise not to kill me!'

Louis in horror at the soda fountain—with Lakewood girlscouts— Coke addicts—nurses—busmen hung on schedule—Police from country precinct, dumbed—and a priest dreaming of pigs on an ancient cliff?

Smelling the air—Louis pointing to emptiness?—Customers vomiting their Cokes—or staring—Louis humiliated—Naomi triumphant—The Announcement of the Plot. Bus arrives, the drivers won't have them on trip to New York.

Phonecalls to Dr. Whatzis, 'She needs a rest,' The mental hospital—State Greystone Doctors—'Bring her here, Mr. Ginsberg.'

Naomi, Naomi—sweating, bulge-eyed, fat, the dress unbuttoned at one side—hair over brow, her stocking hanging evilly on her legs—screaming for a blood transfusion—one righteous hand upraised—a shoe in it—barefoot in the Pharmacy—

The enemies approach—what poisons? Tape recorders? FBI? Zhdanov hiding behind the counter? Trotsky mixing rat bacteria in the back of the store? Uncle Sam in Newark, plotting deathly perfumes in the Negro district? Uncle Ephraim, drunk with murder in the politician's bar, scheming of Hague? Aunt Rose passing water thru the needles of the Spanish Civil War?

till the hired $35 ambulance came from Red Bank——Grabbed her arms—strapped her on the stretcher—moaning, poisoned by imaginaries, vomiting chemicals thru Jersey, begging mercy from Essex County to Morristown—

And back to Greystone where she lay three years—that was the last breakthrough, delivered her to Madhouse again—

On what wards—I walked there later, oft—old catatonic ladies, gray as cloud or ash or walls—sit crooning over floorspace—Chairs—and the wrinkled hags acreep, accusing—begging my 13-year-old mercy—

'Take me home'—I went alone sometimes looking for the lost Naomi, taking Shock—and I'd say, 'No, you're crazy Mama,—Trust the Drs.'—

And Eugene, my brother, her elder son, away studying Law in a furnished room in Newark—

came Paterson-ward next day—and he sat on the broken-down couch in the living room—'We had to send her back to Greystone'—

—his face perplexed, so young, then eyes with tears—then crept weeping all over his face—'What for?' wail vibrating in his cheekbones, eyes closed up, high voice—Eugene's face of pain.

Him faraway, escaped to an Elevator in the Newark Library, his bottle daily milk on windowsill of $5 week furn room downtown at trolley tracks—

He worked 8 hrs. a day for $20/wk—thru Law School years—stayed by himself innocent near negro whorehouses.

Unlaid, poor virgin—writing poems about Ideals and politics

letters to the editor Pat Eve News—(we both wrote, denouncing Senator Borah and Isolationists—and felt mysterious toward Paterson City Hall—

I sneaked inside it once—local Moloch tower with phallus spire & cap o' ornament, strange gothic Poetry that stood on Market Street—replica Lyons' Hotel de Ville—

wings, balcony & scrollwork portals, gateway to the giant city clock, secret map room full of Hawthorne—dark Debs in the Board of Tax—Rembrandt smoking in the gloom—

Silent polished desks in the great committee room—Aldermen? Bd of Finance? Mosca the hairdresser aplot—Crapp the gangster issuing orders from the john—The madmen struggling over Zone, Fire, Cops & Backroom Metaphysics—we're all dead—outside by the bus stop Eugene stared thru childhood—

where the Evangelist preached madly for 3 decades, hard-haired, cracked & true to his mean Bible—chalked Prepare to Meet Thy God on civic pave—

or God is Love on the railroad overpass concrete—he raved like I would rave, the lone Evangelist—Death on City Hall—)

But Gene, young,—been Montclair Teachers College 4 years—taught half year & quit to go ahead in life—afraid of Discipline Problems—dark sex Italian students, raw girls getting laid, no English, sonnets disregarded—and he did not know much—just that he lost—

so broke his life in two and paid for Law—read huge blue books and rode the ancient elevator 13 miles away in Newark & studied up hard for the future

just found the Scream of Naomi on his failure doorstep, for the final time, Naomi gone, us lonely—home—him sitting there—

Then have some chicken soup, Eugene. The Man of Evangel wails in front of City Hall. And this year Lou has poetic loves of suburb middle age—in secret—music from his 1937 book—Sincere—he longs for beauty—

No love since Naomi screamed—since 1923?—now lost in Greystone ward—new shock for her—Electricity, following the 40 Insulin.

And Metrazol had made her fat.

So that a few years later she came home again—we'd much advanced and planned—I waited for that day—my Mother again to cook &—play the piano—sing at mandolin—Lung Stew, & Stenka Razin, & the communist line on the war with Finland—and Louis in debt—suspected to be poisoned money—mysterious capitalisms

—& walked down the long front hall & looked at the furniture. She never remembered it all. Some amnesia. Examined the doilies—and the dining room set was sold—

the Mahogany table—20 years love—gone to the junk man—we still had the piano—and the book of Poe—and the Mandolin, tho needed some string, dusty—

She went to the backroom to lie down in bed and ruminate, or nap, hide—I went in with her, not leave her by herself—lay in bed next to her—shades pulled, dusky, late afternoon—Louis in front room at desk, waiting—perhaps boiling chicken for supper—

'Don't be afraid of me because I'm just coming back home from the mental hospital—I'm your mother—'

Poor love, lost—a fear—I lay there—Said, 'I love you Naomi,'—stiff, next to her arm. I would have cried, was this the comfortless lone union?—Nervous, and she got up soon.

Was she ever satisfied? And—by herself sat on the new couch by the front windows, uneasy—cheek leaning on her hand—narrowing eye—at what fate that day—

Picking her tooth with her nail, lips formed an O, suspicion—thought's old worn vagina—absent sideglance of eye—some evil debt written in the wall, unpaid—& the aged breasts of Newark come near—

May have heard radio gossip thru the wires in her head, controlled by 3 big sticks left in her back by gangsters in amnesia, thru the hospital—caused pain between her shoulders—

Into her head—Roosevelt should know her case, she told me—Afraid to kill her, now, that the government knew their names—traced back to Hitler—wanted to leave Louis' house forever.

One night, sudden attack—her noise in the bathroom—like croaking up her soul—convulsions and red vomit coming out of her mouth—diarrhea water exploding from her behind—on all fours in front of the toilet—urine running between her legs—left retching on the tile floor smeared with her black feces—unfainted—

At forty, varicosed, nude, fat, doomed, hiding outside the apartment door near the elevator calling Police, yelling for her girlfriend Rose to help—

Once locked herself in with razor or iodine—could hear her cough in tears at sink—Lou broke through glass green-painted door, we pulled her out to the bedroom.

Then quiet for months that winter—walks, alone, nearby on Broadway, read Daily Worker—Broke her arm, fell on icy street—

Began to scheme escape from cosmic financial murder plots—later she ran away to the Bronx to her sister Elanor. And there's another saga of late Naomi in New York.

Or thru Elanor or the Workmen's Circle, where she worked, addressing envelopes, she made out—went shopping for Campbell's tomato soup—saved money Louis mailed her—

Later she found a boyfriend, and he was a doctor—Dr. Isaac worked for National Maritime Union—now Italian bald and pudgy old doll—who was himself an orphan—but they kicked him out—Old cruelties—

Sloppier, sat around on bed or chair, in corset dreaming to herself—'I'm hot—I'm getting fat—I used to have such a beautiful figure before I went to the hospital—You should have seen me in Woodbine—' This in a furnished room around the NMU hall, 1943.

Looking at naked baby pictures in the magazine—baby powder advertisements, strained lamb carrots—'I will think nothing but beautiful thoughts.'

Revolving her head round and round on her neck at window light in summertime, in hypnotize, in doven-dream recall—

'I touch his cheek, I touch his cheek, he touches my lips with his hand, I think beautiful thoughts, the baby has a beautiful hand.'—

Or a No-shake of her body, disgust—some thought of Buchenwald—some insulin passes thru her head—a grimace nerve shudder at Involuntary (as shudder when I piss)—bad chemical in her cortex—'No don't think of that. He's a rat.'

Naomi: 'And when we die we become an onion, a cabbage, a carrot, or a squash, a vegetable.' I come downtown from Columbia and agree. She reads the Bible, thinks beautiful thoughts all day.

'Yesterday I saw God. What did he look like? Well, in the afternoon I climbed up a ladder—he has a cheap cabin in the country, like Monroe, N.Y. the chicken farms in the wood. He was a lonely old man with a white beard.

'I cooked supper for him. I made him a nice supper—lentil soup, vegetables, bread & butter—miltz—he sat down at the table and ate, he was sad.

'I told him, Look at all those fightings and killings down there, What's the matter? Why don't you put a stop to it?

'I try, he said—That's all he could do, he looked tired. He's a bachelor so long, and he likes lentil soup.'

Serving me meanwhile, a plate of cold fish—chopped raw cabbage dript with tapwater—smelly tomatoes—week-old health food—grated beets & carrots with leaky juice, warm—more and more disconsolate food—I can't eat it for nausea sometimes—the Charity of her hands stinking with Manhattan, madness, desire to please me, cold undercooked fish—pale red near the bones. Her smells—and oft naked in the room, so that I stare ahead, or turn a book ignoring her.

One time I thought she was trying to make me come lay her—flirting to herself at sink—lay back on huge bed that filled most of the room, dress up round her hips, big slash of hair, scars of operations, pancreas, belly wounds, abortions, appendix, stitching of incisions pulling down in the fat like hideous thick zippers—ragged long lips between her legs—What, even, smell of asshole? I was cold—later revolted a little, not much—seemed perhaps a good idea to try—know the Monster of the Beginning Womb—Perhaps—that way. Would she care? She needs a lover.

Yisborach, v'yistabach, v'yispoar, v'yisroman, v'yisnaseh, v'yishador, v'yishalleh, v'yishallol, sh'meh d'kudsho, b'rich hu.

And Louis reestablishing himself in Paterson grimy apartment in negro district—living in dark rooms—but found himself a girl he later married, falling in love again—tho sere & shy—hurt with 20 years Naomi's mad idealism.

Once I came home, after longtime in N.Y., he's lonely—sitting in the bedroom, he at desk chair turned round to face me—weeps, tears in red eyes under his glasses—

That we'd left him—Gene gone strangely into army—she out on her own in N.Y., almost childish in her furnished room. So Louis walked downtown to postoffice to get mail, taught in highschool—stayed at poetry desk, forlorn—ate grief at Bickford's all these years—are gone.

Eugene got out of the Army, came home changed and lone—cut off his nose in jewish operation—for years stopped girls on Broadway for cups of coffee to get laid—Went to NYU, serious there, to finish Law.—

And Gene lived with her, ate naked fishcakes, cheap, while she got crazier—He got thin, or felt helpless, Naomi striking 1920 poses at the moon, half-naked in the next bed.

bit his nails and studied—was the weird nurse-son—Next year he moved to a room near Columbia—though she wanted to live with her children—

'Listen to your mother's plea, I beg you'—Louis still sending her checks—I was in bughouse that year 8 months—my own visions unmentioned in this here Lament—

But then went half mad—Hitler in her room, she saw his mustache in the sink—afraid of Dr. Isaac now, suspecting that he was in on the Newark plot—went up to Bronx to live near Elanor's Rheumatic Heart—

And Uncle Max never got up before noon, tho Naomi at 6 A.M. was listening to the radio for spies—or searching the windowsill,

for in the empty lot downstairs, an old man creeps with his bag stuffing packages of garbage in his hanging black overcoat.

Max's sister Edie works—17 years bookkeeper at Gimbels—lived downstairs in apartment house, divorced—so Edie took in Naomi on Rochambeau Ave—

Woodlawn Cemetery across the street, vast dale of graves where Poe once—Last stop on Bronx subway—lots of communists in that area.

Who enrolled for painting classes at night in Bronx Adult High School—walked alone under Van Cortlandt Elevated line to class—paints Naomiisms—

Humans sitting on the grass in some Camp No-Worry summers yore—saints with droopy faces and long-ill-fitting pants, from hospital—

Brides in front of Lower East Side with short grooms—lost El trains running over the Babylonian apartment rooftops in the Bronx—

Sad paintings—but she expressed herself. Her mandolin gone, all strings broke in her head, she tried. Toward Beauty? or some old life Message?

But started kicking Elanor, and Elanor had heart trouble—came upstairs and asked her about Spydom for hours,—Elanor frazzled. Max away at office, accounting for cigar stores till at night.

'I am a great woman—am truly a beautiful soul—and because of that they (Hitler, Grandma, Hearst, the Capitalists, Franco, Daily News, the '20s, Mussolini, the living dead) want to shut me up—Buba's the head of a spider network—'

Kicking the girls, Edie & Elanor—Woke Edie at midnite to tell her she was a spy and Elanor a rat. Edie worked all day and couldn't take it—She was organizing the union.—And Elanor began dying, upstairs in bed.

The relatives call me up, she's getting worse—I was the only one left—Went on the subway with Eugene to see her, ate stale fish—

'My sister whispers in the radio—Louis must be in the apartment—his mother tells him what to say—LIARS!—I cooked for my two children—I played the mandolin—'

Last night the nightingale woke me / Last night when all was still / it sang in the golden moonlight / from on the wintry hill. She did.

I pushed her against the door and shouted 'DON'T KICK ELANOR!'—she stared at me—Contempt—die—disbelief her sons are so naive, so dumb—'Elanor is the worst spy! She's taking orders!'

'—No wires in the room!'—I'm yelling at her—last ditch, Eugene listening on the bed—what can he do to escape that fatal Mama—'You've been away from Louis years already—Grandma's too old to walk—'

We're all alive at once then—even me & Gene & Naomi in one mythological Cousinesque room—screaming at each other in the Forever—I in Columbia jacket, she half undressed.

I banging against her head which saw Radios, Sticks, Hitlers—the gamut of Hallucinations—for real—her own universe—no road that goes elsewhere—to my own—No America, not even a world—

That you go as all men, as Van Gogh, as mad Hannah, all the same—to the last doom—Thunder, Spirits, Lightning!

I've seen your grave! O strange Naomi! My own—cracked grave!
Shema Y'Israel—I am Svul Avrum—you—in death?

Your last night in the darkness of the Bronx—I phonecalled—thru
hospital to secret police
    that came, when you and I were alone, shrieking at Elanor in my
ear—who breathed hard in her own bed, got thin—
    Nor will forget, the doorknock, at your fright of spies,—Law
advancing, on my honor—Eternity entering the room—you running to
the bathroom undressed, hiding in protest from the last heroic fate—
    staring at my eyes, betrayed—the final cops of madness rescuing
me—from your foot against the broken heart of Elanor,
    your voice at Edie weary of Gimbels coming home to broken
radio—and Louis needing a poor divorce, he wants to get married soon—
Eugene dreaming, hiding at 125 St., suing negroes for money on crud
furniture, defending black girls—
    Protests from the bathroom—Said you were sane—dressing in a
cotton robe, your shoes, then new, your purse and newspaper clippings—
no—your honesty—
    as you vainly made your lips more real with lipstick, looking in the
mirror to see if the Insanity was Me or a carful of police.
    or Grandma spying at 78—Your vision—Her climbing over the
walls of the cemetery with political kidnapper's bag—or what you saw on
the walls of the Bronx, in pink nightgown at midnight, staring out the
window on the empty lot—
    Ah Rochambeau Ave.—Playground of Phantoms—last apartment
in the Bronx for spies—last home for Elanor or Naomi, here these com-
munist sisters lost their revolution—
    'All right—put on your coat Mrs.—let's go—We have the wagon
downstairs—you want to come with her to the station?'
    The ride then—held Naomi's hand, and held her head to my breast,
I'm taller—kissed her and said I did it for the best—Elanor sick—and Max
with heart condition—Needs—
    To me—'Why did you do this?'—'Yes Mrs., your son will have to
leave you in an hour'—The Ambulance
    came in a few hours—drove off at 4 A.M. to some Bellevue in the
night downtown—gone to the hospital forever. I saw her led away—she
waved, tears in her eyes.

Two years, after a trip to Mexico—bleak in the flat plain near
Brentwood, scrub brush and grass around the unused RR train track to the
crazyhouse—

new brick 20 story central building—lost on the vast lawns of madtown on Long Island—huge cities of the moon.

Asylum spreads out giant wings above the path to a minute black hole—the door—entrance thru crotch—

I went in—smelt funny—the halls again—up elevator—to a glass door on a Women's Ward—to Naomi—Two nurses buxom white—They led her out, Naomi stared—and I gaspt—She'd had a stroke—

Too thin, shrunk on her bones—age come to Naomi—now broken into white hair—loose dress on her skeleton—face sunk, old! withered—cheek of crone—

One hand stiff—heaviness of forties & menopause reduced by one heart stroke, lame now—wrinkles—a scar on her head, the lobotomy—ruin, the hand dipping downwards to death—

O Russian faced, woman on the grass, your long black hair is crowned with flowers, the mandolin is on your knees—

Communist beauty, sit here married in the summer among daisies, promised happiness at hand—

holy mother, now you smile on your love, your world is born anew, children run naked in the field spotted with dandelions,

they eat in the plum tree grove at the end of the meadow and find a cabin where a white-haired negro teaches the mystery of his rainbarrel—

blessed daughter come to America, I long to hear your voice again, remembering your mother's music, in the Song of the Natural Front—

O glorious muse that bore me from the womb, gave suck first mystic life & taught me talk and music, from whose pained head I first took Vision—

Tortured and beaten in the skull—What mad hallucinations of the damned that drive me out of my own skull to seek Eternity till I find Peace for Thee, O Poetry—and for all humankind call on the Origin

Death which is the mother of the universe!—Now wear your nakedness forever, white flowers in your hair, your marriage sealed behind the sky—no revolution might destroy that maidenhood—

O beautiful Garbo of my Karma—all photographs from 1920 in Camp Nicht-Gedeiget here unchanged—with all the teachers from Newark—Nor Elanor be gone, nor Max await his specter—nor Louis retire from this High School—

Back! You! Naomi! Skull on you! Gaunt immortality and revolution come—small broken woman—the ashen indoor eyes of hospitals, ward grayness on skin—

'Are you a spy?' I sat at the sour table, eyes filling with tears—'Who are you? Did Louis send you?—The wires—'

in her hair, as she beat on her head—'I'm not a bad girl—don't murder me!—I hear the ceiling—I raised two children—'

Two years since I'd been there—I started to cry—She stared—nurse broke up the meeting a moment—I went into the bathroom to hide, against the toilet white walls

'The Horror' I weeping—to see her again—'The Horror'—as if she were dead thru funeral rot in—'The Horror!'

I came back she yelled more—they led her away—'You're not Allen—' I watched her face—but she passed by me, not looking—

Opened the door to the ward,—she went thru without a glance back, quiet suddenly—I stared out—she looked old—the verge of the grave—'All the Horror!'

Another year, I left N.Y.—on West Coast in Berkeley cottage dreamed of her soul—that, thru life, in what form it stood in that body, ashen or manic, gone beyond joy—

near its death—with eyes—was my own love in its form, the Naomi, my mother on earth still—sent her long letter—& wrote hymns to the mad—Work of the merciful Lord of Poetry.

that causes the broken grass to be green, or the rock to break in grass—or the Sun to be constant to earth—Sun of all sunflowers and days on bright iron bridges—what shines on old hospitals—as on my yard—

Returning from San Francisco one night, Orlovsky in my room—Whalen in his peaceful chair—a telegram from Gene, Naomi dead—

Outside I bent my head to the ground under the bushes near the garage—knew she was better—

at last—not left to look on Earth alone—2 years of solitude—no one, at age nearing 60—old woman of skulls—once long-tressed Naomi of Bible—

or Ruth who wept in America—Rebecca aged in Newark—David remembering his Harp, now lawyer at Yale

or Srul Avrum—Israel Abraham—myself—to sing in the wilderness toward God—O Elohim!—so to the end—2 days after her death I got her letter—

Strange Prophecies anew! She wrote—'The key is in the window, the key is in the sunlight at the window—I have the key—Get married Allen don't take drugs—the key is in the bars, in the sunlight in the window.

Love,

your mother'

which is Naomi—

Hymmnn

In the world which He has created according to his will Blessed Praised
    Magnified Lauded Exalted the Name of the Holy One Blessed is He!
In the house in Newark Blessed is He! In the madhouse Blessed is He! In
    the house of Death Blessed is He!
Blessed be He in homosexuality! Blessed be He in Paranoia! Blessed be He
    in the city! Blessed be He in the book!
Blessed be He who dwells in the shadow! Blessed be He! Blessed be He!
Blessed be you Naomi in tears! Blessed be you Naomi in fears! Blessed
    Blessed Blessed in sickness!
Blessed be you Naomi in hospitals! Blessed be you Naomi in solitude! Blest
    be your triumph! Blest be your bars! Blest be your last years'
    loneliness!
Blest be your failure! Blest be your stroke! Blest be the close of your
    eye! Blest be the gaunt of your cheek! Blest be your withered
    thighs!
Blessed be Thee Naomi in Death! Blessed be Death! Blessed be Death!
Blessed be He Who leads all sorrow to Heaven! Blessed be He in the end!
Blessed be He who builds Heaven in Darkness! Blessed Blessed Blessed be
    He! Blessed be He! Blessed be Death on us All!

III

Only to have not forgotten the beginning in which she drank cheap sodas
    in the morgues of Newark,
only to have seen her weeping on gray tables in long wards of her universe
only to have known the weird ideas of Hitler at the door, the wires in her
    head, the three big sticks
rammed down her back, the voices in the ceiling shrieking out her ugly
    early lays for 30 years,
only to have seen the time-jumps, memory lapse, the crash of wars, the roar
    and silence of a vast electric shock,
only to have seen her painting crude pictures of Elevateds running over the
    rooftops of the Bronx
her brothers dead in Riverside or Russia, her lone in Long Island writing a
    last letter—and her image in the sunlight in the window
'The key is in the sunlight at the window in the bars the key is in the
    sunlight,'
only to have come to that dark night on iron bed by stroke when the sun
    gone down on Long Island

and the vast Atlantic roars outside the great call of Being to its own
to come back out of the Nightmare—divided creation—with her head lain
      on a pillow of the hospital to die
—in one last glimpse—all Earth one everlasting Light in the familiar
      blackout—no tears for this vision—
But that the key should be left behind—at the window—the key in the
      sunlight—to the living—that can take
that slice of light in hand—and turn the door—and look back see
Creation glistening backwards to the same grave, size of universe,
size of the tick of the hospital's clock on the archway over the white door—

IV
O mother
what have I left out
O mother
what have I forgotten
O mother
farewell
with a long black shoe
farewell
with Communist Party and a broken stocking
farewell
with six dark hairs on the wen of your breast
farewell
with your old dress and long black beard around the vagina
farewell
with your sagging belly
with your fear of Hitler
with your mouth of bad short stories
with your fingers of rotten mandolins
with your arms of fat Paterson porches
with your belly of strikes and smokestacks
with your chin of Trotsky and the Spanish War
with your voice singing for the decaying overbroken workers
with your nose of bad lay with your nose of the smell of pickles of Newark
with your eyes
with your eyes of Russia
with your eyes of no money
with your eyes of false China
with your eyes of Aunt Elanor in an oxygen tent
with your eyes of starving India
with your eyes pissing in the park

with your eyes of America taking a fall
with your eyes of your failure at the piano
with your eyes of your relatives in California
with your eyes of Ma Rainey dying in an aumbulance
with your eyes of Czechoslovakia attacked by robots
with your eyes going to painting class at night in the Bronx
with your eyes of the killer Grandma you see on the horizon from the Fire-
    Escape
with your eyes running naked out of the apartment screaming into the hall
with your eyes being led away by policemen to an ambulance
with your eyes strapped down on the operating table
with your eyes with the pancreas removed
with your eyes of appendix operation
with your eyes of abortion
with your eyes of ovaries removed
with your eyes of shock
with your eyes of lobotomy
with your eyes of divorce
with your eyes of stroke
with your eyes alone
with your eyes
with your eyes
with your Death full of Flowers

V

Caw caw caw crows shriek in the white sun over grave stones in Long
    Island
Lord Lord Lord Naomi underneath this grass my halflife and my own as hers
caw caw my eye be buried in the same Ground where I stand in Angel
Lord Lord great Eye that stares on All and moves in a black cloud
caw caw strange cry of Beings flung up into sky over the waving trees
Lord Lord O Grinder of giant Beyonds my voice in a boundless field in
    Sheol
Caw caw the call of Time rent out of foot and wing an instant in the
    universe
Lord Lord an echo in the sky the wind through ragged leaves the roar of
    memory
caw caw all years my birth a dream caw caw New York the bus the broken
    shoe the vast highschool caw caw all Visions of the Lord
Lord Lord Lord caw caw caw Lord Lord Lord caw caw caw Lord

Paris, December 1957–New York, 1959

Psalm IV

Now I'll record my secret vision, impossible sight of the face of God:
It was no dream, I lay broad waking on a fabulous couch in Harlem
having masturbated for no love, and read half naked an open book of Blake
    on my lap
Lo & behold! I was thoughtless and turned a page and gazed on the living
    Sun-flower
and heard a voice, it was Blake's, reciting in earthen measure:
the voice rose out of the page to my secret ear never heard before—
I lifted my eyes to the window, red walls of buildings flashed outside,
    endless sky sad in Eternity
sunlight gazing on the world, apartments of Harlem standing in the
    universe—
each brick and cornice stained with intelligence like a vast living face—
the great brain unfolding and brooding in wilderness!—Now speaking
    aloud with Blake's voice—
Love! thou patient presence & bone of the body! Father! thy careful
    watching and waiting over my soul!
My son! My son! the endless ages have remembered me! My son! My son!
    Time howled in anguish in my ear!
My son! My son! my father wept and held me in his dead arms.

1960

Magic Psalm

Because this world is on the wing and what cometh no man can know
O Phantom that my mind pursues from year to year descend from heaven
    to this shaking flesh
catch up my fleeting eye in the vast Ray that knows no bounds—
    Inseparable—Master—
Giant outside Time with all its falling leaves—Genius of the Universe—
    Magician in Nothingness where appear red clouds—
Unspeakable King of the roads that are gone—Unintelligible Horse riding
    out of the graveyard—Sunset spread over Cordillera and insect—
    Gnarl Moth—
Griever—Laugh with no mouth, Heart that never had flesh to die—
    Promise that was not made—Reliever, whose blood burns in a
    million animals wounded—
O Mercy, Destroyer of the World, O Mercy, Creator of Breasted Illusions,
    O Mercy, cacophonous warmouthed doveling, Come,
invade my body with the sex of God, choke up my nostrils with corrup-
    tion's infinite caress,
transfigure me to slimy worms of pure sensate transcendency I'm still alive,
croak my voice with uglier than reality, a psychic tomato speaking Thy
    million mouths,
Myriad-tongued my Soul, Monster or Angel, Lover that comes to fuck me
    forever—white gown on the Eyeless Squid—
Asshole of the Universe into which I disappear—Elastic Hand that spoke
    to Crane—Music that passes into the phonograph of years from
    another Millennium—Ear of the buildings of NY—
That which I believe—have seen—seek endlessly in leaf dog eye—fault
    always, lack—which makes me think—
Desire that created me, Desire I hide in my body, Desire all Man know
    Death, Desire surpassing the Babylonian possible world
that makes my flesh shake orgasm of Thy Name which I don't know never
    will never speak—
Speak to Mankind to say the great bell tolls a golden tone on iron balconies
    in every million universe,
I am Thy prophet come home this world to scream an unbearable Name
    thru my 5 senses hideous sixth
that knows Thy Hand on its invisible phallus, covered with electric bulbs
    of death—
Peace, Resolver where I mess up illusion, Softmouth Vagina that enters my
    brain from above, Ark-Dove with a bough of Death.

Drive me crazy, God I'm ready for disintegration of my mind, disgrace me in the eye of the earth,

attack my hairy heart with terror eat my cock Invisible croak of deathfrog leap on me pack of heavy dogs salivating light,

devour my brain One flow of endless consciousness, I'm scared of your promise must make scream my prayer in fear—

Descend O Light Creator & Eater of Mankind, disrupt the world in its madness of bombs and murder,

Volcanos of flesh over London, on Paris a rain of eyes—truckloads of angel-hearts besmearing Kremlin walls—the skullcup of light to New York—

myriad jeweled feet on the terraces of Pekin—veils of electrical gas descending over India—cities of Bacteria invading the brain—the Soul escaping into the rubber waving mouths of Paradise—

This is the Great Call, this is the Tocsin of the Eternal War, this is the cry of Mind slain in Nebulae,

this is the Golden Bell of the Church that has never existed, this is the Boom in the heart of the sunbeam, this is the trumpet of the Worm at Death,

Appeal of the handless castrate grab Alm golden seed of Futurity thru the quake & volcan of the world—

Shovel my feet under the Andes, splatter my brains on the Sphinx, drape my beard and hair over Empire State Building,

cover my belly with hands of moss, fill up my ears with your lightning, blind me with prophetic rainbows

That I taste the shit of Being at last, that I touch Thy genitals in the palmtree,

that the vast Ray of Futurity enter my mouth to sound Thy Creation Forever Unborn, O Beauty invisible to my Century!

that my prayer surpass my understanding, that I lay my vanity at Thy foot, that I no longer fear Judgment over Allen of this world

born in Newark come into Eternity in New York crying again in Peru for human Tongue to psalm the Unspeakable,

that I surpass desire for transcendency and enter the calm water of the universe

that I ride out this wave, not drown forever in the flood of my imagination

that I not be slain thru my own insane magic, this crime be punished in merciful jails of Death,

men understand my speech out of their own Turkish heart, the prophets aid me with Proclamation,

the Seraphim acclaim Thy Name, Thyself at once in one huge Mouth of Universe make meat reply.

June 1960

The End

I am I, old Father Fisheye that begat the ocean, the worm at my cwn ear,
      the serpent turning around a tree,
I sit in the mind of the oak and hide in the rose, I know if any wake up, none
      but my death,
come to me bodies, come to me prophecies, come all foreboding, come
      spirits and visions,
I receive all, I'll die of cancer, I enter the coffin forever, I close my eye, I
      disappear,
I fall on myself in winter snow, I roll in a great wheel through rain, I watch
      fuckers in convulsion,
car screech, furies groaning their basso music, memory fading in the brain,
      men imitating dogs,
I delight in a woman's belly, youth stretching his breasts and thighs to sex,
      the cock sprung inward
gassing its seed on the lips of Yin, the beasts dance in Siam, they sing opera
      in Moscow,
my boys yearn at dusk on stoops, I enter New York, I play my jazz on a
      Chicago Harpsichord,
Love that bore me I bear back to my Origin with no loss, I float over the
      vomiter
thrilled with my deathlessness, thrilled with this endlessness I dice and
      bury,
come Poet shut up eat my word, and taste my mouth in your ear.

New York, 1960

VI
PLANET NEWS: TO EUROPE AND ASIA
(1961–1963)

'O go way man I can
  hypnotize this nation
I can shake the earth's foundation
  with the Maple Leaf Rag.'

To NEAL CASSADY
again
Spirit to Spirit
February 8, 1925–February 4, 1968
'the greater driver'
'secret hero of these poems'

Television Was a Baby Crawling Toward
That Deathchamber

Either we blow ourselves up now and die, like the old tribe of man, arguing
        among neutrons, spit on India, fuck Tibet, stick up America,
        clobber Moscow, die Baltic, have your tuberculosis in Arabia, wink
        not in Enkidu's reverie—
it's a long Train of Associations stopped for gas in the desert & looking for
        drink of old-time H_2O— . . .
I prophesy, we will all prophesy to each other & I give thee happy tidings
        Robert Lowell and Jeanette MacDonald— . . .
The Bardo Thodol extends in the millions of black jello for every dying
        Mechanic—We will make Colossal movies—
We will be a great Tantric Mogul & starify a new Hollywood with our
        unimaginable Flop—Great Paranoia! . . .
I myself saw the sunflower-monkeys of the Moon—spending their dear
        play-money electricity in a homemade tape-record minute of car-
        toony high Sound— . . .
which has been playing out there always for me, whoever can hear enough
        to write it down for a day to let men fiddle in space, blow a tempo-
        rary brass tuba or wave a stick at a physical orchestra
and remember the Wagner-music in his own titty-head Consciousness—
        ah yes that's the message—
That's what I came here to compose, what I knocked off my life to Inscribe
        on my gray metal typewriter . . .
The being roars its own name in the Radio, the Bomb goes off its twenty
        years ago,
I hear thy music O my mystery, my own Poetry's Tongue, my Hallelujah
        Way beyond all mortal inherited Heavens, O my own blind an-
        cient Love in-mind! . . .
The President laughs in his Chair, and swivels his head on his neck
        controlling fangs of Number—
bacteria come numberless, atoms count themselves greatness in their
        pointy Empire— . . .
but there is the Saintly Meat of the Heart—feeling to thee o Peter and all
        my Lords—Decades American loves car-rides and vow-sworn
        faces lain on my breast,—my head on many more naked than my
        own sad hoping flesh—
our feelings! come back to the heart—to the old blind hoping Creator
        home in Mercy, beating everywhere behind machine hand

clothes-man Senator iron powerd or fishqueen fugitive-com'd
lapel—

Here I am—Old Betty Boop whoopsing behind the skull-microphone
wondering what Idiot soap opera horror show we broadcast by
Mistake . . .
hypnotizing millions of legional-eyed detectives to commit mass murder
on the Invisible
which is only a bunch of women weeping hidden behind newspapers in
the Andes, conspired against by Standard Oil . . .
Screech out over the radio that Standard Oil is a bunch of spying Business-
men intent on building one Standard Oil in the whole universe like
an egotistical cancer
and yell on Television to England to watch out for United Fruits they got
Central America by the balls
nobody but them can talk San Salvador, they run big Guatemala puppet
armies, gas Dictators, they're the Crown of Thorns
upon the Consciousness of poor Christ-indian Central America, and
the Pharisees are US Congress & Publicans is the American
People
who have driven righteous bearded faithful pink new Castro 1961 is he
mad? who knows? . . .
AMERICA WILL BE REFUSED ETERNITY BY HER OWN MAD
SON THE BOMB! MEN WORKING IN ELECTRICITY BE
U.S. SADISTS THEIR MAGIC PHANOPOEIAC THRU
MASS MEDIA THE NASTIEST IN THIS FIRST HISTORY!
EVIL SPELLS THRU THE DAILY NEWS! HORRIBLE MASO-
CHISMS THUNK UP BY THE AMERICAN MEDICAL AS-
SOCIATION! DEATH TO JUNKIES THRU THE TREA-
SURY DEPARTMENT! TAXES ON YOUR HATE FOR THIS
HERE WAR!
LEGIONS OF DECENCY BLACKMAIL THY CINEMAL FATE!
CONSPIRACIES CONTROL ALL WHITE MAGICIANS! I
CAN'T TELL YOU MY SECRET STORY ON TV!
Chambers of Commerce misquote Bob Hope who is a grim sex revolution-
ist talking in hysterial code flat awful jokes
Jimmy Durante's kept from screaming to death in the movies by a huge fat
Cardinal, the Spell Man, Black Magician he won't let mad white
Chaplin talk thru the State Megaphone! He takes evil pix with
Swiss financial cunt!
It's the American Medical Association poisoning the poets with their
double-syndicate of heroin cut with money-dust . . .

Human dragons train to fly the air with bomb-claws clutched to breast &
     wires entering their brains thru muffled ears—connected to what
     control tower—jacked to what secret Lab where the macrocosm-
     machine
picks up vibrations of my thought in this poem—the attendant is afraid—
     Is the President listening? is
Evil Eye, the invisible police-cop-secrecy masters Controlling Central
     Intelligence—do they know I took Methedrine, heroin, magic
     mushrooms, & lambchops & guess toward a Prophecy tonight?
No the big dopes all they do is control each other—Doom! in the vast
car America—they're screeching on two mind-wheels on a National
     Curve . . .
wherever and whoever is plugged in by real filaments or wireless or
     whatever magic wordy-synapse to the money-center of the mind
whose Eye is hidden somewhere behind All mass media—what makes
     reporters fear their secret dreamy news—behind the Presiden-
     tial mike & all its starry bunting, front for some mad BIL-
     LIONAIRES
who own United Fruits & Standard Oil and Hearst The Press and Texas
     NBC and someone owns the Radios owns vast Spheres of Air—
     Subliminal Billionaire got
State Legislatures filled with Capital Punishment Fiends because nobody's
     been in love on US soil long enough to realize We who pay the
     Public Hangman make State Murder thru Alien Gas who cause
     any form of hate-doom hanging
do that in public everybody agreed by the neck suffering utmost pangs
     Each citizen himself unloved suicides him, because there's no
     beloved, now in America for All in the gas chamber the whole
     California Legislature . . .
Warlocks, Black magicians burning and cursing the Love-Books, Jack be
     damned, casting spells from the shores of America on the inland
     cities, lacklove-curses on our Eyes which read genital poetry—
O deserts of deprivation for some high school'd gang, lone Cleveland that
     delayed its books of Awe, Chicago struggling to read its maga-
     zines, police and papers yapping over grimy gossip skyscraped
     from some sulphurous yellow cloud drift in from archtank hot
     factories make nebulous explosives near Detroit—smudge got on
     Corso's Rosy Page— . . .
That's when I began vomiting my paranoia when Old National Skullface
     the invisible sixheaded billionaire began brainwashing my stom-
     ach with strange feelers in the *Journal American*—the penis of
     billionaires depositing professional semen in my ear, Fulton Lewis

coming with strychnine jizzum in his voice making an evil suggestion that entered my mouth

while I was sitting there gaping in wild dubiety & astound on my peaceful couch, he said to all the taxidrivers and schoolteachers in brokendown old Blakean America

that Julius and Ethel Rosenberg smelled bad & shd die, he sent to kill them with personal electricity, his power station is the spirit of generation leaving him thru his asshole by Error, that very electric entered Ethel's eye

and his tongue is the prick of a devil he don't even know, a magic capitalist ghosting it on the lam after the Everett Massacre—fucks a Newscaster in the mouth every time he gets on the Microphone—

and those ghost jizzums started my stomach trouble with capital punishment, . . .

It was a big electrocution in every paper and mass medium, Television was a baby crawling toward that deathchamber . . .

But I am the Intolerant One Gasbag from the Morgue & Void, Garbler of all Conceptions that myope my eye & is Uncle Sam asleep in the Funeral Home—?

Bad magic, scram, hide in J. E. Hoover's bathingsuit. Make his pants fall in the ocean, near Miami—

Gangster CRASH! America will be forgotten, the identity files of the FBI slipt into the void-crack, the fingerprints unwhorled—no track where He came from—

Man left no address, not even hair, just disappeared & forgot his big wallstreet on Earth—Uncle I hate the FBI it's all a big dreamy skyscraper somewhere over the Mutual Network—I don't even know who they are—like the Nameless—

Hallooo I am coming end of my Presidency—Everybody's fired—I am a hopeless whitehaired congressman—I lost my last election—landslide for Reader's Digest—not even humans—

Nobody home in town—just offices with many jangling telephones & automatic switchboards keep the message—typewriters return yr calls oft, Yakkata yak & tinbellring—THE POLICE ARE AT THE DOOR— . . .

Goodbye, said the metal Announcer in doors of The Chamber of Commerce—we're merging with NAM forever—and the NAM has no door but's sealed copper 10 foot vault under the Federal Reserve Bldg—

Six billionaires that control America are playing Scrabble with antique Tarot—they've just unearthed another Pyramid—in the bombproof Cellar at Fort Knox

Not even the FBI knows who—They give orders to J. E. Hoover thru the
    metal phonegirl at the Robot Transmitter on top of RCA—you
can see new Fortune officers look like spies from 20 floors below with
    their eyeglasses & gold skulls—silver teeth flashing up the shit-
    mouthed grin—weeping in their martinis! There is no secret to
    the success of the
Six Billionaires that own all Time since the Gnostic Revolt in Aegypto—
    they built the Sphinx to confuse my sex life, Who Fuckd the
    Void?
Why are they starting that war all over again in Laos over Neutral Mind? Is
    the United States CIA army Legions overthrowing somebody like
    Angelica Balabanoff?
Six thousand movietheaters, 100,000,000 television sets, a billion radios,
    wires and wireless crisscrossing hemispheres, semaphore lights
    and morse, all telephones ringing at once connect every mind by
    its ears to one vast consciousness This Time Apocalypse— . . .

Now all sentience broods and listens—contemplative & hair full of rain for
    15 years inside New York—what millions know and hark to hear,
    & death will tell, but—
many strange magicians in buildings listening inside their own heads—
    or clouds over Manhattan Bridge—or strained thru music mes-
    sages . . .
Life is waving, the cosmos is sending a message to itself, its image is
    reproduced endlessly over TV
over the radio the babble of Hitler's and Claudette Colbert's voices got
    mixed up in the bathroom radiator
Hello hello are you the Telephone the Operator's singing we are the
    daughters of the universe
get everybody on the line at once plug in all being ears by laudspeaker,
    newspeak, secret message,
handwritten electronic impulse traveling along rays electric spiderweb
magnetisms shuddering on one note We We We, mustached disc jockeys
    trembling in mantric excitement, . . . the wire services are hysteri-
    cal and send too much message,
they're waiting to bam out the Armageddon, millions of rats reported in
    China, smoke billows out New York's hospital furnace smokestack,
I am writing millions of letters a year, I correspond with hopeful messen-
    gers in Detroit, I am taking drugs
and leap at my postman for more correspondence. Man is leaving the earth
    in a rocket ship, . . .
it makes me crosseyed to think how, the mass media assemble themselves
    like congolese Ants for a purpose

in the massive clay mound an undiscovered huge Queen is born, Africa
    wakes to redeem the old Cosmos,
I am masturbating in my bed, I dreamed a new Stranger touched my heart
    with his eye,
he hides in a sidestreet loft in Hoboken, the heavens have covered East
    Second Street with Snow,
all day I walk in the wilderness over white carpets of City . . . I take power
    over the dead creation,
I am naked in New York, a star breaks thru the blue skull of the sky out the
    window,
I seize the tablets of the Law, the spectral Buddha and the spectral Christ
    turn to a stick of shit in the void, a fearful Idea,
I take the crown of the Idea and place it on my head, and sit a King beside
    the reptile Devas of my Karma—
Eye in every forehead sleeping waxy & the light gone inward—to dream of
    fearful Jaweh or the Atom Bomb—
All these eternal spirits to be wakened, all these bodies touched and healed,
    all these lacklove
suffering the Hate, dumbed under rainbows of Creation, O Man the means
    of Heaven are at hand, thy rocks & my rocks are nothing,
the identity of the Moon is the identity of the flower-thief. I and the Police
    are one in revolutionary Numbness! . . .
Stop Arguing, Cosmos, I give up so I be, I receive a happy letter from Ray
    Bremser exiled from home in New Jersey jail—. . .

That much illusion, and what's visions but visions, and these words filled
    Methedrine—I have a backache & 2 telegrams come midnight
    from messengers that cry to plug in the Electrode Ear to
my skull downstreet, & hear what they got to say, big lives like trees of
    Cancer in Bronx & Long Island—Telephones connect the voids
    island blissy darkness scattered in many manmind—

New York, February 1961

This Form of Life Needs Sex

I will have to accept women
            if I want to continue the race,
      kiss breasts, accept
      strange hairy lips behind
                        buttocks,
Look in questioning womanly eyes
            answer soft cheeks,
bury my loins in the hang of pearplum
            fat tissue
                  I had abhorred
before I give godspasm Babe leap
      forward thru death—
Between me and oblivion an unknown
                  woman stands;
Not the Muse but living meat-phantom,
a mystery scary as my fanged god
            sinking its foot in its gullet &
vomiting its own image out of its ass
—This woman Futurity I am pledge to
                  born not to die,
but issue my own cockbrain replica Me-Hood
            again—For fear of the Blot?
Face of Death, my Female, as I'm sainted
            to my very bone,
I'm fated to find me a maiden for
                  ignorant Fuckery—
flapping my belly & smeared with Saliva
      shamed face flesh & wet,
—have long droopy conversations
      in Cosmical Duty boudoirs,
                  maybe bored?
Or excited New Prospect, discuss
      her, Futurity, my Wife
         My Mother, Death, My only
                  hope, my very Resurrection
Woman
            herself, why have I feared
            to be joined true
      embraced beneath the Panties of Forever

in with the one hole that repelled me 1937 on?
—Pulled down my pants on the porch showing
        my behind to cars passing in rain—
& She be interested, this contact with Silly new Male
        that's sucked my loveman's cock
in Adoration & sheer beggary romance-awe
        gulp-choke Hope of Life come
and buggered myself innumerably boy-yangs
            gloamed inward so my solar plexus
        feel godhead in me like an open door—

Now that's changed my decades body old
tho' admiring male thighs at my brow,
        hard love pulsing thru my ears,
            stern buttocks upraised
                    for my masterful Rape
        that were meant for a private shit
            if the Army were All—
But no more answer to life
            than the muscular statue
        I felt up its marbles
envying Beauty's immortality in the
            museum of Yore—
You can fuck a statue but you can't
        have children
You can joy man to man but the Sperm
        comes back in a trickle at dawn
    in a toilet on the 45th Floor—
& Can't make continuous mystery out of that
        finished performance
                    & ghastly thrill
    that ends as began,
                stupid reptile squeak
        denied life by Fairy Creator
            become Imaginary
        because he decided not to incarnate
            opposite—Old Spook
who didn't want to be a baby & die,
        didn't want to shit and scream
            exposed to bombardment on a
                    Chinese RR track

and grow up to pass his spasm on
        the other half of the Universe—
Like a homosexual capitalist afraid of the masses—
and that's my situation, Folks—

New York, April 12, 1961

Describe: The Rain on Dasaswamedh Ghat

Kali Ma tottering up steps to shelter tin roof, feeling her way to
    curb, around bicycle & leper seated on her way—to piss on a
    broom
left by the Stone Cutters who last night were shaking the street with Boom!
    of Stone blocks unloaded from truck
Forcing the blindman in his gray rags to retreat from his spot in the middle
    of the road where he sleeps & shakes under his blanket
Jai Ram all night telling his beads or sex on a burlap carpet
Past which cows donkeys dogs camels elephants marriage processions
    drummers tourists lepers and bathing devotees
step to the whine of serpent-pipes & roar of car motors around his black
    ears—
Today on a balcony in shorts leaning on iron rail I watched the leper who
    sat hidden behind a bicycle
emerge dragging his buttocks on the gray rainy ground by the glove-
    bandaged stumps of hands,
one foot chopped off below knee, round stump-knob wrapped with black
    rubber
pushing a tin can shiny size of his head with left hand (from which only a
    thumb emerged from leprous swathings)
beside him, lifting it with both ragbound palms down the curb into the
    puddled road,
balancing his body down next to the can & crawling forward on his behind
trailing a heavy rag for seat, and leaving a path thru the street wavering
like the Snail's slime track—imprint of his crawl on the muddy asphalt
    market entrance—stopping
to drag his can along stubbornly konking on the paved surface near the
    water pump—
Where a turban'd workman stared at him moving along—his back
    humped with rags—
and inquired why didn't he put his can to wash in the pump altarplace—
    and why go that way when free rice
Came from the alley back there by the river—As the leper looked up &
    rested, conversing curiously, can by his side approaching a puddle.
Kali had pissed standing up & then felt her way back to the Shop Steps on
    thin brown legs
her hands in the air—feeling with feet for her rag pile on the stone steps'
    wetness—

as a cow busied its mouth chewing her rags left wet on the ground for five
  minutes digesting
Till the comb-&-hair-oil-booth keeper woke & chased her away with a
  stick
Because a dog barked at a madman with dirty wild black hair who rag
  round his midriff & water pot in hand
Stopped in midstreet turned round & gazed up at the balconies, windows,
  shops and city stagery filled with glum activity
Shrugged & said *Jai Shankar!* to the imaginary audience of Me's,
While a white robed Baul Singer carrying his one stringed dried pumpkin
  Guitar
Sat down near the cigarette stand and surveyed his new scene, just arrived
  in the Holy City of Benares.

Benares, February 1963

Describe: The Rain on Dasaswamedh Ghat   **129**

Patna–Benares Express

Whatever it may be whoever it may be
The bloody man all singing all just
However he die
He rode on railroad cars
He woke at dawn, in the white light of a new universe
He couldn't do any different
He the skeleton with eyes
raised himself up from a wooden bench
felt different looking at the fields and palm trees
no money in the bank of dust
no nation but inexpressible gray clouds before sunrise
lost his identity cards in his wallet
in the bald rickshaw by the Maidan in dry Patna
Later stared hopeless waking from drunken sleep
dry mouthed in the RR Station
among sleeping shoeshine men in loincloth on the dirty concrete
Too many bodies thronging these cities now

Benares, May 1963

The Change: *Kyoto–Tokyo Express*

I

Black Magicians
Come home: the pink meat image
  black yellow image with
  ten fingers and two eyes
is gigantic already: the black
  curly pubic hair, the
  blind hollow stomach,
the silent soft open vagina
  rare womb of new birth
cock lone and happy to be home
        again
touched by hands by mouths,
  by hairy lips—

Close the portals of the festival?

Open the portals to what Is,
The mattress covered with sheets,
  soft pillows of skin,
long soft hair and delicate
  palms along the buttocks
  timidly touching,
waiting for a sign, a throb
  softness of balls, rough
  nipples alone in the dark
  met by a weird finger;
Tears allright, and laughter
  allright
I am that I am—

    Closed off from this
The schemes begin, roulette,
  brainwaves, bony dice,
  Stroboscope motorcycles
  Stereoscopic Scaly
   Serpents winding thru
   cloud spaces of
    what is not—

". . . convoluted, lunging upon
a pismire, a conflagration, a—"

II
Shit! Intestines boiling in sand fire
        creep yellow brain cold sweat
        earth unbalanced vomit thru
        tears, snot ganglia buzzing
        the Electric Snake rising hypnotic
        shuffling metal-eyed coils
        whirling rings within wheels
        from asshole up the spine
        Acid in the throat the chest
        a knot trembling Swallow back
        the black furry ball of the great
        Fear

Oh!

The serpent in my bed pitiful
        crawling unwanted babes of
        snake covered with veins and pores
        breathing heavy frightened love
        metallic Bethlehem out the window
        the lost, the lost hungry
        ghosts here alive trapped
        in carpet rooms   How can I
        be sent to Hell
        with my skin and blood

Oh I remember myself so

Gasping, staring at dawn over
        lower Manhattan   the bridges
        covered with rust, the slime
        in my mouth & ass, sucking
        his cock like a baby crying Fuck
        me in my asshole   Make love
        to this rotten slave   Give me the
        power to whip & eat your heart
        I own your belly & your eyes

I speak thru your screaming
mouth Black Mantra Fuck you
Fuck me Mother Brother Friend
old white haired creep shuddering in
the toilet slum bath floorboards—

Oh how wounded, how wounded, I
murder the beautiful chinese women

It will come on the railroad, beneath
the wheels, in drunken hate screaming
thru the skinny machine gun, it will
come out of the mouth of the pilot
the dry lipped diplomat, the hairy
teacher will come out of me
again shitting the meat out of
my ears on my cancer deathbed

Oh crying man crying woman
crying guerrilla shopkeeper
crying dysentery boneface on
the urinal street of the Self

Oh Negro beaten in the eye in my
home, oh black magicians
in white skin robes boiling the
stomachs of your children that
you do not die but shudder in
Serpent & worm shape forever
Powerful minds & superhuman
Roar of volcano & rocket in
Your bowels—

Hail to your fierce desire, your
Godly pride, my Heaven's gate
will not be closed until
we enter all—

All human shapes, all
trembling donkeys & apes, all
lovers turned to ghost
all achers on trains &

taxicab bodies sped away
from date with desire, old movies,
all who were refused—

All which was rejected, the
leper-sexed hungry of
nazi conventions, hollow
cheeked arab marxists of Acco
Crusaders dying of starvation
in the Holy Land—

Seeking the Great Spirit of the
Universe in Terrible Godly
form, O suffering Jews
burned in the hopeless fire
O thin Bengali sadhus adoring
Kali mother hung with
nightmare skulls O Myself
under her pounding
feet!

Yes I am that worm soul under
the heel of the daemon horses
I am that man trembling to die
in vomit & trance in bamboo
eternities belly ripped by
red hands of courteous
chinamen kids—Come sweetly
now back to my Self as I was—

Allen Ginsberg says this: I am
a mass of sores and worms
& baldness & belly & smell
I am false Name the prey
of Yamantaka Devourer of
Strange dreams, the prey of
radiation & Police Hells of Law

I am that I am I am the
man & the Adam of hair in
my loins   This is my spirit and
physical shape I inhabit

this Universe Oh weeping
against what is my
own nature for now

Who would deny his own shape's
loveliness in his
dream moment of bed
Who sees his desire to be
horrible instead of Him

Who is, who cringes, perishes,
is reborn a red Screaming
baby? Who cringes before
that meaty shape in
          Fear?

In this dream I am the Dreamer
and the Dreamed   I am
that I am Ah but I have
always known

oooh for the hate I have spent
in denying my image & cursing
the breasts of illusion—
Screaming at murderers, trembling
between their legs in fear of the
steel pistols of my mortality—

Come, sweet lonely Spirit, back
to your bodies, come great God
back to your only image, come
to your many eyes & breasts,
come thru thought and
motion up all your
arms the great gesture of
Peace & acceptance Abhaya
Mudra Mudra of fearlessness
Mudra of Elephant Calmed &
war-fear ended forever!

The war, the war on Man, the
war on woman, the ghost

assembled armies vanish in
their realms

Chinese American Bardo Thodols
all the seventy hundred hells from
Orleans to Algeria tremble
with tender soldiers weeping

In Russia the young poets rise
to kiss the soul of the revolution
in Vietnam the body is burned
to show the truth of only the
body in Kremlin & White House
the schemers draw back
weeping from their schemes—

In my train seat I renounce
my power, so that I do
live I will die

Over for now the Vomit, cut
up & pincers in the skull,
fear of bones, grasp
against man woman & babe.

Let the dragon of Death
come forth from his
picture in the whirling
white clouds' darkness

And suck dream brains &
claim these lambs for his
meat, and let him feed
and be other than I

Till my turn comes and I
enter that maw and change
to a blind rock covered
with misty ferns that
I am not all now

but a universe of skin and breath
& changing thought and

burning hand & softened
heart in the old bed of
my skin   From this single
birth reborn that I am
to be so—

My own Identity now nameless
neither man nor dragon or
God

but the dreaming Me full
of physical rays' tender
red moons in my belly &
Stars in my eyes circling

And the Sun the Sun the
Sun my visible father
making my body visible
thru my eyes!

Tokyo, July 18, 1963

VII
KING OF MAY:
AMERICA
TO EUROPE
(1963–1965)

I Am a Victim of Telephone

When I lie down to sleep dream the Wishing Well it rings
"Have you a new play for the brokendown theater?"
When I write in my notebook poem it rings
"Buster Keaton is under the brooklyn bridge on Frankfurt and Pearl . . ."
When I unsheath my skin extend my cock toward someone's thighs fat or
      thin, boy or girl
Tingaling—"Please get him out of jail . . . the police are crashing down"
When I lift the soupspoon to my lips, the phone on the floor begins
      purring
"Hello it's me—I'm in the park two broads from Iowa . . . nowhere to sleep
      last night . . . hit 'em in the mouth"
When I muse at smoke crawling over the roof outside my street window
purifying Eternity with my eye observation of gray vaporous columns in
      the sky
ring ring "Hello this is Esquire be a dear and finish your political commit-
      ment manifesto"
When I listen to radio presidents roaring on the convention floor
the phone also chimes in "Rush up to Harlem with us and see the riots"
Always the telephone linked to all the hearts of the world beating at once
crying my husband's gone my boyfriend's busted forever my poetry was
      rejected
won't you come over for money and please won't you write me a piece of
      bullshit
How are you dear can you come to Easthampton we're all here bathing in
      the ocean we're all so lonely
and I lie back on my pallet contemplating $50 phone bill, broke, drowsy,
      anxious, my heart fearful of the fingers dialing, the deaths, the
      singing of telephone bells
ringing at dawn ringing all afternoon ringing up midnight ringing now
      forever.

New York, June 20, 1964

Today

O I am happy! O Swami Shivananda—a smile!
O telephone sweet little black being, what many voices and tongues!
Tonight I'll call up Jack tell him Buster Keaton is under the Brooklyn
    Bridge
by a vast red-brick wall still dead pan alive in red suspenders, portly
    abdomen.
Today I saw movies, publishers, bookstores, checks—wait, I'm still poor
Poor but happy! I saw politicians we wrote a Noise Law!
A Law to free poetry—Poor Plato! Whoops here comes Fascism! I rode in
    a taxi!
I rode a bus, ate hot Italian Sausages, Coca-Cola, a chili-burger, Kool-Aid I
    drank—
All day I did things! I took a nap—didn't I dream about lampshade
    academies and ouch! I am dying?
I stuck a needle in my arm and flooded my head with drowsy bliss . . .
And a hairy bum asked Mr. Keaton for money drink! Oh Buster! No
    answer!
Today I was really amazed! Samuel Beckett had rats eyes and gold round
    glasses—
I didn't say a word—I had my picture taken and read all thru the NY Times
and Daily News, I read everybody's editorials, I protested in my mind I
    have the privilege of being
Mad. Today I did everything, I wore a pink shirt in the street, at home in
    underwear
I marveled Henry Miller's iron sink, how could he remember so clearly?
Hypnagogic vision in Brooklyn 50 years ago—just now my eyeball
troops marched in square mufti battalion dragging prisoners to—
eyelids lifted I saw a blue devil with fifteen eyes on the wall—everything's
    mine, antique Tibetan Tankas, a siamese cat asleep on its side
    relaxed—
I looked out of the window and saw Tonight, it was dark—someone said
    ooo! in Puerto Rican.
But it was light all day, sweating hot—iron eyes blinking at the human
    element—
Irreducible Me today, I bought cigarettes at a machine, I was really worried
about my gross belly independent of philosophy, drama, idealism
    imagery—
My fate and I became one today and today became today—
just like a mystic prophecy—I'll conquer my belly tomorrow

or not, I'll toy with Mr. Choice also for real—today I said "Forever"
        thrice—
and walked under the vast Ladder of Doom, insouciant, not merely innocent
but completely hopeless! In Despair when I woke this morning,
my mouth furry smoked a Lucky Strike first thing when I dialed telephone
        to check on the Building Department—
I considered the License Department as I brushed my teeth with an odd
        toothbrush
some visitor left I lost mine—where? rack my brains it's there
somewhere in the past—with the snubnosed uncle cock from the freak-
        show
The old man familiar today, first time I thought of him in years, in the rain
in Massachusetts but I was a child that summer The pink thing bulged at
        his open thigh fly
he fingered it out to show me—I tarried till startled when the whiskied
        barker
questioned mine I ran out on the boardwalk drizzle confronting the Atlan-
        tic Ocean
—so trotted around the silent moody blocks home speechless
to mother father vaginal jelly rubber instruments discovered in the
        closet—
a stealthy memory makes hackles rise—"He inserts his penis into her
        vagina"—
What a weird explanation! I who collected matchbook covers like J. P.
        Morgan
gloating over sodden discoveries in the wet gutter—O happy grubby
        sewers of Revere—distasteful riches—
hopeless treasure I threw away in a week when I realized it was endless to
        complete—
next year gathered all the heat in my loins to spurt my white surprise drops
        into the wet brown wood under a
steamy shower, I used the toilet paper cardboard skeleton tube
to rub and thrill around my unconscious own shaft—playing with myself
        unbeknownst to the entire population of Far Rockaway—
remembered it all today—many years thinking of Kali Ma and other
        matters—
a big surprise it was Me—Dear Reader, I seem strange to myself—
You recognize everything all over again where you are, it's wonderful
to be introduced to strangers who know you already—
like being Famous—a reverberation of Eternal Consciousness—
Today heraldic of Today, archetypal mimeograph machines reprinting
        everybody's poetry,

like finishing a book of surrealism which I haven't read for years—
Benjamin Péret & René Crevel heroic for real—the old New Conscious-
ness reminded
me today—how busy I was, how fatal like a man in the madhouse, dis-
tracted
with presence of dishes of food to eat—Today's *stringbeans in the moon-
light*"
Like today I brought home blueberry pie for the first time in years—
Also today bit by a mosquito (to be precise, toward dawn)
(toward dusk ate marshmallows at the News Stand and drank huge cold
grape soda eyeing:
this afternoon's *Journal* headline FBI IN HARLEM, what kind of Nasty
old Epic
Afternoons I imagine!) Another event, a $10 bill in my hands, debt re-
paid,
a café espresso smaller event—Feeling rich I bought a secondhand record
of Gertrude Stein's actual Voice—
My day was Harmonious—Though I heard no mechanic music—
I noticed some Nazi propaganda—I wrote down my dream about Earth
dying—I wanted to telephone Long Island—I stood on a street
corner and didn't know where to go—
I telephoned the Civil Liberties Union—discussed the Junk Problem &
Supreme Court—
I thought I was planting suggestions in everybody's Me-ity—
thought a few minutes of Blake—his quatrains—I climbed four flights &
stood at Fainlight's Chinatown door locked up—I'm being
mysterious—
What does this mean? Don't ask me today, I'm still thinking,
Trying to remember what happened while it's still happening—
I wrote a "poem," I scribbled quotation marks everywhere over Fate
passing by
Sometimes I felt noble, sometimes I felt ugly, I spoke to man and woman
from *Times* & *Time*, summarized hugely—plots, cinematic glories, I
boasted a little, subtly—
Was I seen thru? Too much happened to see thru All—
I was never alone except for two blocks by the park, nor was I unhappy—
I blessed my Guru, I felt like a shyster—told Ed how much I liked being
made love to by delicate girl hands—
It's true, more girls should do that to us, we chalked up another mark what's
wrong
and told everybody to register to vote this November—I stopped on the
street and shook hands—

I took a crap once this day—How extraordinary it all goes! recollected, a
     lifetime!
Imagine writing autobiography what a wealth of Detail to enlist!
I see the contents of future magazines—just a peek Today being hurried—
Today is slowly ending—I will step back into it and disappear.

New York, July 21, 1964

KRAL MAJALES

And the Communists have nothing to offer but fat cheeks and
  eyeglasses and lying policemen
and the Capitalists proffer Napalm and money in green suitcases
  to the Naked,
and the Communists create heavy industry but the heart is also
  heavy
and the beautiful engineers are all dead, the secret technicians
  conspire for their own glamor
in the Future, in the Future, but now drink vodka and lament the
  Security Forces,
and the Capitalists drink gin and whiskey on airplanes but let
  Indian brown millions starve
and when Communist and Capitalist assholes tangle the Just man
  is arrested or robbed or had his head cut off,
but not like Kabir, and the cigarette cough of the Just man above
  the clouds
in the bright sunshine is a salute to the health of the blue sky.
For I was arrested thrice in Prague, once for singing drunk on
  Narodni street,
once knocked down on the midnight pavement by a mustached
  agent who screamed out *BOUZERANT*,
once for losing my notebooks of unusual sex politics dream opinions,
and I was sent from Havana by plane by detectives in green
  uniform,
and I was sent from Prague by plane by detectives in Czecho-
  slovakian business suits,
Cardplayers out of Cezanne, the two strange dolls that entered
  Joseph K's room at morn
also entered mine, and ate at my table, and examined my scribbles,
and followed me night and morn from the houses of lovers to the
  cafés of Centrum—
And I am the King of May, which is the power of sexual youth,
and I am the King of May, which is industry in eloquence and
  action in amour,
and I am the King of May, which is long hair of Adam and the
  Beard of my own body
and I am the King of May, which is Kral Majales in the Czecho-
  slovakian tongue,
and I am the King of May, which is old Human poesy, and 100,000
  people chose my name,
and I am the King of May, and in a few minutes I will land at
  London Airport,
and I am the King of May, naturally, for I am of Slavic parentage
  and a Buddhist Jew
who worships the Sacred Heart of Christ the blue body of Krishna
  the straight back of Ram
The Beads of Chango the Nigerian   singing Shiva Shiva in a
  manner which I have invented,
and the King of May is a middleeuropean honor, mine in the XX
  century
despite space ships and the Time Machine, because I heard the
  voice of Blake in a vision,
and repeat that voice. And I am the King of May that sleeps with
  teenagers laughing.
And I am the King of May, that I may be expelled from my
  Kingdom with Honor, as of old,
To shew the difference between Caesar's Kingdom and the King-
  dom of the May of Man—
and I am the King of May, tho paranoid, for the Kingdom of May
  is too beautiful to last for more than a month—
and I am the King of May because I touched my finger to my
  forehead saluting
a luminous heavy girl with trembling hands who said "one moment
  Mr. Ginsberg"
before a fat young Plainclothesman stepped between our bodies—
  I was going to England—
and I am the King of May, returning to see Bunhill Fields and walk
  on Hampstead Heath,
and I am the King of May, in a giant jetplane touching Albion's
  airfield trembling in fear
as the plane roars to a landing on the grey concrete, shakes &
  expells air,
and rolls slowly to a stop under the clouds with part of blue heaven
  still visible.
And tho I am the King of May, the Marxists have beat me upon
  the street, kept me up all night in Police Station, followed
  me thru Springtime Prague, detained me in secret and
  deported me from our kingdom by airplane.
Thus I have written this poem on a jet seat in mid Heaven.

Robert LaVigne

May 7, 1965   *Allen Ginsberg*   oyez

146   *King of May: America to Europe (1963–1965)*

Kral Majales

And the Communists have nothing to offer but fat cheeks and eyeglasses
and lying policemen
and the Capitalists proffer Napalm and money in green suitcases to the
Naked,
and the Communists create heavy industry but the heart is also heavy
and the beautiful engineers are all dead, the secret technicians conspire for
their own glamour
in the Future, in the Future, but now drink vodka and lament the Security
Forces,
and the Capitalists drink gin and whiskey on airplanes but let Indian brown
millions starve
and when Communist and Capitalist assholes tangle the Just man is ar-
rested or robbed or had his head cut off,
but not like Kabir, and the cigarette cough of the Just man above the clouds
in the bright sunshine is a salute to the health of the blue sky.
For I was arrested thrice in Prague, once for singing drunk on Narodni
street,
once knocked down on the midnight pavement by a mustached agent who
screamed out BOUZERANT,
once for losing my notebooks of unusual sex politics dream opinions,
and I was sent from Havana by plane by detectives in green uniform,
and I was sent from Prague by plane by detectives in Czechoslovakian
business suits,
Cardplayers out of Cézanne, the two strange dolls that entered Joseph K's
room at morn
also entered mine, and ate at my table, and examined my scribbles,
and followed me night and morn from the houses of lovers to the cafés of
Centrum—
And I am the King of May, which is the power of sexual youth,
and I am the King of May, which is industry in eloquence and action in
amour,
and I am the King of May, which is long hair of Adam and the Beard of my
own body
and I am the King of May, which is Kral Majales in the Czechoslovakian
tongue,
and I am the King of May, which is old Human poesy, and 100,000 people
chose my name,
and I am the King of May, and in a few minutes I will land at London
Airport,

and I am the King of May, naturally, for I am of Slavic parentage and a
  Buddhist Jew

who worships the Sacred Heart of Christ the blue body of Krishna the
  straight back of Ram

the beads of Chango the Nigerian singing Shiva Shiva in a manner which I
  have invented,

and the King of May is a middleeuropean honor, mine in the XX century

despite space ships and the Time Machine, because I heard the voice of
  Blake in a vision,

and repeat that voice. And I am King of May that sleeps with teenagers
  laughing.

And I am the King of May, that I may be expelled from my Kingdom with
  Honor, as of old,

To show the difference between Caesar's Kingdom and the Kingdom of
  the May of Man—

And I am the King of May, tho' paranoid, for the Kingdom of May is too
  beautiful to last for more than a month—

and I am the King of May because I touched my finger to my forehead
  saluting

a luminous heavy girl trembling hands who said "one moment Mr. Gins-
  berg"

before a fat young Plainclothesman stepped between our bodies—I was
  going to England—

and I am the King of May, returning to see Bunhill Fields and walk on
  Hampstead Heath,

and I am the King of May, in a giant jetplane touching Albion's airfield
  trembling in fear

as the plane roars to a landing on the gray concrete, shakes & expels air,

and rolls slowly to a stop under the clouds with part of blue heaven still
  visible.

And *tho'* I am the King of May, the Marxists have beat me upon the street,
  kept me up all night in Police Station, followed me thru Spring-
  time Prague, detained me in secret and deported me from our
  kingdom by airplane.

Thus I have written this poem on a jet seat in mid Heaven.

May 7, 1965

Guru

It is the moon that disappears
It is the stars that hide not I
It's the City that vanishes, I stay
with my forgotten shoes,
my invisible stocking
It is the call of a bell

Primrose Hill, May 1965

Who Be Kind To

Be kind to your self, it is only one
        and perishable
of many on the planet, thou art that
one that wishes a soft finger tracing the
        line of feeling from nipple to pubes—
one that wishes a tongue to kiss your armpit,
        a lip to kiss your cheek inside your
        whiteness thigh—
Be kind to yourself Harry, because unkindness
        comes when the body explodes
napalm cancer and the deathbed in Vietnam
is a strange place to dream of   trees
        leaning over and angry American faces
grinning with sleepwalk terror over your
        last eye—
Be kind to yourself, because the bliss of your own
        kindness will flood the police tomorrow,
because the cow weeps in the field and the
        mouse weeps in the cat hole—
Be kind to this place, which is your present
        habitation, with derrick and radar tower
        and flower in the ancient brook—
Be kind to your neighbor who weeps
        solid tears on the television sofa,
he has no other home, and hears nothing
        but the hard voice of telephones
Click, buzz, switch channel and the inspired
        melodrama disappears
and he's left alone for the night, he disappears
        in bed—
Be kind to your disappearing mother and
        father gazing out the terrace window
        as milk truck and hearse turn the corner
Be kind to the politician weeping in the galleries
        of Whitehall, Kremlin, White House
        Louvre and Phoenix City
aged, large nosed, angry, nervously dialing
        the bald voice box connected to

electrodes underground converging thru
    wires vaster than a kitten's eye can see
on the mushroom shaped fear-lobe under
    the ear of Sleeping Dr. Einstein
crawling with worms, crawling with worms, crawling
    with worms the hour has come—
Sick, dissatisfied, unloved, the bulky
    foreheads of Captain Premier President
    Sir Comrade Fear!
Be kind to the fearful one at your side
    Who's remembering the Lamentations
    of the bible
the prophecies of the Crucified Adam   Son
    of all the porters and char men of
                Bell   gravia—
Be kind to your self who weeps under
    the Moscow moon and hide your bliss hairs
    under raincoat and suede Levi's—
For this is the joy to be born, the kindness
    received thru strange eyeglasses on
    a bus thru Kensington,
the finger touch of the Londoner on your thumb,
    that borrows light from your cigarette,
the morning smile at Newcastle Central
    station, when longhair Tom blond husband
    greets the bearded stranger of telephones—
the boom bom that bounces in the joyful
    bowels as the Liverpool Minstrels of
    CavernSink
raise up their joyful voices and guitars
    in electric Afric hurrah
    for Jerusalem—
The saints come marching in, Twist &
    Shout, and Gates of Eden are named
    in Albion again
Hope sings a black psalm from Nigeria,
    and a white psalm echoes in Detroit
    and reechoes amplified from Nottingham to Prague
and a Chinese psalm will be heard, if we all
    live out our lives for the next 6 decades—
Be kind to the Chinese psalm in the red transistor
    in your breast—

Be kind to the Monk in the 5 Spot who plays
      lone chord-bangs on his vast piano
lost in space on a bench and hearing himself
      in the nightclub universe—
Be kind to the heroes that have lost their
      names in the newspaper
and hear only their own supplication for
      the peaceful kiss of sex in the giant
      auditoriums of the planet,
nameless voices crying for kindness in the orchestra,
screaming in anguish that bliss come true
      and sparrows sing another hundred years
      to white haired babes
and poets be fools of their own desire—O Anacreon
      and angelic Shelley!
Guide these new-nippled generations on space
      ships to Mars' next universe
The prayer is to man and girl, the only
      gods, the only lords of Kingdoms of
      Feeling, Christs of their own
      living ribs—
Bicycle chain and machine gun, fear sneer
      & smell cold logic of the Dream Bomb
have come to Saigon, Johannesburg,
      Dominica City, Phnom Penh, Pentagon
      Paris and Lhasa—
Be kind to the universe of Self that
      trembles and shudders and thrills
      in XX Century,
that opens its eyes and belly and breast
      chained with flesh to feel
      the myriad flowers of bliss
      that I Am to Thee—
A dream! a Dream! I don't want to be alone!
      I want to know that I am loved!
I want the orgy of our flesh, orgy
      of all eyes happy, orgy of the soul
      kissing and blessing its mortal-grown
      body,
orgy of tenderness beneath the neck, orgy of
      kindness to thigh and vagina
Desire given with meat hand

and cock, desire taken with
mouth and ass, desire returned
to the last sigh!
Tonite let's all make love in London
as if it were 2001 the years
of thrilling god—
And be kind to the poor soul that cries in
a crack of the pavement because he
has no body—
Prayers to the ghosts and demons, the
lackloves of Capitals & Congresses
who make sadistic noises
on the radio—
Statue destroyers & tank captains, unhappy
murderers in Mekong & Stanleyville,
That a new kind of man has come to his bliss
to end the cold war he has borne
against his own kind flesh
since the days of the snake.

June 8, 1965

VIII
THE FALL
OF AMERICA
(1965–1971)

'. . . same electric lightning South
follows this train
Apocalypse prophesied—
the fall of America
signalled from Heaven—'

To WALT WHITMAN

"Intense and loving comradeship, the personal and passionate attachment of man to man—which, hard to define, underlies the lessons and ideals of the profound saviors of every land and age, and which seems to promise, when thoroughly develop'd, cultivated and recognised in manners and literature, the most substantial hope and safety of the future of these States, will then be fully express'd.

"It is to the development, identification, and general prevalence of that fervid comradeship, (the adhesive love, at least rivaling the amative love hitherto possessing imaginative literature, if not going beyond it,) that I look for the counterbalance and offset of our materialistic and vulgar American democracy, and for the spiritualization thereof. Many will say it is a dream, and will not follow my inferences: but I confidently expect a time when there will be seen, running like a half-hid warp through all the myriad audible and visible worldly interests of America, threads of manly friendship, fond and loving, pure and sweet, strong and life-long, carried to degrees hitherto unknown—not only giving tone to individual character, and making it unprecedentedly emotional, muscular, heroic, and refined, but having the deepest relations to general politics. I say democracy infers such loving comradeship, as its most inevitable twin or counterpart, without which it will be incomplete, in vain, and incapable of perpetuating itself."

DEMOCRATIC VISTAS, 1871

First Party at Ken Kesey's with Hell's Angels

Cool black night thru the redwoods
cars parked outside in shade
behind the gate, stars dim above
the ravine, a fire burning by the side
porch and a few tired souls hunched over
in black leather jackets. In the huge
wooden house, a yellow chandelier
at 3 A.M. the blast of loudspeakers
hi-fi Rolling Stones Ray Charles Beatles
Jumping Joe Jackson and twenty youths
dancing to the vibration thru the floor,
a little weed in the bathroom, girls in scarlet
tights, one muscular smooth skinned man
sweating dancing for hours, beer cans
bent littering the yard, a hanged man
sculpture dangling from a high creek branch,
children sleeping softly in their bedroom bunks.
And 4 police cars parked outside the painted
gate, red lights revolving in the leaves.

December 1965

These States: into L.A.

... Overpopulation, overpopulation
        Give me 3 acres of land
        Give my brother how much?
                Each man have fine estate?
                settle giant Communes?
LSD Shakti-snake settles like gas into Consciousness
        —Brightest Venus I've ever seen
Canyon floor road, near
        bursting tides
    & caves they'd slept in earlier years
                covered with green water
                height of a man.
    A stranger walked that ground.
        Five years ago we picnicked
                in this place.
Auto track by a mud log, Bixby Creek
    wove channels
                thru the shifting sands.
I saw the ghost of Neal
        pass by, Ferlinghetti's ghost
    The ghost of Homer roaring at the surf
        barking & wagging his tail
    My own footprint at the sea's lips
        white foam to the rock where I sang Harekrishna
sand garden drying, kelp
        standing head upward in sunlight.
                Dinosaur hard, scabrous
    overgrown with seaweed tendrils,
                Professors of rock ...

Where's Stravinsky? Theda Bara? Chaplin? Harpo Marx?
    Where's Laurel and his Hardy?
            Laughing phantoms
            going to the grave—
Last time this town   I saw them in movies
    Ending *The Road to Utopia* 'O Carib Isle!'
    Laurel aged & white-haired Hardy
        Hydrogen Comic smoke billowing
            up from their Kingdom—

Grauman's Chinese Theater's drab sidewalk front's
　　concrete footprints, stood there
　　　　　stupid, anal, exciting
　　　　　　　　upside down, Crosseyed moviestar'd
　　I craned my neck at Myrna Loy & Shirley Temple shoe-marks—

Raccoon crouched at road-edge, praying—
　　　　　　　　　　　　Carlights pass—
Merry Christmas to Mr. & Mrs.
　　　　　　　　Chiang Kai Shek
Merry Christmas to President Johnson & pray for Health
Merry Christmas to McNamara, State Secretary Rusk,
　　　　　Khrushchev hid in his apartment house,
　　　　　　　　to Kosygin's name, to Ho Chi Minh grown old,
Merry Christmas to rosycheeked Mao Tze Tung
　　　Happy New Year Chou En Lai & Laurel and Hardy
Merry Christmas to the Pope
　　　　　　& to the Dalai Lama Rebbe Lubovitcher
　　to the highest Priests of Benin,
　　to the Chiefs of the Faery Churches—
Merry Christmas to the Four Shankaracharyas,
　　to all Naga Sadhus, Bauls & Chanting Dervishes from Egypt to
　　　　　　　　　　　　　　　Malaya— . . .
　　　　　Good Cheer Happy Kalpa
for Dominica Vietnam Congo China India America
　　　　　Tho England rang with the Beatles!
　　　"healing all that was oppressed with the Devil."
　& at Santa Barbara exit
　　　　　the Preacher hollered in tongues
　　　　　YOUR NAME IS WRITTEN IN HEAVEN
Aquamarine lights revolving along the highway,
　　　　　night stars over L.A., exit trees,
　　turquoise brilliance shining on sidestreets—

　　　　　　　　　　　　　　　　Xmas Eve 1965

Wichita Vortex Sutra

I
... Kansas! Kansas! Shuddering at last!
                    PERSON appearing in Kansas!
        angry telephone calls to the University
        Police dumbfounded leaning on
                            their radiocar hoods
        While Poets chant to Allah in the roadhouse Showboat!
Blue eyed children dance and hold thy Hand O aged Walt
        who came from Lawrence to Topeka to envision
                    Iron interlaced upon the city plain—
        Telegraph wires strung from city to city O Melville!
                    Television brightening thy *rills of Kansas lone*
I come,
        lone man from the void, riding a bus
        hypnotized by red tail lights on the straight
                            space road ahead—
        & the Methodist minister with cracked eyes
                            leaning over the table
                    quoting Kierkegaard "death of God"
                            a million dollars
        in the bank   owns all West Wichita
                            come to Nothing!
                    Prajnaparamita Sutra over coffee—Vortex
        of telephone radio aircraft assembly frame ammunition
        petroleum nightclub Newspaper streets illuminated by Bright
                            EMPTINESS—

Thy sins are forgiven, Wichita!
                    Thy lonesomeness annulled, O Kansas dear!
                    as the western Twang prophesied
        thru banjo, when lone cowboy walked the railroad track
                    past an empty station toward the sun
        sinking giant-bulbed orange down the box canyon—
        Music strung over his back
        and empty handed   singing on this planet earth
                    I'm a lonely Dog, O Mother!

Come, Nebraska, sing & dance with me—
    Come lovers of Lincoln and Omaha,
           hear my soft voice at last
As Babes need the chemical touch of flesh in pink infancy
    lest they die Idiot returning to Inhuman—
                  Nothing—
So, tender lipt adolescent girl, pale youth,
          give me back my soft kiss
    Hold me in your innocent arms,
        accept my tears as yours to harvest
        equal   in nature to the Wheat
        that made your bodies' muscular bones
        broad shouldered, boy bicept—
        from leaning on cows & drinking Milk
            in Midwest Solitude—
No more fear of tenderness, much delight in weeping, ecstasy
    in singing, laughter rises that confounds
        staring Idiot mayors
          and stony politicians eyeing
          Thy breast,
             O Man of America, be born!
Truth breaks through!
    How big is the prick of the President?
        How big is Cardinal Vietnam?
How little the prince of the FBI, unmarried all these years!
    How big are all the Public Figures?
  What kind of flesh hangs, hidden behind their Images? . . .

                     February 15, 1966

II
Face the Nation
Thru Hickman's rolling earth hills
        icy winter
            gray sky   bare trees lining the road
    South to Wichita
      you're in the Pepsi Generation   Signum enroute
Aiken Republican on the radio   60,000
     Northvietnamese troops now infiltrated but over 250,000

South Vietnamese   armed men
our Enemy—
Not Hanoi our enemy
Not China our enemy
The Viet Cong!
McNamara made a "bad guess"
"Bad Guess?" chorused the Reporters.
Yes, no more than a Bad Guess, in 1962
"8000 American Troops handle the
Situation"
Bad Guess
in 1954, 80% of the
Vietnamese people would've voted for Ho Chi Minh
wrote Ike   years later   *Mandate for Change*
A bad guess in the Pentagon
And the Hawks were guessing all along
Bomb China's 200,000,000
cried Stennis from Mississippi
I guess it was 3 weeks ago
Holmes Alexander in Albuquerque Journal
Provincial newsman
said I guess we better begin to do that Now,
his typewriter clacking in his aged office
on a side street   under Sandia Mountain?
Half the world away from China
Johnson got some bad advice   Republican Aiken sang
to the Newsmen over the radio
The General guessed they'd stop infiltrating the South
if they bombed the North—
So I guess they bombed!
Pale Indochinese boys came thronging thru the jungle
in increased numbers
to the scene of TERROR!
While the triangle-roofed Farmer's Grain Elevator
sat quietly by the side of the road
along the railroad track
American Eagle beating its wings over Asia
million dollar helicopters
a billion dollars worth of Marines
who loved *Aunt Betty*

Drawn from the shores and farms shaking
from the high schools to the landing barge
blowing the air thru their cheeks with fear
in *Life* on Television
Put it this way on the radio
Put it this way in television language
Use the words
language, language:
"A bad guess"

Put it this way in headlines
Omaha World Herald—*Rusk Says Toughness*
Essential For Peace
Put it this way
Lincoln Nebraska morning Star—
Vietnam War Brings Prosperity
Put it *this* way
Declared McNamara   speaking language
Asserted Maxwell Taylor
General, Consultant to White House
Viet Cong losses leveling up three five zero zero per month
Front page testimony February '66
Here in Nebraska same as Kansas same known in Saigon
in Peking, in Moscow, same known
by the youths of Liverpool three five zero zero
the latest quotation in the human meat market—
Father I cannot tell a lie!

A black horse bends its head to the stubble
beside the silver stream winding thru the woods
by an antique red barn on the outskirts of Beatrice—
Quietness, quietness
over this countryside
except for unmistakable signals on radio
followed by the honkytonk tinkle
of a city piano
to calm the nerves of taxpaying housewives of a Sunday morn.
Has anyone looked in the eyes of the dead?
U.S. Army recruiting service sign *Careers With A Future*
Is anyone living to look for future forgiveness?
Water hoses frozen on the street, the

Crowd gathered to see a strange happening garage—
Red flames on Sunday morning
in a quiet town!
Has anyone looked in the eyes of the wounded?
Have we seen but paper faces, Life Magazine?
Are screaming faces made of dots,
electric dots on Television—
fuzzy decibels registering
the mammal voiced howl
from the outskirts of Saigon to console model picture tubes
in Beatrice, in Hutchinson, in El Dorado
in historic Abilene
O inconsolable!

Stop, and eat more flesh.
"We will negotiate anywhere anytime"
said the giant President
Kansas City Times 2/14/66: "Word reached U.S. authorities that
Thailand's leaders feared that in Honolulu Johnson might have tried to
persuade South Vietnam's rulers to ease their stand against negotiating
with the Viet Cong.
American officials said these fears were groundless and Humphrey
was telling the Thais so."
AP dispatch
The last week's paper is Amnesia.

Three five zero zero is numerals
Headline language poetry, nine decades after Democratic Vistas
and the Prophecy of the Good Gray Poet
Our nation "of the fabled damned"
or else . . .
Language, language
Ezra Pound the Chinese Written Character for truth
defined as man standing by his word
Word picture: forked creature
Man
standing by a box, birds flying out
representing mouth speech
Ham Steak please waitress, in the warm café.
Different from a bad guess.

The war is language,
language abused
for Advertisement,
language used
like magic for power on the planet:
Black Magic language,
formulas for reality—
Communism is a 9 letter word
used by inferior magicians with
the wrong alchemical formula for transforming earth into gold
—funky warlocks operating on guesswork,
handmedown mandrake terminology
that never worked in 1956
for gray-domed Dulles,
brooding over at State,
that never worked for Ike who knelt to take
the magic wafer in his mouth
from Dulles' hand
inside the church in Washington:
Communion of bum magicians
congress of failures from Kansas & Missouri
working with the wrong equations
Sorcerer's Apprentices who lost control
of the simplest broomstick in the world:
Language
O longhaired magician come home take care of your dumb helper
before the radiation deluge floods your livingroom,
your magic errandboy's
just made a bad guess again
that's lasted a whole decade.

NBCBSUPAPINSLIFE
Time Mutual presents
World's Largest Camp Comedy:
Magic In Vietnam—
reality turned inside out
changing its sex in the Mass Media
for 30 days, TV den and bedroom farce
Flashing pictures Senate Foreign Relations Committee room
Generals faces flashing on and off screen

                                        mouthing language
State Secretary speaking nothing but language
McNamara declining to speak public language
        The President talking language,
                        Senators reinterpreting language
        General Taylor *Limited Objectives*
                                Owls from Pennsylvania
                Clark's Face *Open Ended*
                        Dove's *Apocalypse*
                        Morse's hairy ears
Stennis orating in Mississippi
                half billion chinamen crowding into the
                                        polling booth,
                Clean shaven Gen. Gavin's image
                                imagining *Enclaves*
                Tactical Bombing the magic formula for
                a silver haired Symington:
Ancient Chinese apothegm:
                Old in vain.
        Hawks swooping thru the newspapers
                talons visible
        wings outspread in the giant updraft of hot air
                        loosing their dry screech in the skies
                                over the Capitol
Napalm and black clouds emerging in newsprint
        Flesh soft as a Kansas girl's
                        ripped open by metal explosion—
        three five zero zero   on the other side of the planet
                caught in barbed wire, fire ball
                bullet shock, bayonet electricity
        bomb blast terrific in skull & belly, shrapneled throbbing meat
While this American nation argues war:
                conflicting language, language
                        proliferating in airwaves
        filling the farmhouse ear, filling
                the City Manager's head in his oaken office
                the professor's head in his bed at midnight
                the pupil's head at the movies
                        blond haired, his heart throbbing with desire
                        for the girlish image bodied on the screen:
                        or smoking cigarettes
                        and watching Captain Kangaroo

166   *The Fall of America (1965–1971)*

                    that fabled damned of nations
                    prophecy come true—
Though the highway's straight,
        dipping downward through low hills,
        rising narrow on the far horizon
                black cows browse in caked fields
                    ponds in the hollows lie frozen,
                            quietness.
Is this the land that started war on China?
        This be the soil that thought Cold War for decades?
        Are these nervous naked trees & farmhouses
                            the vortex
                            of oriental anxiety molecules
        that've imagined   American Foreign Policy
            and magick'd up paranoia in Peking
                    and curtains of living blood
                        surrounding far Saigon?
Are these the towns where the language emerged
        from the mouths here
                    that makes a Hell of riots in Dominica
        sustains the aging tyranny of Chiang in silent Taipeh city
        Paid for the lost French war in Algeria
                overthrew the Guatemalan polis in '54
        maintaining United Fruit's banana greed
                            another thirteen years
                for the secret prestige of the Dulles family lawfirm?

Here's Marysville—
        a black railroad engine in the children's park,
                    at rest—
and the Track Crossing
        with Cotton Belt flatcars
                    carrying autos west from Dallas
        Delaware & Hudson gondolas filled with power stuff—
        a line of boxcars far east as the eye can see
                    carrying battle goods to cross the Rockies
                into the hands of rich longshoremen loading
                            ships on the Pacific—
                Oakland Army Terminal lights
                        blue illumined all night now—
Crash of couplings and the great American train
                moves on carrying its cushioned load of metal doom

Union Pacific linked together with your Hoosier Line
            followed by passive Wabash
                        rolling behind
            all Erie carrying cargo in the rear,
            Central Georgia's rust colored truck proclaiming
                        The Right Way, concluding
the awesome poem writ by the train
            across northern Kansas,
        land which gave right of way
        to the massing of metal meant for explosion
                        in Indochina—
Passing thru Waterville,
            Electronic machinery in the bus humming prophecy—
            paper signs blowing in cold wind,
                        mid-Sunday afternoon's silence in town
            under frost-gray sky
                        that covers the horizon—
That the rest of earth is unseen,
                        an outer universe invisible,
            Unknown except thru
                        language
                            airprint
                                magic images
    or prophecy of the secret
                heart the same
                in Waterville as Saigon one human form:
            When a woman's heart bursts in Waterville
                        a woman screams equal in Hanoi—
On to Wichita to prophesy! O frightful Bard!
        into the heart of the vortex
            where anxiety rings
                    the University with millionaire pressure,
            lonely crank telephone voices sighing in dread,
    and students waken trembling in their beds
            with dreams of a new truth warm as meat,
            little girls suspecting their elders of murder
                        committed by remote control machinery,
            boys with sexual bellies aroused
                        chilled in the heart by the mailman
            with a letter from an aging white haired General

Director of selection for service in Deathwar
            all this black language
                        writ by machine!
                O hopeless Fathers and Teachers
                in Hué   do you know
                            the same woe too?

I'm an old man now, and a lonesome man in Kansas
        but not afraid
                to speak my lonesomeness in a car,
            because not only my lonesomeness
                it's Ours, all over America,
                            O tender fellows—
                & spoken lonesomeness is Prophecy
                in the moon 100 years ago or in
                        the middle of Kansas now.
It's not the vast plains mute our mouths
                    that fill at midnite with ecstatic language
            when our trembling bodies hold each other
                    breast to breast on a mattress—
        Not the empty sky that hides
                    the feeling from our faces
    nor our skirts and trousers that conceal
            the bodylove emanating in a glow of beloved skin,
                white smooth abdomen down to the hair
                            between our legs,
        It's not a God that bore us that forbid
            our Being, like a sunny rose
                    all red with naked joy
            between our eyes & bellies, yes
All we do is for this frightened thing
            we call Love, want and lack—
    fear that we aren't the one whose body could be
        beloved of all the brides of Kansas City,
        kissed all over by every boy of Wichita—
    O but how many in their solitude weep aloud like me—
        On the bridge over Republican River
            almost in tears to know
                        how to speak the right language—
        on the frosty broad road

uphill between highway embankments
I search for the language
that is also yours—
almost all our language has been taxed by war.
Radio antennae high tension
wires ranging from Junction City across the plains—
highway cloverleaf sunk in a vast meadow
lanes curving past Abilene
to Denver filled with old
heroes of love—
to Wichita where McClure's mind
burst into animal beauty
drunk, getting laid in a car
in a neon misted street
15 years ago—
to Independence where the old man's still alive
who loosed the bomb that's slaved all human consciousness
and made the body universe a place of fear—
Now, speeding along the empty plain,
no giant demon machine
visible on the horizon
but tiny human trees and wooden houses at the sky's edge
I claim my birthright!
reborn forever as long as Man
in Kansas or other universe—Joy
reborn after the vast sadness of War Gods!
A lone man talking to myself, no house in the brown vastness to hear,
imaging the throng of Selves
that make this nation one body of Prophecy
languaged by Declaration as Pursuit of
Happiness!
I call all Powers of imagination
to my side in this auto to make Prophecy,
all Lords
of human kingdoms to come
Shambu Bharti Baba naked covered with ash
Khaki Baba fat-bellied mad with the dogs
Dehorahava Baba who moans Oh how wounded, How wounded
Sitaram Onkar Das Thakur who commands
give up your desire

Satyananda who raises two thumbs in tranquillity
        Kali Pada Guha Roy whose yoga drops before the void
                Shivananda who touches the breast and says OM
Srimata Krishnaji of Brindaban who says take for your guru
        William Blake the invisible father of English visions
        Sri Ramakrishna master of ecstasy eyes
                half closed who only cries for his mother
Chaitanya arms upraised singing & dancing his own praise
        merciful Chango judging our bodies
                Durga-Ma covered with blood
                        destroyer of battlefield illusions
                million-faced Tathagata gone past suffering
        Preserver Harekrishna returning in the age of pain
Sacred Heart my Christ acceptable
                Allah the Compassionate One
                        Jaweh Righteous One
                        all Knowledge-Princes of Earth-man, all
        ancient Seraphim of heavenly Desire, Devas, yogis
                & holymen I chant to—
                        Come to my lone presence
                                into this Vortex named Kansas,
I lift my voice aloud,
        make Mantra of American language now,
                I here declare the end of the War!
Let the States tremble,
        let the Nation weep,
                let Congress legislate its own delight
                        let the President execute his own desire—
this Act done by my own voice,
published to my own senses,
                        blissfully received by my own form
        approved with pleasure by my sensations
                manifestation of my very thought
                accomplished in my own imagination
                        all realms within my consciousness fulfilled
        60 miles from Wichita
                        near El Dorado,
                                The Golden One,
in chill earthly mist
        houseless brown farmland plains rolling heavenward

                                        in every direction
one midwinter afternoon Sunday called the day of the Lord—
        Pure Spring Water gathered in one tower
                where Florence is
                        set on a hill,
                stop for tea & gas

        Cars passing their messages along country crossroads
                to populaces cement-networked on flatness,
                                giant white mist on earth
                and a Wichita Eagle-Beacon headlines
                "Kennedy Urges Cong Get Chair in Negotiations"
The War is gone,
        Language emerging on the motel news stand,
                        the right magic
                Formula, the language known
        in the back of the mind before, now in black print
                        daily consciousness
Eagle News Services Saigon—
        Headline Surrounded Vietcong Charge Into Fire Fight
                the suffering not yet ended
                        for others
                The last spasms of the dragon of pain
                        shoot thru the muscles
                        a crackling around the eyeballs
                        of a sensitive yellow boy by a muddy wall
Continued from page one   area
        after the Marines killed 256 Vietcong captured 31
        ten day operation Harvest Moon last December
                        Language language
        U.S. Military Spokesmen
                        Language language
                                Cong death toll
                has soared to 100 in First Air Cavalry
                Division's Sector of
                        Language language
                        Operation White Wing near Bong Son
Some of the
        Language language
                        Communist
                        Language language soldiers

charged so desperately
    they were struck with six or seven bullets before they fell
    Language Language M 60 Machine Guns
                    Language language in La Drang Valley
    the terrain is rougher infested with leeches and scorpions
                    The war was over several hours ago!
Oh at last again the radio opens
    blue Invitations!
                    Angelic Dylan singing across the nation
                    "When all your children start to resent you
                    Won't you come see me, Queen Jane?"
    His youthful voice making glad
                    the brown endless meadows
    His tenderness penetrating aether,
            soft prayer on the airwaves,
                    Language language, and sweet music too
                    even unto thee,
                            hairy flatness!
                    even unto thee
                                despairing Burns!

Future speeding on swift wheels
                    straight to the heart of Wichita!
Now radio voices cry population hunger world
                    of unhappy people
            waiting for Man to be born
                    O man in America!
    you certainly smell good
                    the radio says
    passing mysterious families of winking towers
    grouped round a quonset-hut on a hillock—
            feed storage or military fear factory here?
Sensitive City, Ooh! Hamburger & Skelley's Gas
                    lights feed man and machine,
    Kansas Electric Substation aluminum robot
            signals thru thin antennae towers
            above the empty football field
                                at Sunday dusk
to a solitary derrick that pumps oil from the unconscious
                    working night & day
    & factory gas-flares edge a huge golf course

             where tired businessmen can come and play—
Cloverleaf, Merging Traffic East Wichita turnoff
                    McConnell Airforce Base
                              nourishing the city—
         Lights rising in the suburbs
         Supermarket Texaco brilliance starred
                    over streetlamp vertebrae on Kellogg,
              green jeweled traffic lights
                    confronting the windshield,
Centertown ganglion entered!
                    Crowds of autos moving with their lightshine,
                    signbulbs winking in the driver's eyeball—
         The human nest collected, neon lit,
                              and sunburst signed
                    for business as usual, except on the Lord's Day—
         Redeemer Lutheran's three crosses lit on the lawn
                         reminder of our sins
         and Titsworth offers insurance on Hydraulic
         by De Voors Guard's Mortuary for outmoded bodies
                         of the human vehicle
                    which no Titsworth of insurance will customize for resale—
So home, traveler, past the newspaper language factory
         under Union Station railroad bridge on Douglas
         to the center of the Vortex, calmly returned
                    to Hotel Eaton—
Carry Nation began the war on Vietnam here
                    with an angry smashing ax
                         attacking Wine—
         Here fifty years ago, by her violence
began a vortex of hatred that defoliated the Mekong Delta—
         Proud Wichita! vain Wichita
              cast the first stone!—
                         That murdered my mother
                who died of the communist anticommunist psychosis
                    in the madhouse one decade long ago
      complaining about wires of masscommunication in her head
                    and phantom political voices in the air
                         besmirching her girlish character.
         Many another has suffered death and madness
                in the Vortex from Hydraulic
                    to the end of 17th—enough!

The war is over now—
    Except for the souls
               held prisoner in Niggertown
still pining for love of your tender white bodies O children of Wichita!

February 14, 1966

Kansas City to Saint Louis

... Funky barn, black hills approaching Fulton
    where Churchill rang down the Curtain
        on Consciousness
   and set a chill which overspread the world
     one icy day in Missouri
        not far from the Ozarks—
Provincial ears heard the Spenglerian Iron
         Terror Pronouncement
     Magnificent Language, they said,
       for country ears—
St Louis calling St Louis calling
    Twenty years ago,
       Thirty years ago
        the Burroughs School
Pink cheeked Kenney with fine blond hair,
    his almond eyes aristocrat
      gazed,
    Morphy teaching English & Rimbaud
     at midnight to the fauns
W.S.B. leather cheeked, sardonic
     waiting for change of consciousness,
       unnamed in those days—
    coffee, vodka, night for needles,
    young bodies
      beautiful unknown to themselves
     running around St Louis
  on a Friday evening
    getting drunk in awe & honor of the
     terrific future these
red dry trees at sunset go thru two decades later
     They could've seen
  the animal branches, wrinkled to the sky
    & known the gnarled prophecy to come,
if they'd opened their eyes outa the whiskey-haze
      in Mississippi riverfront bars
    and gone into the country with a knapsack to
        smell the ground.
     Oh grandfather maple and elm!
Antique leafy old oak of Kingdom City in the purple light

come down, year after year,
                to the tune
                        of mellow pianos.
Salute, silent wise ones,
                Cranking powers of the ground,
        awkward arms of knowledge
        reaching blind above the gas station
                by the high TV antennae
        Stay silent, ugly Teachers,
let me & the Radio yell about Vietnam and mustard gas . . .

The hero surviving his own murder,
        his own suicide, his own
                        addiction, surviving his own
        poetry, surviving his own
                        disappearance from the scene—
returned in new faces, shining
        through the tears of new eyes.
                New small adolescent hands
                        on tiny breasts,
                pale silken skin at the thighs,
                        and the cherry-prick raises hard
                                innocent heat pointed up
                                from the muscular belly
of basketball highschool English class spiritual Victory,
        made clean at midnight in the bathtub of old City,
                                hair combed for love—
millionaire body from Clayton or spade queen from E St Louis
                laughing together in the TWA lounge
Blue-lit airfields into St Louis,
        past billboards ruddy neon,
                looking for old hero renewed,
                a new decade—
Hill-wink of houses,
        Monotone road gray bridging the streets
        thin bones of aluminum sentineled dark
        on the suburban hump bearing high wires
                        for thought to traverse
                river & wood, from hero to hero—

Crane all's well, the wanderer returns
                from the west with his Powers,

the Shaman with his beard
                in full strength,
the longhaired Crank with subtle humorous voice
                  enters city after city
          to kiss the eyes of your high school sailors
          and make laughing Blessing
               for a new Age in America
   spaced with concrete but Souled by yourself
               with Desire,
or like yourself of perfect Heart, adorable
          and adoring its own millioned population
              one by one self-wakened
    under the radiant signs
        of Power stations stacked above the river
    highway spanning highway,
                  bridged from suburb to suburb.

March 1966

Uptown

Yellow-lit Budweiser signs over oaken bars,
"I've seen everything"—the bartender handing me change of $10,
I stared at him amiably eyes thru an obvious Adamic beard—
with Montana musicians homeless in Manhattan, teenage
curly hair themselves—we sat at the antique booth & gossiped,
Madame Grady's literary salon a curious value in New York—
"If I had my way I'd cut off your hair and send you to Vietnam"—
"Bless you then" I replied to a hatted thin citizen hurrying to the barroom
        door
upon wet dark Amsterdam Avenue decades later—
"And if I couldn't do that I'd cut your throat" he snarled farewell,
and "Bless you sir" I added as he went to his fate in the rain, dapper Irishman.

April 1966

Iron Horse

I

... And ninety-nine soldiers piled on the train at Amarillo—
    Hadn't read the paper four weeks
                training Air Force
                  Pneumohydraulics—
Ninety-nine soldiers entering the train
            and all so friendly
      Only a month
                hair clipped & insulted
    They weren't too sad,
    glad going to some electronics field near Chicago
—Been taking courses in Propaganda,
      How not to believe what they were told
                  by the enemy,
Young fellas that some of them had long hair
          before they came to the heated camp
       friendly, over hamburgers
                Volunteered
    assignments behind the line of Great Machines
                that drop Napalm,
    milking
                the Calf of Gold.
    Three months from now
               Vietnam, they said.

Walking the length of the train,
    Lounge Car with Time Magazine
          Amarillo Globe, US News & World Report
       Reader's Digest Coronet Universal Railroad Schedule,
       everyone on the same track,
           bound leatherette read on sofas,
      America heartland passing flat
          trees rising in night—
    Dining Car
          negro waiters negro porters
    negro sandwichmen negro bartenders white jacketed
     kindly old big-assed Gents half bald,
Going, sir, California to Chicago
             feeding the Soldiers.

Blue eyed children   climbing chair backs
                staring at my beard, gay.

A consensus around card table beer—
    "It's my country,
              better fight 'em over there than here,"
        afraid to say "No it's crazy
                    everybody's insane—
                            This country's Wrong,
                the Universe, Illusion."

        Soldiers gathered round
                    saying—"my country
    and they say I gotta fight,
            I have no choice,
                    we're in it too deep to pull out,
                                    if we lose,
            there's no stopping the Chinese communists,
                    We're fightin the communists, aren't we?
                    Isn't that what it's about?"
Flatland,
        emptiness,
            ninety nine soldiers graduated Basic Training
                    eating hamburgers—
                "you learn to eat fast
                you learn to be insulted without caring
                you gotta do what your country expects—"
    even the bright talkative orphan farm boy
    whose auto parts father wanted 'im to grow up military
    "almost et by a male hog up to his shoulders"
        4 hours punching at power steering tractor
                brakes front & hind foot
                        giant insect specialized—
The whole populace fed by News
few dissenting on this train, I the lone beard who don't like
                                Vietnam War—
        Ninety nine airforce boys
            lined up with their pants down forever . . .

    Lightning's blue glare fills Oklahoma plains,
    the train rolls east
            casting yellow shadow on grass
                            Twenty years ago

                    approaching Texas
                              I saw
                                   sheet lightning
                                        cover Heaven's corners
                    Feed Storage Elevators in gray rain mist,
                              checkerboard light over sky-roof
          same electric lightning South
                    follows this train
                              Apocalypse prophesied—
                    the Fall of America
                              signaled from Heaven—

          Ninety nine soldiers in uniform paid by the Government
                                             to Believe—
          ninety nine soldiers escaping the draft for an Army job,
          ninety nine soldiers shaved
                                   with nowhere to go but where told,
          ninety nine soldiers seeing lightning flash
                                        a thousand years ago
          Ten thousand Chinese marching on the plains
             all turned their heads to Heaven at once to see the Moon.
          An old man catching fireflies on the porch at night
             watched the Herd Boy cross the Milky Way
                                   to meet the Weaving Girl . . .
                                   How can we war against that?
                                   How can we war against that? . . .

          Too late, too late
                    the Iron Horse hurrying to war,
                              too late for laments
                                   too late for warning—
          I'm a stranger alone in my country again.
          Better to find a house in the veldt,
          better a finca in Brazil—
                    Green corn here healthy under sky
                    & telephone wires carry news as before,
             radio bulletins & television images
                                        build War—
                    American Fighter Comic Books
                                   on coach seat.
          Better a house hidden in trees
                              Mississippi bank

                   high cliff protected from flood
Better an acre down Big Sur
            morning path, ocean shining
                  first day's blue world
Better a farm in backland Oregon,
                  roads near Glacier Peak
Better withdraw from the Newspaper world
Better withdraw from the electric world
Better retire before war cuts my head off,
                        not like Kabir—
      Better to buy a Garden of Love
      Better protect the lamb in some valley
      Better go way from taxicab radio cities
                              screaming President,
                  Better to stop smoking
Better to stop jerking off in trains
Better to stop seducing white bellied boys
Better to stop publishing Prophecy—
            Better to meditate under a tree
            Better become a nun in the forest
            Better turn flapjacks in Omaha
                  than be a prophet on the electric Networks—
There's nothing left for this country but doom
There's nothing left for this country but death
                  Their faces are so plain
                  their thoughts so simple,
                        their machinery so strong—
            Their arms reach out 10,000 miles with lethal gas
                  Their metaphor so mixed with machinery
                  No one knows where flesh ends and
                        the robot Polaris begins—
"Waves of United States jetplanes struck at North Vietnam
            again today in the face of . . ."
                  Associated Press July 21st—
                  A summer's day in Illinois! . . .

II

Bus outbound from Chicago Greyhound basement
        green neon beneath streets Route 94
        Giant fire's orange tongues & black smoke
                pouring out   that roof,
        little gay pie truck passing the wall—
        Brick & trees E. London, antique attics
                      mixed with smokestacks
  Apartments apartments square windows set like Moscow
apartments red brick for multimillion population
        out where industries raise craned necks
Gas station lights, old old old old traveler
        "put a tiger in yr tank—"
        Fulbright sang on the Senate floor
        Against the President's Asian War
          Chicago's acrid fumes in the bus
                A-1 Outdoor Theatre
           'gainst horned factory horizon,
          tender steeples ringing Metropolis
Thicker thicker, factories
          crowd iron cancer on the city's throat—
                Aethereal roses
                      distant gas flares
              twin flue burning at horizon
        Night falling on the bus
                  steady ear roar
          between Chicago and New York
Wanderer, whither next?
        See Palenque dream again,
        long hair in America,
        cut it for Tehuantepec—
          Peter's golden locks grown gray,
          quiet meditation in Oaxaca's
                old backyard,
      Tonalá or Angel Port warm nights
          no telephone, the War
                  rages North
          Police break down the Cross
          Crowds screaming in the streets— . . .

Jack you remember the afternoon
        Xochimilco with Fairies?

Green paradise boats
        flower laden poled upriver
    Pulque in the poop
       stringed music in air—
                drunkenness, & happiness
      anonymous
          fellows without care from America—
            Now war moves my mind—
Villahermosa full of purple flowers
Mérida hath cathedral & cheap hotels
        —boat to Isla Cozumel
    Julius can wander thru Fijijiapan
    forgetting his dog peso Nicotinic Acid—
Bus seat white light shines on Mexico map,
      quietness, quietness over countryside
        palmfrond insects, cactus ganja
& Washington's Police 5 thousand miles away?
Ray Charles singing from hospital
        "Let's   go get stoned."

Durango-Mazatlán road's built over
      Sierra Madre's moon valleys now
Children with quartz jewels climbing highway cliff-edge
        Jack you bought crystals & beer—

    Old houses in Panama City
      La Barranca gray canyon under Guadalajara,
          Tepic for more candy.

I wanna go out in a car
    not leave word where I'm going—
        travel ahead.
Or Himalayas in Spring
    following the pilgrim's path
       10,000 Hindus
          to Shiva temples North
     Rishikesh & Laxman Jula
     Homage to Shivananda,
         the Guru heart—
thru green canyons, Ganges gorge—
    carrying a waterpot
    to Kedernath & Badrinath

        & Gangotri in the ice
     —Manasarovar forbidden,
        Kailash forbidden,
      the Chinese eat Tibet.

Howl for them that suffer broken bone
          homeless on moody balconies
   Jack's voice returning to me over & over
             with prophecy
 "Howl for boys sleeping hungry on tables in cafés with their long hair
        to the sea" in Hidalgo de Parral,
              Hermosillo & Tetuán— . . .

Baghavan Sri Ramana Maharshi
      in his photo has a fine white halo of hair,
      thin man with a small beard
           silver short-cropped skull-fur
   His head tilted to one side,
      mild smile, intelligent eyes
      "The Jivan-Mukta is not a Person."

Morning sunrise over Tussie Hills,
   earth covered with emerald-dark fur.
       Cliffs to climb, a little wilderness,
         a little solitude,
       and a long valley you could call a home.
   Came thru here with Peter before & noticed
            green forest,
   What a place to walk & look
          thru cellular consciousness
   —Near Nealyton or Dry Run
     Waterfall or Meadow Gap, or Willow Hill.
Sunrays filtering thru clouds like a negative photograph,
      smoky bus window, passengers asleep
      over Susquehanna River's morning mist . . .
In my twenties I would've enjoyed running around these
             green woods naked.
In my twenties I would've enjoyed making love naked
        by these brooks.

Who's the enemy, year after year?
    War after war, who's the enemy?
What's the weapon, battle after battle?
What's the news, defeat after defeat?
What's the picture, decade after decade?
        Television shows blood,
          print broken arms burning skin photographs,
            wounded bodies revealed on the screen
Cut Sound out of television you won't tell who's Victim
Cut Language off the Visual you'll never know
          Who's Aggressor—
            cut commentary from Newscast
            you'll see a mass of madmen at murder.
Chicago train soldiers chatted over beer
They, too, vowed to fight the Cottenpickin Communists
        and give their own bodies to the fray.
Where've they learnt the lesson? Grammarschool
        taught 'em Newspaper Language?
D'they buy it at Safeway with Reader's Digest? . . .

    "Seeing objects and conceiving God in them are mental processes, but
that is not seeing God, because He is within.
    "Who am I? . . . You're in truth a pure spirit   but you identify it with
a body . . ."

       The war is Appearances, this poetry Appearances
                   . . . measured thru Newspapers
       All Phantoms of Sound
         All landscapes have become Phantom—
         giant New York ahead'll perish with my mind.
           "understand that the Self is not a Void"
not this, not that,
        Not my anger, not War Vietnam
        Maha Yoga a phantom
           Blue car swerves close to the bus
           —not the Self.
      Ramana Maharshi, whittle myself a walkingstick,
          waterspray irrigating the fields
              That's not the Self—
    hard-on spring in loins
        rocking in highway chair,
           poignant flesh spasm not it Self,

                body's speaking there,
                & feeling, that's not Self
       Who says No, says Yes—not Self.
Phelps Dodge's giant white building
           highway side, not Self . . .

MAKE NO IMAGE

Mohammedans say
      Jews have no painting
            Buddha's Nameless
                Alone is Alone,
    all screaming of soldiers
                crying on wars
       speech politics massing armies
              is false-feigning show—
Calm senses, seek self, forget
       thine own adjurations
             Who are you?
      to mass world armies in planet war?
McGraw-Hill building green grown old, car fumes &
    Manhattan tattered, summer heat,
        sweltering noon's odd patina
          on city walls,
        Greyhound exhaust terminal,
                  trip begun,
   taxi-honk toward East River where
        Peter waits working

             July 22–23, 1966

City Midnight Junk Strains

for Frank O'Hara

Switch on lights yellow as the sun
                    in the bedroom . . .
The gaudy poet dead   Frank O'Hara's bones
                under cemetery grass
An emptiness at 8 P.M. in the Cedar Bar
        Throngs of drunken
                guys talking about paint
        & lofts, and Pennsylvania youth.
                Kline attacked by his heart
& chattering Frank
                stopped forever—
    Faithful drunken adorers, mourn.
                The busfare's a nickel more
        past his old apartment 9th Street by the park.
Delicate Peter loved his praise,
        I wait for the things he says
                    about me—
    Did he think me an Angel
        as angel I am still talking into earth's microphone willy nilly
    —to come back as words ghostly hued
                    by early death
    but written so bodied
                mature in another decade.
Chatty prophet
                of yr own loves, personal
                memory feeling fellow
        Poet of building-glass
I see you walking you said with your tie
        flopped over your shoulder   in the wind down 5th Ave
            under the handsome breasted workmen
                on their scaffolds ascending Time
                    & washing the windows of Life
—off to a date with martinis & a blond
            beloved poet far from home
                —with thee and Thy sacred Metropolis
        in the enormous bliss   of a long afternoon
        where death is the shadow

                    cast by Rockefeller Center
                            over your intimate street.
Who were you, black suited, hurrying to meet,
        Unsatisfied one?
                            Unmistakable,
                                        Darling date
for the charming solitary   young poet with a big cock
                    who could fuck you all night long
                            till you never came,
        trying your torture on his   obliging fond body
        eager to satisfy god's whim that made you
                    Innocent,   as you are.
I tried   your boys and found them ready
        sweet and amiable
                    collected gentlemen
                            with large sofa apartments
        lonesome to please   for pure language;
and you mixed with money
                    because you knew enough language to be rich
                            if you wanted your walls to be empty—
Deep philosophical terms dear Edwin Denby serious as Herbert Read
        with silvery hair   announcing your dead gift
to the grave crowd   whose historic op art   frisson was
the new sculpture your big blue wounded body made in the Universe
        when you went away   to Fire Island for the weekend
        tipsy with a family of decade-olden friends

Peter stares out the window   at robbers
        the Lower East Side   distracted in Amphetamine
I stare into my head   & look for your / broken roman nose
        your wet mouth-smell of martinis
                    & a big artistic tipsy kiss.
   40's only half a life   to have filled
                with so many fine parties and evenings'
                interesting drinks together with one
                            faded friend or new
                            understanding social cat . . .
I want to be there in your garden party in the clouds
                    all of us naked
strumming our harps and reading each other   new poetry
        in the boring celestial
                    Friendship Committee Museum.

You're in a bad mood?
                    Take an Aspirin.
                              In the Dumps?
                                   I'm falling asleep
                                        safe in your thoughtful arms.
Someone uncontrolled by History would have to own Heaven,
                                        on earth as it is.
I hope you satisfied your childhood love
     Your puberty fantasy   your sailor punishment on your knees
                              your mouth-suck
Elegant insistency
                    on the honking self-prophetic Personal
                    as Curator of funny emotions to the mob,
Trembling One, whenever possible. I see New York thru your eyes
     and hear of one funeral a year nowadays—
                              from Billie Holiday's time
                    appreciated more and more
a common ear
                    for our deep gossip.

July 29, 1966

Autumn Gold: New England Fall

Auto Poetry to Hanover, New Hampshire

. . . Autumn again, you wouldn't know in the city
Gotta come out in a car see the birds
      flock by the yellow bush—
In Autumn, in autumn, this part of the planet's
      famous for red leaves—
Difficult for Man on earth to 'scape the snares of delusion—
    All wrong, the thought process screamed at
                    from Infancy,
The Self built with myriad thoughts
      from football to I Am That I Am,
Difficult to stop breathing factory smoke,
Difficult to step out of clothes,
      hard to forget the green parka—
Trees scream & drop
      bright Leaves,
Yea Trees scream & drop bright leaves,
Difficult to get out of bed in the morning
      in the slums—
Even sex happiness a long drawn-out scheme
      To keep the mind moving—

Big gray truck rolling down highway
      to unload wares—
Bony white branches of birch relieved of their burden
—overpass, overpass, overpass
    crossing the road, more traffic
    between the cities,
        More sex carried near and far—
      Blinking tail lights
    To the Veterans hospital where we can all collapse,
Forget Pleasure and Ambition,
      be tranquil and let leaves
      blush, turned on
by the lightningbolt doctrine that rings
              telephones
    interrupting my pleasurable humiliating dream
      in the locker room
        last nite?—

Weeping Willow, what's your catastrophe?
        Red Red oak, oh, what's your worry?
Hairy Mammal whaddya want,
            What more than a little graveyard
                    near the lake by airport road,
Electric towers marching to Hartford,
        Buildingtops spiked in sky,
            asphalt factory cloverleafs spread over meadows
Smoke thru wires, Connecticut River concrete wall'd
        past city central gastanks, glass boat bldgs,
                    downtown, ten blocks square,
North, North on the highway, soon outa town,
                            green fields . . .

President Johnson in a plane toward Hawaii,
        Fighter Escort above & below
                    air roaring—
Radiostatic electric crackle from the
                        center of communications:
        I broadcast thru Time,
                He, with all his wires & wireless,
                        only an Instant— . . .

Entering Whately,
                Senses amazed on the hills,
                bright vegetable populations
                        hueing rocks nameless yellow,
        veils of bright Maya over New England,
        Veil of Autumn leaves laid over the Land,
Transparent blue veil over senses,
                    Language in the sky—
And in the city, brick veils,
        curtains of windows,
            Wall Street's stage drops,
        Honkytonk scenery—
        or slum-building wall scrawled
                "Bourgeois Elements must go"— . . .

All the cows gathered to the feed truck in the middle of the pasture,
        shaking their tails, hungry for the yellow Fitten Ration
                that fills the belly
                        and makes the eyes shine
                                & mouth go Mooooo.

Autumn Gold: New England Fall   **193**

Then they lie down in the hollow green meadow to die—
In old Deerfield, Indian Tribes & Quakers
      have come & tried
                        To conquer Maya-Time—
Thanksgiving pumpkins
            remain by the highway,
                  signaling yearly Magic
                        plump from the ground . . .

Gold gold red gold yellow gold older than painted cities,
      Gold over Connecticut River cliffs
      Gold by Iron railroad,
            gold running down riverbank,
      Gold in eye, gold on hills,
            golden trees surrounding the barn—
Silent tiny golden hills, Maya-Joy in Autumn
                  Speeding 70 MPH.

                                          October 17, 1966

Wales Visitation

White fog lifting & falling on mountain-brow
    Trees moving in rivers of wind
                    The clouds arise
  as on a wave, gigantic eddy lifting mist
    above teeming ferns exquisitely swayed
                    along a green crag
    glimpsed thru mullioned glass in valley raine—

Bardic, O Self, Visitacione, tell naught
  but what seen by one man in a vale in Albion,
    of the folk, whose physical sciences end in Ecology,
        the wisdom of earthly relations,
    of mouths & eyes interknit ten centuries visible
        orchards of mind language manifest human,
  of the satanic thistle that raises its horned symmetry
  flowering above sister grass-daisies' pink tiny
        bloomlets angelic as lightbulbs—

Remember 160 miles from London's symmetrical thorned tower
    & network of TV pictures flashing bearded your Self
  the lambs on the tree-nooked hillside this day bleating
  heard in Blake's old ear, & the silent thought of Wordsworth in eld
                Stillness
  clouds passing through skeleton arches of Tintern Abbey—
    Bard Nameless as the Vast, babble to Vastness!

All the Valley quivered, one extended motion, wind
        undulating on mossy hills
  a giant wash that sank white fog delicately down red runnels
        on the mountainside
  whose leaf-branch tendrils moved asway
        in granitic undertow down—
and lifted the floating Nebulous upward, and lifted the arms of the trees
  and lifted the grasses an instant in balance
    and lifted the lambs to hold still
  and lifted the green of the hill, in one solemn wave

A solid mass of Heaven, mist-infused, ebbs thru the vale,
  a wavelet of Immensity, lapping gigantic through Llanthony Valley,

the length of all England, valley upon valley under Heaven's ocean
                              tonned with cloud-hang,
        —Heaven balanced on a grassblade.
Roar of the mountain wind slow, sigh of the body,
        One Being on the mountainside stirring gently
                Exquisite scales trembling everywhere in balance,
one motion thru the cloudy sky-floor shifting on the million feet of
                                          daisies,
one Majesty the motion that stirred wet grass quivering
        to the farthest tendril of white fog poured down
                through shivering flowers on the mountain's head—

No imperfection in the budded mountain,
        Valleys breathe, heaven and earth move together,
   daisies push inches of yellow air, vegetables tremble,
                        grass shimmers green
sheep speckle the mountainside, revolving their jaws with empty eyes,
                horses dance in the warm rain,
        tree-lined canals network live farmland,
                blueberries fringe stone walls on hawthorn'd hills,
        pheasants croak on meadows haired with fern—

Out, out on the hillside, into the ocean sound, into delicate gusts of wet
                                          air,
Fall on the ground, O great Wetness, O Mother, No harm on your body!
Stare close, no imperfection in the grass,
                each flower Buddha-eye, repeating the story,
                        myriad-formed—
Kneel before the foxglove raising green buds, mauve bells dropped
        doubled down the stem trembling antennae,
   & look in the eyes of the branded lambs that stare
        breathing stockstill under dripping hawthorn—
I lay down mixing my beard with the wet hair of the mountainside,
        smelling the brown vagina-moist ground, harmless,
                tasting the violet thistle-hair, sweetness—
One being so balanced, so vast, that its softest breath
        moves every floweret in the stillness on the valley floor,
   trembles lamb-hair hung gossamer rain-beaded in the grass,
lifts trees on their roots, birds in the great draught
        hiding their strength in the rain, bearing same weight,

Groan thru breast and neck, a great Oh! to earth heart
                Calling our Presence together

The great secret is no secret
        Senses fit the winds,
                Visible is visible,
rain-mist curtains wave through the bearded vale,
        gray atoms wet the wind's kabbala
Crosslegged on a rock in dusk rain,
        rubber booted in soft grass, mind moveless,
  breath trembles in white daisies by the roadside,
                Heaven breath and my own symmetric
Airs wavering thru antlered green fern
drawn in my navel, same breath as breathes thru Capel-Y-Ffn,
        Sounds of Aleph and Aum
                through forests of gristle,
        my skull and Lord Hereford's Knob equal,
                All Albion one.

What did I notice? Particulars! The
        vision of the great One is myriad—
  smoke curls upward from ashtray,
        house fire burned low,
The night, still wet & moody black heaven
                starless
        upward in motion with wet wind.

                    July 29, 1967 (LSD)–August 3, 1967 (London)

Elegy for Neal Cassady

OK Neal
    aethereal Spirit
        bright as moving air
        blue as city dawn
happy as light   released by the Day
      over the city's new buildings—

Maya's Giant bricks rise rebuilt
              in Lower East Side
    windows shine in milky smog.
        Appearance unnecessary now.

Peter sleeps alone next room, sad.
Are you reincarnate? Can ya hear me talkin?
If anyone had strength to hear the invisible,
And drive thru Maya Wall
    you *had* it—
            What're you now, Spirit?
That were spirit in body—

The body's cremate
        by Railroad track
      San Miguel de Allende Desert,
        outside town,
      Spirit become spirit,
        or robot reduced to Ashes.

Tender Spirit, thank you for touching me with tender hands
When you were young, in a beautiful body,
    Such a pure touch it was Hope beyond Maya-meat,
    What you are now,
           Impersonal, tender—
you showed me your muscle/warmth/over twenty years ago
when I lay trembling at your breast
          put your arm around my neck,
—we stood together in a bare room on 103d St.
Listening to a wooden Radio,
          with our eyes closed

Eternal redness of Shabda
                    lamped in our brains
at Illinois Jacquet's Saxophone Shuddering,
        prophetic Honk of Louis Jordan,
        Honeydrippers, Open The Door Richard
                    To Christ's Apocalypse—
The buildings're insubstantial—
That's my New York Vision
                    outside eastern apartment offices
            where telephone rang last night
                    and stranger's friendly Denver Voice
asked me, had I heard the news from the West?

Some gathering Bust, Eugene Oregon or Hollywood Impends
                    I had premonition.
"No" I said—"been away all week,"
        "you havent heard the News from the West,
                    Neal Cassady is dead—"
        Peter's dove-voic'd Oh! on the other line, listening.

Your picture stares cheerful, tearful, strain'd,
                    a candle burns,
            green stick incense by household gods.
Military Tyranny overtakes Universities, your Prophecy
        approaching its kindest sense brings us
                                Down
            to the Great Year's awakening.
Kesey's in Oregon writing novel language
                    family farm alone.
Hadja no more to do? Was your work all done?
        Had ya seen your first grandson?
                Why'dja leave us all here?
        Has the battle been won?

I'm a phantom skeleton with teeth, skull
        resting on a pillow
            calling your spirit
        god echo consciousness, murmuring
            sadly to myself.

Lament in dawnlight's not needed,
                the world is released,

desire fulfilled, your history over,
                    story told, Karma resolved,
                                        prayers completed
vision manifest, new consciousness fulfilled,
                    spirit returned in a circle,
world left standing empty, buses roaring through streets—
          garbage scattered on pavements galore—
Grandeur solidified, phantom-familiar fate
                    returned to Auto-dawn,
                              your destiny fallen on RR track
My body breathes easy,
                    I lie alone,
                              living
After friendship fades from flesh forms—
heavy happiness hangs in heart,
                    I could talk to you forever,
                              The pleasure inexhaustible,
                                   discourse of spirit to spirit,
                                              O Spirit.
Sir spirit, forgive me my sins,
Sir spirit give me your blessing again,
Sir Spirit forgive my phantom body's demands,
Sir Spirit thanks for your kindness past,
Sir Spirit in Heaven, What difference was yr mortal form,
          What further this great show of Space?
          Speedy passions generations of
                    Question? agonic Texas Nightrides?
                    psychedelic bus hejira-jazz,
          Green auto poetries, inspired roads?
Sad, Jack in Lowell saw the phantom most—
          lonelier than all, except your noble Self.
Sir Spirit, an' I drift alone:
                    Oh deep sigh.

                                   February 10, 1968, 5–5:30 A.M.

Kiss Ass

Kissass is the Part of Peace
America will have to Kissass Mother Earth
Whites have to Kissass Blacks, for Peace & Pleasure,
Only Pathway to Peace, Kissass

Houston, April 24, 1968

Please Master

Please master can I touch your cheek
please master can I kneel at your feet
please master can I loosen your blue pants
please master can I gaze at your golden haired belly
please master can I gently take down your shorts
please master can I have your thighs bare to my eyes
please master can I take off my clothes below your chair
please master can I kiss your ankles and soul
please master can I touch lips to your hard muscle hairless thigh
please master can I lay my ear pressed to your stomach
please master can I wrap my arms around your white ass
please master can I lick your groin curled with blond soft fur
please master can I touch my tongue to your rosy asshole
please master may I pass my face to your balls,
please master, please look into my eyes,
please master order me down on the floor,
please master tell me to lick your thick shaft
please master put your rough hands on my bald hairy skull
please master press my mouth to your prick-heart
please master press my face into your belly, pull me slowly strong thumbed
till your dumb hardness fills my throat to the base
till I swallow & taste your delicate flesh-hot prick barrel veined Please
Master push my shoulders away and stare in my eye, & make me bend over
        the table
please master grab my thighs and lift my ass to your waist
please master your hand's rough stroke on my neck your palm down my
        backside
please master push me up, my feet on chairs, till my hole feels the breath of
        your spit and your thumb stroke
please master make me say Please Master Fuck me now Please
Master grease my balls and hairmouth with sweet vaselines
please master stroke your shaft with white creams
please master touch your cock head to my wrinkled self-hole
please master push it in gently, your elbows enwrapped round my breast
your arms passing down to my belly, my penis you touch w / your fingers
please master shove it in me a little, a little, a little,
please master sink your droor thing down my behind
& please master make me wiggle my rear to eat up the prick trunk
till my asshalfs cuddle your thighs, my back bent over,

till I'm alone sticking out, your sword stuck throbbing in me
please master pull out and slowly roll into the bottom
please master lunge it again, and withdraw to the tip
please please master fuck me again with your self, please fuck me Please
Master drive down till it hurts me the softness the
Softness please master make love to my ass, give body to center, & fuck me
          for good like a girl,
tenderly clasp me please master I take me to thee,
& drive in my belly your selfsame sweet heat-rood
you fingered in solitude Denver or Brooklyn or fucked in a maiden in Paris
          carlots
please master drive me thy vehicle, body of love dops, sweat fuck
body of tenderness, Give me your dog fuck faster
please master make me go moan on the table
Go moan O please master do fuck me like that
in your rhythm thrill-plunge & pull-back-bounce & push down
till I loosen my asshole a dog on the table yelping with terror delight to be
          loved
Please master call me a dog, an ass beast, a wet asshole,
& fuck me more violent, my eyes hid with your palms round my skull
& plunge down in a brutal hard lash thru soft drip-fish
& throb thru five seconds to spurt out your semen heat
over & over, bamming it in while I cry out your name I do love you
please Master.

                                                    May 1968

On Neal's Ashes

Delicate eyes that blinked blue Rockies all ash
nipples, Ribs I touched w / my thumb are ash
mouth my tongue touched once or twice all ash
bony cheeks soft on my belly are cinder, ash
earlobes & eyelids, youthful cock tip, curly pubis
breast warmth, man palm, high school thigh,
baseball bicept arm, asshole anneal'd to silken skin
           all ashes, all ashes again.

August 1968

Rain-wet asphalt heat, garbage curbed cans overflowing

I hauled down lifeless matresses to sidewalk refuse-piles,
old rugs stept on from Paterson to Lower East Side filled with bed-bugs,
gray pillows, couch seats treasured from the street laid back on the street
—out, to hear Murder-tale, 3rd Street cyclists attacked tonite—
Bopping along in the rain, Chaos fallen over City roofs,
shrouds of chemical vapour drifting over building-tops—
Get the *Times*, Nixon says peace reflected from the Moon,
but I found no boy body to sleep with all night on pavements 3 A.M.
        home in sweating drizzle—
Those mattresses soggy lying by full five garbagepails—
Barbara, Mareta, Peter Steven Rosebud slept on these Pillows years ago,
forgotten names, also made love to me, I had these mattresses four years
        on my floor—
Gerard, Jimmy, many months, even blond Gordon later,
Paul with the beautiful big cock, that teenage boy that lived in
        Pennsylvania,
forgotten numbers, young dream loves and lovers, earthly bellies—
many strong youths with eyes closed, come sighing and helping me
        come—
Desires already forgotten, tender persons used and kissed goodbye
and all the times I came to myself alone in the dark dreaming of Neal or
        Billy Budd
—nameless angels of half-life—heart beating & eyes weeping for lovely
        phantoms—
Back from the Gem Spa, into the hallway, a glance behind
and sudden farewell to the bedbug-ridden mattresses piled soggy in dark
        rain.

August 2, 1969

Memory Gardens

       covered with yellow leaves
         in morning rain

—Quel Deluge
      he threw up his hands
         & wrote the Universe dont exist
           & died to prove it.

Full Moon over Ozone Park
      Airport Bus rushing thru dusk to
           Manhattan,
Jack the Wizard in his
             grave at Lowell
for the first nite—
That Jack thru whose eyes I
      saw
      smog glory light
        gold over Mannahatta's spires
      will never see these
        chimneys smoking
anymore over statues of Mary
        in the graveyard . . .
Eternal fixity, the big headed
      wax painted Buddha doll
        pale resting incoffined—

Empty-skulled New
        York streets
Starveling phantoms
      filling city—
Wax dolls walking park
        Ave,
Light gleam in eye glass
Voice echoing thru Microphones
Grand Central Sailor's
      arrival 2 decades later
        feeling melancholy—
Nostalgia for Innocent World
      War II—

A million corpses running
        across 42d street
Glass buildings rising higher
                transparent
                        aluminum—
artificial trees, robot sofas,
        Ignorant cars—
One Way Street to Heaven . . .

Flying to Maine in a trail of black smoke . . .
Empire State in Heaven Sun Set Red,
        White mist in old October
over the billion trees of Bronx—
                There's too much to see—
Jack saw sun set red over Hudson horizon
        Two three decades back . . .

Northport, in the trees, Jack drank
        rot gut & made haiku of birds
                tweetling on his porch rail at dawn—
Fell down and saw Death's golden lite
        in Florida garden a decade ago.
Now taken utterly, soul upward,
        & body down in wood coffin
                & concrete slab-box.
I threw a kissed handful of damp earth
        down on the stone lid
                & sighed
        looking in Creeley's one eye,
Peter sweet holding a flower
        Gregory toothless bending his
                knuckle to Cinema machine— . . .

Well, while I'm here I'll
        do the work—
    and what's the Work?
            To ease the pain of living.
    Everything else, drunken
            dumbshow.

October 22–29, 1969

Milarepa Taste

Who am I? Saliva,
    vegetable soup,
        empty mouth?

Hot roach, breathe smoke
    suck in, hold, exhale—
        light as ashes.

September on Jessore Road

feet   Mil - lions   of   ba - bies   in   pain

Mil - lions   of   moth - ers   in   rain   Mil - lions   of   broth - ers   in

woe - Mil - lions   of   child - ren

no - where   to   go

Millions of babies watching the skies
Bellies swollen, with big round eyes
On Jessore Road—long bamboo huts
Noplace to shit but sand channel ruts

Millions of fathers in rain
Millions of mothers in pain
Millions of brothers in woe
Millions of sisters nowhere to go

One Million aunts are dying for bread
One Million uncles lamenting the dead
Grandfather millions homeless and sad
Grandmother millions silently mad

Millions of daughters walk in the mud
Millions of children wash in the flood
A Million girls vomit & groan
Millions of families hopeless alone

Millions of souls Nineteenseventyone
homeless on Jessore road under gray sun
A million are dead, the millions who can
Walk toward Calcutta from East Pakistan

Taxi September along Jessore Road
Oxcart skeletons drag charcoal load
past watery fields thru rain flood ruts
Dung cakes on treetrunks, plastic-roof huts

Wet processions   Families walk
Stunted boys   big heads dont talk
Look bony skulls   & silent round eyes
Starving black angels in human disguise

Mother squats weeping & points to her sons
Standing thin legged   like elderly nuns
small bodied   hands to their mouths in prayer
Five months small food   since they settled there

on one floor mat   with a small empty pot
Father lifts up his hands at their lot
Tears come to their mother's eye
Pain makes mother Maya cry

Two children together   in palmroof shade
Stare at me   no word is said
Rice ration, lentils   one time a week
Milk powder for warweary infants meek

No vegetable money or work for the man
Rice lasts four days   eat while they can
Then children starve   three days in a row
and vomit their next food   unless they eat slow.

On Jessore road   Mother wept at my knees
Bengali tongue   cried mister Please
Identity card   torn up on the floor
Husband still waits   at the camp office door

Baby at play I was washing the flood
Now they won't give us any more food
The pieces are here in my celluloid purse
Innocent baby play   our death curse

Two policemen surrounded   by thousands of boys
Crowded waiting   their daily bread joys
Carry big whistles   & long bamboo sticks
to whack them in line   They play hungry tricks

Breaking the line   and jumping in front
Into the circle   sneaks one skinny runt
Two brothers dance forward   on the mud stage
The guards blow their whistles   & chase them in rage

Why are these infants   massed in this place
Laughing in play   & pushing for space
Why do they wait here so cheerful   & dread
Why this is the House where they give children bread

The man in the bread door   Cries & comes out
Thousands of boys & girls   Take up his shout
Is it joy? is it prayer?   "No more bread today"
Thousands of Children at once scream   "Hooray!"

Run home to tents   where elders await
Messenger children   with bread from the state
No bread more today! & no place to squat
Painful baby, sick shit he has got.

Malnutrition skulls thousands for months
Dysentery drains   bowels all at once
Nurse shows disease card   Enterostrep
Suspension is wanting   or else chlorostrep

Refugee camps   in hospital shacks
Newborn lay naked   on mothers' thin laps
Monkeysized week-old   Rheumatic babe eye
Gastroenteritis Blood Poison   thousands must die

September Jessore   Road rickshaw
50,000 souls   in one camp I saw
Rows of bamboo   huts in the flood
Open drains, & wet families waiting for food

Border trucks flooded, food cant get past,
American Angel machine   please come fast!
Where is Ambassador Bunker today?
Are his Helios machinegunning children at play?

Where are the helicopters of U.S. AID?
Smuggling dope in Bangkok's green shade.
Where is America's Air Force of Light?
Bombing North Laos all day and all night?

Where are the President's Armies of Gold?
Billionaire Navies   merciful Bold?
Bringing us medicine   food and relief?
Napalming North Vietnam   and causing more grief?

Where are our tears? Who weeps for this pain?
Where can these families go in the rain?
Jessore Road's children close their big eyes
Where will we sleep when Our Father dies?

Whom shall we pray to for rice and for care?
Who can bring bread to this shit flood foul'd lair?
Millions of children alone in the rain!
Millions of children weeping in pain!

Ring O ye tongues of the world for their woe
Ring out ye voices for Love we dont know
Ring out ye bells of electrical pain
Ring in the conscious American brain

How many children are we who are lost
Whose are these daughters we see turn to ghost?
What are our souls that we have lost care?
Ring out ye musics and weep if you dare—

Cries in the mud by the thatch'd house sand drain
Sleeps in huge pipes in the wet shit-field rain
waits by the pump well, Woe to the world!
whose children still starve   in their mothers' arms curled.

Is this what I did to myself in the past?
What shall I do Sunil Poet I asked?
Move on and leave them without any coins?
What should I care for the love of my loins?

What should we care for our cities and cars?
What shall we buy with our Food Stamps on Mars?
How many millions sit down in New York
& sup this night's table on bone & roast pork?

How many million beer cans are tossed
in Oceans of Mother? How much does She cost?
Cigar gasolines and   asphalt car dreams
Stinking the world and dimming star beams—

Finish the war in your breast   with a sigh
Come taste the tears   in your own Human eye
Pity us millions of phantoms you see
Starved in Samsara   on planet TV

How many millions of children die more
before our Good Mothers perceive the Great Lord?
How many good fathers pay tax to rebuild
Armed forces that boast   the children they've killed?

How many souls walk through Maya in pain
How many babes   in illusory rain?
How many families   hollow eyed lost?
How many grandmothers   turning to ghost?

How many loves who never get bread?
How many Aunts with holes in their head?
How many sisters skulls on the ground?
How many grandfathers   make no more sound?

How many fathers in woe
How many sons   nowhere to go?
How many daughters   nothing to eat?
How many uncles   with swollen sick feet?

Millions of babies in pain
Millions of mothers in rain
Millions of brothers in woe
Millions of children   nowhere to go

New York, November 14–16, 1971

IX

MIND
BREATHS
ALL OVER
THE PLACE
(1972–1977)

Sad Dust Glories　(1972–1974)
Ego Confessions　(1974–1977)

'Time after time for such a journey none but iron pens
Can write And adamantine leaves receive nor can the man who goes
The journey obstinate refuse to write time after time'

'Meeting, the two friends laugh aloud;
In the grove, fallen leaves are many.'

To VAJRACARYA
Chögyam Trungpa, Rinpoche
Poet

"Guru Death your words are true
Teacher Death I do thank you
For inspiring me to sing this Blues"

To LARRY FERLINGHETTI
Fellow
Poet

Editor

Vomit Express

I'm going down to Puerto Rico
I'm going down on the midnite plane
I'm going down on the Vomit Express
I'm going down with my suitcase pain

You can take an ancient vacation
Fly over Florida's blue end
Rise up out of this madhouse nation
I'm going down with my oldest tender friend
        I'm going down, etc.

We know each other now 20 years
Seen murders and we wept tears
Now we're goina take ourselves a little bit of Free Time
Wandering round southern Poverty Clime

Start flyin with those poor old sick ladies
Everybody in plane crowded & drunk & they're crazy
Flying home to die in the wobbly air
All night long they wanted the cheapest fare

Land there dawn on the airfield I never been there
Except once walking around on the airfield in the great wet heat
Walk out & smell that old mother lode of shit from the tropics
Stomach growl Love   O friends beware—

Me & my friend no we won't even drink
& I won't eat meat   I won't fuck around
Gonna walk the streets alone cars all blink & wink
Taxi buses & U.S. gas all around

Start with poetry at the University meet kids
Look at their breasts touch their hands kiss their heads
Sing from the heart maybe the Four Buddhist Noble Truths
Existence is suffering, it ends when you're dead

Go out & walk up on the mountain   see the green rain
Imagine that forest vines get lost
Sit crosslegged meditate on old love pain
Watch every old love turn to ghost

See raindrops in the jungle Rainbows ants & men
Brown legs walk around on mud roads
Far from U.S. Smog War again
Sit down Empty Mind   vomit my holy load

Come back to earth, walk streets in shock
Smoke some grass & eat some cock
Kiss the mouth of the sweetest boy I can see
Who shows me his white teeth & brown skin joy

Go find my old friend   we'll go to the museum
Talk about politics with the cats and ask for revolution
Get back on the plane   & chant high in the sky
Back to Earth to New York Garbage streets fly

Im gonna come back with Frightens in the heart
At New York's electric eternity here
Pull the airconditioner plug from the wall
Sit down with my straight spine and Pray!

I'm going down to Puerto Rico
I'm going down on the midnight plane
I'm going down on the Vomit Express
I'm going down with my suitcase pain.

November 17, 1971

Jimmy Berman Rag

Moderato G

Who zat Jim - mie Ber - man I
heard you drop his name? Whad d' - ze got to say
what pap- ers is he sel- lin'? I
don't know if he's the guy I met or aint the same
Well that Jim- mie Ber man is a
boy that is worth tel - lin'.

Whozat Jimmie Berman
I heard you drop his name?
Whadd'ze got to say
what papers is he sellin?
I dont know if he's the guy
I met or aint the same—
Well that Jimmie Berman was
a boy that is worth tellin':

Jimmie Berman on the corner
Sold the New York Times
Jimmie Berman in New York
He had a long long Climb—

Started as a shoeshine boy
Ended on Times Square—
Jimmie Berman whatzat rose
You got settin' in your hair?

Jimmie Berman what's your sex
Why ya hang round here all day?
Jimmie Berman What Love Next
O What (God) do you pray?

Who you wanna sleep with tonite Jimmie Boy
Would'ya like—Come with me?
Jimmy Berman—O my love.
Oh what misery—

Jimmie Berman do you feel
the same as what I do
Jimmy Berman wont you come home
And make love with me too?

Jimmie Berman I'll take my clothes off
Lay me down in bed
Jimmy Berman drop your pants
I'll give you some good head

Eighteen year old Jimmie!
The Boy is my delight!
Eighteen year old Jimmy
I'll love him day and night!

Now I know I'm getting kinda old
To chase poor Jimmy's tail
But I wont tell your other loves—
It be too long a tale.

Jimmy Berman please love me
I'll throw myself at your feet—
Jimmy Berman I'll give you money O
Wont that be neat!

Jimmie Berman just give me
your heart and yeah your soul
Jimmy Berman please come home
With me I would be whole

Jimmie Berman on the street
Waitin for his god!
Jimmy Berman as I pass
Gives me a holy nod.

Jimmy Berman he has watched
And seen the Strangers pass—
Jimmy Berman he gave up—
He wants no more of ass.

Jimmy Berman does yoga
He smokes a little grass.
Jimmie Berman's back is straight,
He knows what to bypass—

Jimmy Berman dont take Junk
He dont shoot speed neither
Jimmie Berman's got a healthy mind
And Jimmy Berman is Ours—

Jimmy Berman, Jimmy Berman
I will say Goodbye
Jimmy Berman Jimmy Berman
Love you till I die—

Jimmy Berman Jimmy Berman
Wave to me as well—
Jimmy Berman Jimmy Berman
We've abolished Hell!

November 17, 1971

4 AM Blues

I'm a-lone   That's how I'm going to   die.

Oh when you gonna
                    lie down by my side
When the spirit hits you
                    please lie down by my side
Three nights you didnt come home
                    I slept by myself & sighed

O when you gonna
                    look me in the eyes
When the spirit hits you
                    look me in the eyes
Oh honey come hug me
                    take me by surprise

Take me by surprise
                    come home, lie down by my side
Away three days
                    Sometimes I cried
Lie here alone
                    Heart open wide

Gone another night
                    Hand on my heart close my eye
You dont want me in your arms
                    dont want to hear me sigh
That's how I'm alone,
                    That's how I'm going to die.

December 20, 1971
(Traum Folk Concert)

New York Blues

Moderate swing

Walking blues (andante)

I live in an apartment, sink leaks thru the walls
Lower Eastside full of bedbugs. Junkies in the halls
House been broken into. Tibetan Tankas stole
Speed freaks took my statues, made my love a fool
Speed freaks took my statues, made my love a fool

Days I came home tired   nights I needed sleep
Cockroaches crawled in bed with me   my brain began to creep
My work was never done,   my rest'll never begin
I'll be dead and buried and never pleasure win
    I'll be dead and buried and never pleasure win

Lover boy threw meat at me   cursed the day we met
Speed freaks and bedbugs   New York City's what you get
Someday they'll build subways   get rid of all the cars
Cops kill all the bedbugs   speed freaks land on Mars
    Cops kill all the bedbugs   speed freaks land on Mars

December 1971

NY Youth Call Annunciation

Moderato

Come all you Jew - ish boy friends that live here in New York For years we have been read - ing your de - li - ca - tes - sen talk Now it's time to - en - ter in - to bod - ies and to scream Now's the time to wake up from the in - ter - nation al dream Two kin O come ye chil - dren that grew up New York a - round your ears This cen - tu - ry ends with Brim-stone or else your ten - der tears Ga - ther vi - gor in heart sweet in - tel - lect is

yours · · · when spi - rit · stif - fens your spine

On - ly e - mot - tion en - dures

Come all you Jewish boy friends
      that live here in New York
For years we have been reading
      your delicatessen talk
Now it's time to enter
      our bodies and to scream
Now's the time to wake up from
      the International Dream

Two generations ye've hidden
      your light & your sex
Your parents starved to master matter & your
      consciousness perplex
Now all these matter-junkies
      are lost in Moloch's maw
You're left alone in Universe
      your habits to withdraw

Come all ye black boys
      that live on New York's streets
Slaved for decades in Harlem
      Beat & jailed by police
Rise up ye rainbow consciousness
      over Manhattan Isle
Let Loose the joy of mastery ye've
      conquered the white style—

Come all ye Puerto Rican cats
      exiled from tropic sun

To labor in the ice and soot of
                              poisonous Capitalism
Beat your drums & chang guitars
                              Proclaim your softest joy
You will not drink from white beer cans
                              nor be his junkey Boy

Come all ye AmerIndians
                              that drink in Brooklyn's bars
Let loose your ancient Buffalo cry
                              chant under Sand Street's stars
Redeem the Mental Nation
                              Wake the Great Mother's corpse
Human bodies ye are still
                              Whatever Iron warps—

Come O poet Italians
                              long scared of the Syndicate
Secret death and blackmail
                              made your brains work late
Sing over rooftops your
                              ancient Cumaean blues
Dance with your Afric Brothers
                              the world's old tender news

Come out yer Greeks & Russians
                              Ye Arabs & ye Slavs
Boogie woogie down Broadway
                              weep tears of many loves
America was lost
                              ye children found her again
Squatting on the planet
                              belly full of metal sin

Highways full of speed
                              Brain city full of junk
Television blew her mind
                              her eyes are plastic gunk
Every little scream she made
                              was cause for planet war
O soulful Eastern boys & girls
                              lead home our Mother Whore

White boys of Manhattan
        White girls of New York
Come gather all together
        your Loves for the Great Work
Kneel down adore your brothers
        & sisters of the soul & skin
Lay hands on all your bodies
        your touch makes the world kin

O come ye children that grew up
        New York around your ears
This century ends with Brimstone
        or else your tender tears
Gather vigor in heart
        sweet intellect is yours
When spirit stiffens your spine
        Only emotion endures

December 20, 1971

Come Back Christmas: Blues Stanza

Slow Rubato

C

Ra - di - at - or cock - roach

wav - ing your arms at the wall

F

what' - ll I feed you

C G

I don't eat meat at all Go tell the bed bug he

C

bet - ter stay out in the hall

RADIATOR COCKROACH
          WAVING YOUR HORNS AT THE WALL
WHAT'LL I FEED YOU
          I DONT EAT MEAT AT ALL
GO TELL THE BEDBUG
          HE BETTER STAY OUT IN THE HALL

December 1971
(At St. Mark's Church)

Slack Key Guitar

Sweet Oahu
   Got petroleum
         Superhighways
               Glass hotels.

Old Hawaii's
   buried under
         Steamboat Museum's
               Sugar Hells—

Bishop Estates
   Leases homesites
         to the Kaiser
               Industry

& the Military
   Highway's closed off
         to the ocean
               over Kole Kole.

                                        March 1, 1972

Reef Mantra

... Blue Starfish
        Violet minnow.
                Sea cucumber
                        Coral tide ...

March 3, 1972

Bus Ride Ballad Road to Suva

O ho for the bus that rolls down the dirt road
O ho the green sunlight that holds the dust cloud
O ho for the thin-mustached boy with his wound
O ho for banana trees crowding the ground!

O ho the Australian lad drest in red
O ho the Ferlinghetti, beard on his head.
O ho for the roar of the motor uphill
O ho for the leathery grass standing still!

O ho the palm islands that rise from blue sea
O ho the breezy sky that hangs over me
O ho the dirt road that gives us a way
To Fiji, Port Suva, we go there today!

O ho the black ladies so big and so fat
From eating the Taro-root, pink hair, no hat,
O ho the clean Indian wives in white cloth
O ho the green frog that ate the black moth!

O ho misty hills all Sun-shining we've seen
O ho palm-roof huts with doorsteps grass green
O ho the black cow head bent on the field—
Here by the old banyan, bus stops squeaky-wheeled!

The Fiji boy opens the beer with his teeth
The bottle sits down on the floor by his feet.
A cowrie-shell purse & Pall Mall cigarette—
Low tide by the ocean road, sand is still wet!

Green craggy M'Benga sits on the low sea
Her men walk thru fire for you & for me,
O ho that last night the round Kava bowl
Numbed my mouth tasting the island's strange soul!

O ho for hibiscus, mail pouch on the nail,
O ho for the palm frond that waves at the whale,
O ho tin roof deserts & drain pipes in rows—
Pacific Development Corp. only knows!

O ho blessed freedom on Fiji's green land
O ho virgin hills coconuts in your hand,
O ho bless the pawpaw & orchid that grows—
O ho bless the Englishman's leftover Rose!

But curst be the Murchesson Company cranks
Capitalists hiding behind Hong Kong's banks,
Curst be Pan Am & the Hotel Airways.
Their business is ruin for Edens always.

The wind that flaps the banana leaf Ho!
Cocks that peck in the garden & crow,
O ho for the switchbacks on red dirt hill sides
Cows walk by the jungle & grazing abide!

We roll over mountains, rocks clank in the dust,
Stop for bananas and pee as we must,
O ho the blue ocean! What green peak we passed?
Down there the white houses of Suva at last!

March 4, 1972
(1–4–1–5–1 Chord Changes)

Xmas Gift

I met Einstein in a dream
Springtime on Princeton lawn grass
I kneeled down & kissed his young thumb
like a ruddy pope
his face fresh broad cheeked rosy
"I invented a universe separate,
something like a Virgin"—
"Yes, the creature gives birth to itself,"
I quoted from Mescaline
We sat down open air universal summer
to eat lunch, professors' wives
at the Tennis Court Club,
our meeting eternal, as expected,
my gesture to kiss his fist
unexpectedly saintly
considering the Atom Bomb I didn't mention.

New York, December 24, 1972

Ayers Rock / Uluru Song

When the red pond fills fish appear

When the red pond dries fish disappear.

Everything built on the desert crumbles to dust.

Electric cable transmission wires swept down.

The lizard people came out of the rock.

The red Kangaroo people forgot their own song.

Only a man with four sticks can cross the Simpson Desert.

One rain turns red dust green with leaves.

One raindrop begins the universe.

When the raindrop dries, worlds come to their end.

Central Australia, March 23, 1972

Everybody Sing

Moderato

Ev'-ry - bo - dy's just a lit - tle bit
ho - mo - sex - u - al whe - ther they like it or
not Ev' - ry bo - dy feels a lit - tle bit of
love for the boys e - ven if they al - most for -
got Ev' - ry nev - er get laid by a
la - dy or a maid who
won't be scared of your thighs No you'll
nev - er get laid but with mon - ey you paid to
buy off your wo - man with

Repeat six times

lies No you'll nev - er get laid and see free - ly dis - played the God - dess that comes in dis - guise So if you're in troub - le and you don't like your doub - le why dont - cha come see me? I'll take you by the hand and love you through the land and ease your ten - der mi - se - ry

Everybody's just a little
bit homo sexual
whether they like it or not
Everybody feels a little bit
of love for the boys
even if they almost forgot

Everybody goes   a little
        bit sweet hearted
            for a poor freckled sun faced lad
Y'all give him   a little
        bit of your soul
            like a girl that's never been had

Now everybody everybody
        everybody knows
            how thrilling a kiss can be
right on the mouth
        no thought no doubt
            from that singing boy from Tennessee—

Everybody knows   what it
        is to fall in love
            with the football hero bold
But so everybody's thoughts
        never do get lost
            God remembers when you're growing old.

Everybody's born   just a
        little bit gay
            a little bit fairy, and a dog
Everybody's born a lordly
        King of May and a
            little bit even of a hawg.

So if you can't get with your
        natural human
            and dont want no part queer
You line yourself up against
        the wall with your ghosts
            and shoot to kill your fear.

You can empty your revolver
        in any woman's pants
            or any man's mouth you despise
You can call whore names
        or play fairy games
            Plutonium burning in your eyes.

But you'll never get laid
          by a lady or a maid
                    who won't be scared of your thighs
No you'll never get laid
          but with money you paid
                    to buy off your woman with lies,
No you'll never get laid
          and see freely displayed
                    the Goddess that comes in disguise—

So if you're in trouble
          and dont like your double
                    why dontcha come see me?
I'll take you by the hand
          and love you through the land
                    and ease your tender misery.

February 4, 1973

Prayer Blues

Mind Breaths All Over the Place (1972–1977)

When you break your leg
             there's nothing to stand on
Break your leg
             There's nothing to stand on
Break yr bones,
             nothing to stand on
Break up your body
             Nowhere to be.

Jesus Christ
             Nowhere to be
Jesus Christ
             Show me
Jesus Christ
             show me the way to go home
Jesus Christ
             Show mercy to me.

Jesus Christ
             Didn't they break yr bones
Jesus Christ
             Didn't you weep & you groan
Up on the cross
             Didn't you feel alone?
O crown of thorns,
             Hear sweet Jesus' moans.

Jesus is His name   (Jesus Christ)
             As good   as any   (Jesus Christ)
Yes Jackie dear   Jesus' name
             is good   as any   (Jesus Christ)
When your body's in pain   (Shift the load to the Lord)
             and your heart is empty   (Shift the load to the Lord)
O sacred Heart   (Jesus Christ)
             One God is plenty   (Shift the load to the Lord)

Lord Jesus Come   (Jesus Christ)
             Come in my heart   (Shift the load to the Lord)
Lord Jesus Come   (Jesus Christ)
             Come in my heart   (Shift the load to the Lord)

Lord Jesus Come   (Jesus Christ)
            Come in my heart   (Load to the Lord)
Lord Jeeesus
            Come in my heart

There aint noone left   I can
            Come to in my bones
There aint nobody left
            I can come to in my bones
There aint noone here   I can
            come to in my bones
Aint no One anywhere   I can
            come to with my bone

Get rid of it all fast   (Jesus Christ)
            Credit cards in the sun   (Load O Lord)
Unload   Unload!
            house & books   everyone   (Load to the Lord)
Sell it all! Give it all away   your
            farm's no longer funny   (Jesus Christ)
Dump your ego
            & ruin Wall Street's money! (Shift the load to the Lord)

Shift the load to God   (Shift the load to the Lord)
            Let Him worry 'bout the Books   (Load to the Lord)
Give it up ! Let be!   Lord you'll love
            the President's looks   (Shift the load to the Lord)
Throw it all away   Begone! to
            Washington's Generals & crooks   (Load to the Lord)
Dont be so smart!   Get lost!   Last Supper,
            too many cooks!   (Shift the load to the Lord)

Shift the load to the Lord   (Shift the load to the Lord)
            Let Him worry about the War   (Load to the Lord)
Shift the Load to the Lord!   (Shift the load to the Lord)
            I cant fight any more!   (Load to the Lord)
Shift the load to the Lord!   (Shift the Load to the Lord)
            The Soul is a Whore!   (Load to the Lord!)
Shift the load to the Lord!   (Shift the load to the Lord!)
            My soul is no more!   (Om Ah Hūṃ)

Jesus Christ   (Shift the Load to the Lord)
        Take away my pain   (Shift the Load to the Lord)
Jesus Christ   (Shift the load to the Lord)
        Forgive me again   (Shift the load to the Lord)
Please Master   (Load to the Lord)
        You can have my Fame   (Load to the Lord)
JOD HE VOV HE
        I submit to your Name.

February 1973

Broken Bone Blues

Moderato

Bro- ken | Bone Bone Bone | All o - ver the Ground Bro - ken Bone Bone Bone | Ev' - ry - where the sound of Bro - ken bone bone bone | Ev' - ry - one brought down Ev' - ry - one brought | down to bro - ken

> "Naropa, your clay pitcher of a body,
> believing in an I, deserves to be
> broken . . ."
> —MARPA, *NAROPA* (GUENTHER
> TRANSL., OXFORD '63)

Broken Bone Bone Bone
   All over the Ground
Broken   Bone   Bone   Bone
   Everywhere the Sound
of Broken Bone Bone Bone
   Everyone brought down
   Everyone brought down

to broken   Bone Bone Bone
    Broken head & bony crown
Broken Bone Bone Bone
    Broken guru-king & clown
Broken Bone Bone Bone
    To the Boneyard I am bound
    To the Boneyard I am bound

Broken heart   Broken toe
    Broken Soul   Broken nose
Broken heaven   Broken woe
    Broken body into broken
Earth must go
    into broken
                earth must go.

When my bones all break
    I must feel my way to Death
When all my bones break
    when my meat starts to scrape
Through Death I will escape
    to Heaven through my heart
    to Heaven thru my heart's breath

Broke my leg under my knee
    Broke my heart   broke my greed
Broke my body like a dog
    Like a scared dog indeed
Broke my dumb body
    so God could see me
    So God could see me he broke my body.

Broken Bones O Lord
    I'll give my house away
Broken bones O Guru
    It was never mine anyway
Broken Bones O Buddha
    Take my skull today
    Or Take back my skull someday

Break   Break   Break
   O bones every where
Break   Break   Break
   O Soul in the black air
Break   Break   Break
  My body, Guru take care.
    My body, Guru take good care.

Take your time O Lord
   Break my bones ten times ten
Take your time O Death
   And you can tell me when
Farewell swift body dream
   Guru bless me again,
   Come down Guru, bless me again
   & I'll come back & bless you again.

February 1973

Under the world there's a lot of ass, a lot of cunt

a lot of mouths and cocks,
under the world there's a lot of come, and a lot of saliva dripping into
      brooks,
There's a lot of Shit under the world, flowing beneath cities into rivers,
a lot of urine floating under the world,
a lot of snot in the world's industrial nostrils, sweat under the world's iron
      arm, blood
gushing out of the world's breast,
endless lakes of tears, seas of sick vomit rushing between hemispheres
floating toward Sargasso, old oily rags and brake fluids, human gasoline—
Under the world there's pain, fractured thighs, napalm burning in black
      hair, phosphorus eating elbows to bone
insecticides contaminating oceantide, plastic dolls floating across Atlantic,
Toy soldiers crowding the Pacific, B-52 bombers choking jungle air with
      vaportrails and brilliant flares
Robot drones careening over rice terraces dropping cluster grenades,
      plastic pellets spray into flesh, dragontooth mines & jellied fires
      fall on straw roofs and water buffalos,
perforating village huts with barbed shrapnel, trenchpits filled with fuel-
      gas-poison'd explosive powders—
Under the world there's broken skulls, crushed feet, cut eyeballs, severed
      fingers, slashed jaws,
Dysentery; homeless millions, tortured hearts, empty souls.

April 1973

Returning to the Country for a Brief Visit

Annotations to Amitendranath Tagore's Sung Poetry

"In later days, remembering this I shall certainly go mad."

Reading Sung poems, I think of my poems to Neal
dead few years now, Jack underground
invisible—their faces rise in my mind.
Did I write truthfully of them? In later times
I saw them little, not much difference they're dead.
They live in books and memory, strong as on earth.

"I do not know who is hoarding all this rare work."

Old One the dog stretches stiff legged,
soon he'll be underground. Spring's first fat bee
buzzes yellow over the new grass and dead leaves.

What's this little brown insect walking zigzag
across the sunny white page of Su Tung-p'o's poem?
Fly away, tiny mite, even your life is tender—
I lift the book and blow you into the dazzling void.

"You live apart on rivers and seas . . ."

You live in apartments by rivers and seas
Spring comes, waters flow murky, the salt wave's covered with oily dung
Sun rises, smokestacks cover the roofs with black mist
winds blow, city skies are clear blue all afternoon
but at night the full moon hesitates behind brick.
How will all these millions of people worship the Great Mother?
When all these millions of people die, will they recognize the Great
     Father?

Cherry Valley, April 20, 1973

Night Gleam

Over and over thru the dull material world the call is made
over and over thru the dull material world I make the call
O English folk, in Sussex night, thru black beech tree branches
the full moon shone at three AM, I stood in under wear on the lawn—
I saw a mustached English man I loved, with athlete's breast and farmer's
      arms,
I lay in bed that night   many loves beating in my heart
sleepless hearing songs of generations electric returning intelligent
      memory
to my frame, and so went to dwell again in my heart
and worship the Lovers there, love's teachers, youths and poets who live
      forever
in the secret heart, in the dark night, in the full moon, year after year
over & over thru the dull material world the call is made.

July 16, 1973

Mind Breaths All Over the Place (1972–1977)

Mind Breaths

Thus crosslegged on round pillow sat in Teton Space—
I breathed upon the aluminum microphone-stand a body's length away
I breathed upon the teacher's throne, the wooden chair with yellow pillow
I breathed further, past the sake cup half emptied by the breathing guru
Breathed upon the green sprigged thick-leaved plant in a flowerpot
Breathed upon the vast plateglass shining back th' assembled sitting San-
      gha in the meditation cafeteria
my breath thru nostril floated out to the moth of evening beating into
      window'd illumination
breathed outward over aspen twigs trembling September's top yellow
      leaves twilit at mountain foot
breathed over the mountain, over snowpowdered crags ringed under slow-
      breathed cloud-mass white spumes
windy across Tetons to Idaho, gray ranges under blue space swept
with delicate snow flurries, breaths Westward
mountain grass trembling in tiny winds toward Wasatch
Breezes south late autumn in Salt Lake's wooden temple streets,
white salt dust lifted swirling by the thick leaden lake, dust carried up over
      Kennecott's pit onto the massive Unit Rig,
out towards Reno's neon, dollar bills skittering downstreet along the curb,
up into Sierras oak leaves blown down by fall cold chills
over peaktops snowy gales beginning,
a breath of prayer down on Kitkitdizze's horngreen leaves close to ground,
over Gary's tile roof, over temple pillar, tents and manzanita arbors in
      Sierra pine foothills—
a breath falls over Sacramento Valley, roar of wind down the sixlane
      freeway across Bay Bridge
uproar of papers floating over Montgomery Street, pigeons flutter down
      before sunset from Washington Park's white churchsteeple—
Golden Gate waters whitecapped scudding on Pacific spreads
over Hawaii a balmy wind thru Hotel palmtrees, a moist warmth swept
      over the airbase, a dank breeze in Guam's rotten Customs shed,
clear winds breathe on Fiji's palm & coral shores, by wooden hotels in Suva
      town flags flutter, taxis whoosh by Friday night's black prom-
      enaders under the rock & roll discotheque window upstairs beat-
      ing with English neon—
on a breeze into Sydney, and across hillside grass where mushrooms lie low
      on Cow-Flops in Queensland, down Adelaide's alleys a flutter of
      music from Brian Moore's Dobro carried in the wind—

up thru Darwin Land, out Gove Peninsula green ocean breeze, clack of
     Yerkalla village song sticks by the trembling wave

Yea and a wind over mercurial waters of Japan North East, a hollow
     wooden gong echoes in Kyoto's temple hall below the graveyard's
     wavy grass

A foghorn blowing in the China Sea, torrential rains over Saigon, bombers
     float over Cambodia, visioned tiny from stone Avelokitesvera's
     many-faced towers Angkor Wat in windy night,

a puff of opium out of a mouth yellowed in Bangkok, a puff of hashish
     flowing thick out of a bearded saddhu's nostrils & eyes in Nim-
     tallah Burning Ghat,

wood smoke flowing in wind across Hooghly Bridge, incense wafted under
     the Bo Tree in Bodh Gaya, in Benares woodpiles burn at Manikar-
     nika returning incensed souls to Shiva,

wind dallies in the amorous leaves of Brindaban, still air on the vast mosque
     floor above Old Delhi's alleyways,

wind blowing over Kausani town's stone wall, Himalayan peaktops ranged
     hundreds of miles along snowy horizon, prayer flags flutter over
     Almora's wood brown housetops,

trade winds carry dhows thru Indian Ocean to Mombasa or down to Dar
     'Salaam's riverside sail port, palms sway & sailors wrapped in
     cotton sleep on log decks—

Soft breezes up thru Red Sea to Eilat's dry hotels, paper leaflets scatter by
     the Wailing Wall, drifting into the Sepulchre

Mediterranean zephyrs leaving Tel Aviv, over Crete, Lassithi Plains' wind-
     mills still turn the centuries near Zeus' birth cave

Piraeus wave-lashed, Venice lagoon's waters blown up over the floor of San
     Marco, Piazza flooded and mud on the marble porch, gondolas
     bobbing up & down choppy waters at the Zattere,

chill September fluttering thru Milan's Arcade, cold bones & overcoats
     flapping in St. Peter's Square,

down Appian Way silence by gravesites, stelae stolid on a lonely grass path,
     the breath of an old man laboring up road—

Across Scylla & Charybdis, Sicilian tobacco smoke wafted across the boat
     deck,

into Marseilles coalstacks black fumes float into clouds, steamer's white
     drift-spume down wind all the way to Tangier,

a breath of red-tinged Autumn in Provence, boats slow on the Seine, the
     lady wraps her cloak tight round her bodice on toppa Eiffel
     Tower's iron head—

across the Channel rough black-green waves, in London's Piccadilly beer-
     cans roll on concrete neath Eros' silver breast, the Sunday Times
     lifts and settles on wet fountain steps—

over Iona Isle blue day and balmy Inner Hebrides breeze, fog drifts across
    Atlantic,
Labrador white frozen blowing cold, down New York's canyons manila
    paper bags scurry toward Wall from Lower East side—
a breath over my Father's head in his apartment on Park Avenue Paterson,
a cold September breeze down from East Hill, Cherry Valley's maples
    tremble red,
out thru Chicago Windy City the vast breath of Consciousness dissolves,
    smokestacks and autos drift expensive fumes ribboned across rail-
    road tracks,
Westward, a single breath blows across the plains, Nebraska's fields har-
    vested & stubble bending delicate in evening airs
up Rockies, from Denver's Cherry Creekbed another zephyr risen,
across Pike's Peak an icy blast at sunset, Wind River peaktops flowing
    toward the Tetons,
a breath returns vast gliding grass flats cow-dotted into Jackson Hole, into
    a corner of the plains,
up the asphalt road and mud parking lot, a breeze of restless September, up
    wood stairways in the wind
into the cafeteria at Teton Village under the red tram lift
a calm breath, a silent breath, a slow breath breathes outward from the
    nostrils.

September 28, 1973

Stay Away from the White House

Mind Breaths All Over the Place (1972–1977)

Av-en-ue C & Tenth streeet make your mind i cy clear Come

down to earth Merry X - mas I

wish you a Hap py New Year

Stay away from the White House
   Stay away I wish you well
Stay away from the White House
   Stay away I wish you well
Stay away from the White House
   Or you'll go to Diamond Hell

Stay away from New York City
   It costs money to live there
Stay away from the country
   The banks own all the air
Stay away from their electric
   It'll whiten your beard hair

Stay away from smoking cigarettes
   Stay away stay away
Stay your hand off your Marlboro
   Stay away stay away
Stay away from nicotine & beer
   It'll make you old and gay

Stay away from screwing broomsticks
   It'll give you syphilis
Stay away from knocking up rubber dolls
   even if they got big tits
Stay away from 14 year old boys
   makem once they call it quits

Stay away Stay away O yes yes stay away
from eating chemical donuts for breakfast yesterday
Stay away from living death   tho the Army gives good pay

Stay away from Capitalism and the bosses' CIA
Stay away from Oil Industry   they rob your energy
Stay away from Secret Policeman
                    when he calls you out to play

Yea stay away from Satan in the good old USA
Stay away from eating meatballs
                    while the Wall Street Dodgers play
Stay away from the White House this year,
                    wish you a fine day.

Stay away Stay away away from all that jive
rippen off the niggers just to keep the band alive
Yes rippen off the nigger, how white musicians thrive

Stay away from all them jewboys with their Zionist delights
Stay away from all them Christians calling all them jewboys Kikes
Stay away from all them prophets, they'll get you into fights

And Moslem Fundamentalists murder on their mind
Stay away from State Department they bow and scrape you blind
Stay away from Rockefeller he blows up an oily wind

Stay away from Richard Nixon he'll get you all in jail
He'll kick you and he'll punch you & he'll make your vision fail
and while he's got you staying away
                    from the White House   he will wail

"O Stay away from my White House I got it all my own
You can hear it in the basement
                    all them singing Plumbers groan
Stay away O all you Democrats except the Hawks I've flown" . . .

Stay away from Nirvana   your ambition makes you blind
Stay away from   Deva Loka,   you can only grasp the wind
Stay away from every Heaven   you'll wake up in suffering Mind

Come down! Yeeeaah!   Come down to earth right here
on Avenue C & Tenth street   make your mind icy clear
Come down to Earth Merry Xmas   I wish you a Happy New Year

December 25, 1973

Jaweh and Allah Battle

Jaweh with Atom Bomb
    Allah cuts throat of Infidels
Jaweh's armies beat down neighboring tribes
Will Red Sea waters close & drown th'armies of Allah?

Israel's tribes worshipping the Golden Calf
        Moses broke the Tablets of Law.

Zalmon Schacter Lubovitcher Rebbe what you say
    Stone Commandments broken on the ground
   Sufi Sam whaddya say
     Shall Prophet's companions dance circled
round Synagogue while Jews doven bearded electric?

Both Gods Terrible! Awful Jaweh Allah!
       Both hook-nosed-gods, circumcised.
Jaweh Allah which unreal?
              Which stronger Illusion?
                 Which stronger Army?
        Which gives most frightening command?
  What God maintain egohood in Eden? Which be Nameless?
        Which enter Abyss of Light?
Worlds of Gods, jealous Warriors, Humans, Animals & Flowers,
     Hungry Ghosts, even Hell Beings all die,
   Snake cock and pig eat each other's tails & perish
All Jews all Moslems'll die All Israelis all Arabs
Cairo's angry millions Jerusalem's multitudes
   suffer Death's dream Armies in battle!
Yea let Tribes wander to tin camps at cold Europe's walls?
Yea let the Million sit in desert shantytowns with tin cups?
I'm a Jew cries Allah! Buddha circumcised!
        Snake sneaking an apple to Eden—
     Alien, Wanderer, Caller of the Great Call!
What Prophet born on this ground
       bound me Eternal to Palestine
   circled by Armies tanks, droning bomber motors,
      radar electric computers?
What Mind directed Stern Gang Irgun Al Fatah

Black September?
Meyer Lansky? Nixon Shah? Gangster? Premier? King?
one-eyed General Dayan?
Golda Meir & Kissinger bound me with Arms?
HITLER AND STALIN SENT ME HERE!
WEIZMANN & BEN-GURION SENT ME HERE!
NASSER AND SADAT SENT ME HERE!
ARAFAT SENT ME HERE! MESSIAH SENT ME HERE!
GOD SENT ME HERE!
Buchenwald sent me here! Vietnam sent me here!
Mylai sent me here!
Lidice sent me here!
My mother sent me here!
I WAS BORN HERE IN ISRAEL, Arab
circumcised, my father had a coffee shop in Jerusalem
One day the Soldiers came & told me to walk down road
my hands up
walk away leave my house business forever!
The Israelis sent me here!
Solomon's Temple the Pyramids & Sphinx sent me here!
JAWEH AND ALLAH SENT ME HERE!
Abraham will take me to his bosom!
Mohammed will guide me to Paradise!
Christ sent me here to be crucified!
Buddha will wipe us out and destroy the world.
The New York Times and Cairo Editorialist Heykal sent me here!
Commentary and *Palestine Review* sent me here!
The International Zionist Conspiracy sent me here!
Syrian Politicians sent me here! Heroic Pan-Arab
Nationalists sent me here!
They're sending Armies to my side—
The Americans & Russians are sending bombing planes tanks
Chinese Egyptians Syrians help me battle for my righteous
house my Soul's dirt Spirit's Nation body's
boundaries & Self's territory my
Zionist homeland my Palestine inheritance
The Capitalist Communist & Third World Peoples'
Republics Dictatorships Police States Socialisms & Democracies
are all sending Deadly Weapons to our aid!
We shall triumph over the Enemy!
Maintain our Separate Identity! Proud
History evermore!

Defend our own bodies here this Holy Land! This hill
Golgotha never forget, never relinquish
inhabit thru Eternity
under Allah Christ Yaweh forever one God
Shema Yisroel Adonoi Eluhenu Adonoi Echad!
La ilah illa' Allah hu!

OY! AH! HU! OY! AH! HU!
SHALOM! SHANTIH! SALAAM!

New York, January 13, 1974

Hardon Blues

Mind Breaths All Over the Place (1972–1977)

some   day   it - 'll   all   be

gone

Blues is like a hardon   comes right in your mouth
Blues is like a hardon,   it comes in your mouth
never know when its coming   in your North or in yr South

Yea Blues like a hardon, leads you down the road
Blues like a hardon, your standing on the road
Lord I gotta stop here, get rid of my weary load

Blues is like a hardon, it takes you far from home
Go out in night time, in streets & subways roam
looking for a lover like the blues who won't let you alone

Blues is like a hardon, I got a case of Blues
aint got clap or H.I.V.   just got my hardon blues
If you were sitting here in bed with me you'd be the one I choose

Blues is like a hardon, I can't leave it alone
Sitting in my bed in Boulder, all I can do is groan
If I dont get it off right now, someday it'll all be gone.

August 16, 1974

Sad Dust Glories

To the Dead

Teacher
bring me to heaven
or leave me alone.
Why make me work so hard
when everything's spread around
open, like forest's poison oak
                    turned red
empty sleepingbags hanging from
            a dead branch.

When I sit
I see dust motes in my eye
Ponderosa needles trembling
                shine green
in blue sky.
Wind sound passes thru
                pine tops, distant
windy waves flutter black
                oak leaves
and leave them still
like my mind
which forgets
why the bluejay across the woods'
                    clearing
squawks, mid afternoon.

Wind makes sound
    in tree tops
like express trains like city
            machinery
Slow dances high up, huge
branches wave back &
                forth sensitive
needlechairs bob their heads

      —it's too human, it's not
          human
It's treetops, whatever they think,
It's me, whatever I think,
It's the wind talking.

September 1974

Ego Confession

I want to be known as the most brilliant man in America
Introduced to Gyalwa Karmapa heir of the Whispered Transmission
      Crazy Wisdom Practice Lineage
as the secret young wise man who visited him and winked anonymously
      decade ago in Gangtok
Prepared the way for Dharma in America without mentioning Dharma—
      scribbled laughter
Who saw Blake and abandoned God
To whom the Messianic Fink sent messages darkest hour sleeping on steel
      sheets "somewhere in the Federal Prison system" Weathermen
      got no Moscow Gold
who went backstage to Cecil Taylor serious chat chord structure & Time in
      a nightclub
who fucked a rose-lipped rock star in a tiny bedroom slum watched by a
      statue of Vajrasattva—
and overthrew the CIA with a silent thought—
Old Bohemians many years hence in Viennese beergardens'll recall
his many young lovers with astonishing faces and iron breasts
gnostic apparatus and magical observation of rainbow-lit spiderwebs
extraordinary cooking, lung stew & Spaghetti a la Vongole and recipe for
      salad dressing 3 parts oil one part vinegar much garlic and honey a
      spoonful
his extraordinary ego, at service of Dharma and completely empty
unafraid of its own self's spectre
parroting gossip of gurus and geniuses famous for their reticence—
Who sang a blues made rock stars weep and moved an old black guitarist to
      laughter in Memphis—
I want to be the spectacle of Poesy triumphant over trickery of the world
Omniscient breathing its own breath thru War tear gas spy hallucination
whose common sense astonished gaga Gurus and rich Artistes—
who called the Justice department & threaten'd to Blow the Whistle
Stopt Wars, turned back petrochemical Industries' Captains to grieve &
      groan in bed
Chopped wood, built forest houses & established farms
distributed monies to poor poets & nourished imaginative genius of the
      land
Sat silent in jazz roar writing poetry with an ink pen—
wasn't afraid of God or Death after his 48th year—

let his brains turn to water under Laughing Gas his gold molar pulled by
      futuristic dentists
Seaman knew ocean's surface a year
carpenter late learned bevel and mattock
son, conversed with elder Pound & treated his father gently
—All empty all for show, all for the sake of Poesy
to set surpassing example of sanity as measure for late generations
Exemplify Muse Power to the young avert future suicide
accepting his own lie & the gaps between lies with equal good humor
Solitary in worlds full of insects & singing birds all solitary
—who had no subject but himself in many disguises
some outside his own body including empty air-filled space forests &
      cities—
Even climbed mountains to create his mountain, with ice ax & crampons &
      ropes, over Glaciers—

San Francisco, October 1974

Mugging

I

Tonite I walked out of my red apartment door on East tenth street's dusk—
Walked out of my home ten years, walked out in my honking neighbor-
    hood
Tonite at seven walked out past garbage cans chained to concrete anchors
Walked under black painted fire escapes, giant castiron plate covering a
    hole in ground
—Crossed the street, traffic lite red, thirteen bus roaring by liquor store,
past corner pharmacy iron grated, past Coca Cola & Mylai posters fading
    scraped on brick
Past Chinese Laundry wood door'd, & broken cement stoop steps For
    Rent hall painted green & purple Puerto Rican style
Along E. 10th's glass splattered pavement, kid blacks & Spanish oiled hair
    adolescents' crowded house fronts—
Ah, tonite I walked out on my block NY City under humid summer sky
    Halloween,
thinking what happened Timothy Leary joining brain police for a season?
thinking what's all this Weathermen, secrecy & selfrighteousness beyond
    reason—F.B.I. plots?
Walked past a taxicab controlling the bottle strewn curb—
past young fellows with their umbrella handles & canes leaning against a
    ravaged Buick
—and as I looked at the crowd of kids on the stoop—a boy stepped up, put
    his arm around my neck
tenderly I thought for a moment, squeezed harder, his umbrella handle
    against my skull,
and his friends took my arm, a young brown companion tripped his foot
    'gainst my ankle—
as I went down shouting Om Ah Hūṃ to gangs of lovers on the stoop
    watching
slowly appreciating, why this is a raid, these strangers mean strange busi-
    ness
with what—my pockets, bald head, broken-healed-bone leg, my softshoes,
    my heart—
Have they knives? Om Ah Hūṃ —Have they sharp metal wood to shove in
    eye ear ass? Om Ah Hūṃ

& slowly reclined on the pavement, struggling to keep my woolen bag of
        poetry address calendar & Leary-lawyer notes hung from my
        shoulder
dragged in my neat orlon shirt over the crossbar of a broken metal door
dragged slowly onto the fire-soiled floor an abandoned store, laundry
        candy counter 1929—
now a mess of papers & pillows & plastic car seat covers cracked
        cockroach-corpsed ground—
my wallet back pocket passed over the iron foot step guard
and fell out, stole by God Muggers' lost fingers, Strange—
Couldn't tell—snakeskin wallet actually plastic, 70 dollars my bank money
        for a week,
old broken wallet—and dreary plastic contents—Amex card & Manf.
        Hanover Trust Credit too—business card from Mr. Spears British
        Home Minister Drug Squad—my draft card—membership
        ACLU & Naropa Institute Instructor's identification
Om Ah Hūṃ   I continued chanting Om Ah Hūṃ
Putting my palm on the neck of an 18 year old boy fingering my back
        pocket crying "Where's the money"
"Om Ah Hūṃ   there isn't any"
My card Chief Boo-Hoo Neo American Church New Jersey & Lower East
        Side
Om Ah Hūṃ   —what not forgotten crowded wallet—Mobil Credit,
        Shell? old lovers addresses on cardboard pieces, booksellers call-
        ing cards—
—"Shut up or we'll murder you"—"Om Ah Hūṃ   take it easy"
Lying on the floor shall I shout more loud?—the metal door closed on
        blackness
one boy felt my broken healed ankle, looking for hundred dollar bills
        behind my stocking weren't even there—a third boy untied my
        Seiko Hong Kong watch rough from right wrist leaving a clasp-
        prick skin tiny bruise
"Shut up and we'll get out of here"—and so they left,
as I rose from the cardboard mattress thinking Om Ah Hūṃ   didn't stop
        em enough,
the tone of voice too loud—my shoulder bag with 10,000 dollars full of
        poetry left on the broken floor—

November 2, 1974

Dope Fiend Blues

Yes I'm a dope fiend, I dont believe your laws
Hey Mr Policeman I'm a dope fiend, take that
                                    joint out of your jaws
I'm a dopefiend and I'm getting out of jail because

I'm a dopefiend sitting in my bedroom high
I didn't even light up no muggles, dont know why
I'm just naturally a dopefiend under empty sky

Yes I'm a dopefiend I dont sniff cocaine
I hear the walls ringing   my nose is still in pain
It's snowing all round NY City gimme a 2 penny plain

Oho I'm a dopefiend shoulda seen me usta mainline
Yah seen me shoulda shoot that white heroine
useta get the chills   but never burnt down my mind

Hey hey Oh Lord Dope Fiend I dropped LSD
I seen Manhattan's towers stick up in Eternity
Ten years ago you shoulda took the elevator up with me,
                              Holy!

Ha Ha I'm a dopefiend niggerlovin Commie Fagot Queen
I'm a beatnick hippie longhair but a square I never been
But if you Mother see my picture in the paper
                              she say I look clean

Hey I'm a dopefiend I'm a dopefiend I breathe sweet clean air
I dont shoot speed in my arm never more I'm a dopefiend everywhere
I'm a dopefiend in the policeman's eyes Yeah They wouldnt dare

to bust me for dopefiend I dont carry any shit around
I'm just a dopefiend by nature I like to sit on the ground
all naked with my clothes on   make a blue mantra sound

I'm a dopefiend I'm a dopefiend gonna bust this nation's mind
I'm gonna put LSD in your prayers & laughing gas in the wind
Aether & Peyote gonna drive Mt Rainier blind—

I'm a dopefiend I roll my soul in friendly grass
Dopefiend Dopefiend I carry Nothing   but Dharma up my ass
Yeaas all you dopefiends hear me!   out there in the middle class!

Hey rich dopefiend when you gonna change the laws?
Hey poor dopefiend join the Dharma party because
They gonna legalise existence, everybody ride a big white horse.

December 31, 1974

Guru Blues

I cant find anyone to show me what to do
I cant find anyone
                It's maken me so blue
that I cant find anyone
                anyone but you
O I cant find anyone that knows me
                        good as you
Yeah I cant find anyone,
                only you Guru

I cant find anyone that's visited the past
I cant find anyone
                That's willing to be last
to take me up to heaven
                They're going to hell so fast
O I cant find anyone to blow me
                in the grass
Yeah I cant find anyone,
                fuck me in the ass

I cant find anyone
                That isn't drinking wine
I cant find a teacher
                That isnt loaded blind
I cant find anyone
                that isnt out of his mind
on ideas on Fears or the tears
                cops leave behind
Yeah I cant find anyone dont want to
                police the wind—

I cant find anyone that wants to meditate
Nobody wants to work, or play with a steady state
Economy, nobody wants
                the earth to celebrate
a world of conscious mercy, a world we could create
If we all sat down and decided not to be great.

I look in the White House, theres no one talks to me
I look in the Congress
                    dont know Eternity
The Supreme Court
                    is fighting with the Sea
They're sitting now deciding on
                    the old death penalty
and the Rosenbergs' children
                    have written their story

And what's the public doing
                    but drinking beer in cans
and what's the children screwing with
                    but cars to go to dance
and what's the music playing
                    Plutonium in your pants
Yeah the mass is crazed for energy
                    to fill our metal wants
and the capitalists are
                    angry at the communistic ants—

O I cant find anyone
                    to help me sing my song
to spread the Sacred Dharma
                    our suffering's been so long
my ignorance   my ego
                    keeps banging the angry gong
But I gotta find someone
                    Who's willing to be wrong
& stay on Earth & see the worth
                    of a road endlessly long

No I cant find anyone to talk to me with sense
I cant find anyone to cross the bony fence
I cant find anyone to work
                    the work's immense
It's the effort just to get here where we are
                    with common sense
The world of joy is empty, the real world is so dense—

I can't find anyone to show me what to do
I cant find anyone
                    It's maken me so blue
I cant find anyone
                    anyone but you
O I cant find anyone that knows me
                              good as you
Yeah I cant find anyone,
                    only you Guru

Dream, April 24, 1975

Sickness Blues

Lord Lord I got the sickness blues, I must've done something wrong
There ain't no Lord to call on, now my youth is gone

Sickness blues, don't want to screw no more
Sickness blues, can't get it up no more
Tears come in my eyes, feel like an old tired whore

I went to see the doctor, he shot me with poison germs
I got out of the hospital, my head was full of worms

All I can think is Death, father's getting old
He can't walk half a block, his feet feel cold

I went down to Santa Fe take vacation there
Indians selling turquoise in dobe huts in Taos Pueblo Square
Got headache in La Fonda, I could get sick anywhere

Must be my bad karma, making these pretty boys
Hungry ghosts chasing me, because I been chasing joys
Lying here in bed alone, playing with my toys

I musta been doing something wrong meat & cigarettes
Bow down before my lord, 100 thousand regrets
All my poems down in hell, that's what pride begets

Sick and angry, lying in my hospital bed
Doctor Doctor bring morphine before I'm totally dead
Sick and angry at the national universe O my aching head

Someday I'm gonna get out of here, go somewhere alone
Yeah I'm going to leave this town with noise of rattling bone
I got the sickness blues, you'll miss me when I'm gone

Boulder, July 19, 1975

Gospel Noble Truths

Born in this world   Sit   you sit down
You got to suffer   Breathe when you breathe
Everything changes   Lie down   you lie down
You got   no soul   Walk where you walk

Try to be gay   Talk when you talk
Ignorant   happy   Cry when you cry
You get the blues   Lie down   you lie down
You eat jellyroll   Die when you die

There is one Way   Look when you look
You take the high road   Hear what you hear
In your big Wheel   Taste what you taste   here
8 steps you fly   Smell what you smell

Look at the View   Touch what you touch
Right to horizon   Think what you think
Talk to the sky   Let go Let it go   Slow
Act like you talk   Earth Heaven & Hell

Work like the sun   Die when you die
Shine in your heaven   Die when you die
See what you done   Lie down   you lie down
Come down & walk   Die when you die

New York Subway, October 17, 1975

Lay Down Yr Mountain

Mind Breaths All Over the Place (1972–1977)

Lay down   Lay down yr mountain   Lay down God
Lay down   Lay down your music   Love lay down

Lay down   Lay down yr hatred   Lay yrself down
Lay down   Lay down your nation   Lay your foot on the rock

Lay down yr whole creation   Lay yr mind down
Lay down   Lay down yr empire   Lay your whole world down

Lay down your soul forever   Lay your vision down
Lay down yr bright body   Down your golden heavy crown

Lay down   Lay down yr magic hey!   Alchemist lay it down clear
Lay down your practice precisely   Lay down yr wisdom dear

Lay down yr skillful camera   Lay down yr image right
Lay down your brilliant image   Lay down light

Lay down   your ignorance   Roll yr wheel once more
Lay down yr empty suffering   Lay down yr Lion's Roar

October 31, 1975

Don't Grow Old

I

Wasted arms, feeble knees
    80 years old, hair thin and white
        cheek bonier than I'd remembered—
head bowed on his neck, eyes opened
    now and then, he listened—
    I read my father Wordsworth's *Intimations of Immortality*
"*. . . trailing clouds of glory do we come*
    from God, who is our home . . ."
        "That's beautiful," he said, "but it's not true."

"When I was a boy, we had a house
    on Boyd Street, Newark—the backyard
        was a big empty lot full of bushes and tall grass,
    I always wondered what was behind those trees.
When I grew older, I walked around the block,
    and found out what was back there—
        it was a glue factory."

                        May 18, 1976

II

Twenty-eight years before on the living room couch he'd stared at me, I
    said
"I want to see a psychiatrist—I have sexual difficulties—homosexuality"
I'd come home from troubled years as a student. This was the weekend I
    would talk with him.
A look startled his face, "You mean you like to take men's penises in your
    mouth?"
Equally startled, "No, no," I lied, "that isn't what it means."

Now he lay naked in the bath, hot water draining beneath his shanks.
Strong shouldered Peter, once ambulance attendant, raised him up
in the tiled room. We toweled him dry, arms under his, bathrobe over his
    shoulder—
he tottered thru the door to his carpeted bedroom
sat on the soft mattress edge, exhausted, and coughed up watery phlegm.
We lifted his swollen feet talcum'd white, put them thru pajama legs,
tied the cord round his waist, and held the nightshirt sleeve open for his
    hand, slow.

Mouth drawn in, his false teeth in a dish, he turned his head round
looking up at Peter to smile ruefully, "Don't ever grow old."

III

At my urging, my eldest nephew came
to keep his grandfather company, maybe sleep overnight in the apartment.
He had no job, and was homeless anyway.
All afternoon he read the papers and looked at old movies.
Later dusk, television silent, we sat on a soft-pillowed couch,
Louis sat in his easy-chair that swiveled and could lean back—
"So what kind of job are you looking for?"
"Dishwashing, but someone told me it makes your hands' skin scaly red."
"And what about officeboy?" His grandson finished highschool with marks
  too poor for college.
"It's unhealthy inside airconditioned buildings under fluorescent light."
The dying man looked at him, nodding at the specimen.
He began his advice. "You might be a taxidriver, but what if a car crashed
  into you? They say you can get mugged too.
Or you could get a job as a sailor, but the ship could sink, you could get
  drowned.
Maybe you should try a career in the grocery business, but a box of bananas
  could slip from the shelf,
you could hurt your head. Or if you were a waiter, you could slip and fall
  down with a loaded tray, & have to pay for the broken glasses.
Maybe you should be a carpenter, but your thumb might get hit by a
  hammer.
Or a lifeguard—but the undertow at Belmar beach is dangerous, and you
  could catch a cold.
Or a doctor, but sometimes you could cut your hand with a scalpel that had
  germs, you could get sick & die."

Later, in bed after twilight, glasses off, he said to his wife
"Why doesn't he comb his hair? It falls all over his eyes, how can he see?
Tell him to go home soon. I'm too tired."

Amherst, October 5, 1978

IV

Will that happen to me?
Of course, it'll happen to thee.

Will my arms wither away?
Yes yr arm hair will turn gray.

Will my knees grow weak & collapse?
Your knees will need crutches perhaps.

Will my chest get thin?
Your breasts will be hanging skin.

Where will go—my teeth?
You'll keep the ones beneath.

What'll happen to my bones?
They'll get mixed up with stones.

June 1976

Father Death Blues

V

Hey Father Death, I'm flying home
Hey poor man, you're all alone
Hey old daddy, I know where I'm going

Father Death, Don't cry any more
Mama's there, underneath the floor
Brother Death, please mind the store

Old Aunty Death   Don't hide your bones
Old Uncle Death   I hear your groans
O Sister Death   how sweet your moans

O Children Deaths go breathe your breaths
Sobbing breasts'll case your Deaths
Pain is gone, tears take the rest

Genius Death   your art is done
Lover Death your body's gone
Father Death   I'm coming home

Guru Death your words are true
Teacher Death I do thank you
For inspiring me to sing this Blues

Buddha Death, I wake with you
Dharma Death, your mind is new
Sangha Death, we'll work it through

Suffering is what was born
Ignorance made me forlorn
Tearful truths I cannot scorn

Father Breath once more farewell
Birth you gave was no thing ill
My heart is still, as time will tell.

July 8, 1976 (Over Lake Michigan)

Contest of Bards

For Jonathan Robbins

I

THE ARGUMENT: Old bard lived in solitary stone house at ocean edge three decades retired from the world, Young poet arrives naked interrupting his studies & announces his own prophetic dreams to replace the old Bard's boring verities. Young poet had dreamed old poet's scene & its hidden secret, an Eternal Rune cut in stone at the hearth-front hidden under porphyry bard-throne. Young bard tries to seduce old Boner with his energy & insight, & makes him crawl down on the floor to read the secret riddle Rhyme.

The youth the color of the hills laughed delighted at his Vanity
and cried, "Under the hearth stone's a rune, old Bard of Familiarity . . .
Learn in your age what True Magicians spelled for all Futurity,
Cut in the vanity of rock before your feeble hand grasped iron Pen
Or feather fancy tickled your gross ear: There have been sages here
before you, and I am after to outlive your gloomy miserous
hospitality. I loved you Ungrateful Unimaginative Bard . . .
And Came over hills thru small cities to companion your steadfast study . . .
Take eyes off your own veined hands and worm thoughts, lower
Your watery selfish infatuate eyes from my breast to my feet
& read me aloud in Bardic Voice, that Voice of Rock you boast so well so
        many decades,
Yea Face inland to the fields and railroads skyscrapers & Viaducts.
Youths maddened by Afric jukeboxes & maidens simpering at Picture
        shows
Read thru smoky air to a hopeless hundred million fools!" . . .

Startled, the wool-wrapped bard looked up at eyes mocking shining into
        his own:
Looked down at the boy's neck unwrinkled white unlike his own: the breast
thin muscled unawakened silken flesh: the belly with a corse of tawny hair
rosed round the pricked virgin-budding genitals, shining in hearth light,
thighs ready and careless like a strong Child's, playful walking & dancing
        tho awkward,
Thick calves with new hair light to the foot long as a man's . . .
His eyes fell down to the messenger's foot, toes spread firm on the runed
        lintel:

The Rune

Where the years have gone,   where the clouds have flown
             Where the rainbow shone
We vanish,   and we make no moan

Where the sun will blind   the delighting mind
             in a diamond wind
We appear,   our beauty refined.

Icy intellect,   fi'ry Beauty wreck
             but Love's castled speck
of Moonbeam,   nor is Truth correct.

Wise bodies leave here   with the mind's false cheer,
             Eternity near
as Beauty,   where we disappear.

When sufferings come,   when all tongues lie dumb
             when Bliss is all numb
with knowledge,   a bony white sum,

We die neither blest   nor with curse confessed
             wanting Earth's worst Best:
But return,   where all Beauties rest.

January 17–22, 1977

II

THE ARGUMENT: The Rune having been discovered by the Boy to the Man, the messenger commands the Hermit Sage to go out into the world with him, seek the ancient unearthly Beauty the riddle indicated. The old man gets mad, he says he's near death, has lost Desire. The boy reads his mind and lies down with the sage to make love. At dawn he gets up says he's disgusted with the body, condemns the sage to Chastity, demands the hermit leave his cell forever, and promises to lead him to the land of Poetry in the Sky. Exasperated, the old bard reveals the secret of the mysterious riddle.

. . . "Will you obey my will and follow me through a riot of cities, to
      delicate-porched countryhouses
& rich polished-marble mansions, where we'll sport with Princes & Mil-
      lionaires
and make fun of the world's kings and Presidents Pomps & Limousines all
      present in their Unbeauty?
Come leave your stupid business of seashells & seawrack, gathering wrin-
      kles of the sea?
Come with your pearls and banks of Ambergris hidden under yr bed & in
      yr stone closets?
Come wrapped with seaweed round your belly & Neptunic laurel moist on
      yr skull's half century?
Carry yr vowelic conch & give blast midnights in Midcity canyons Wall
      Street to Washington,
Granite Pillars echoing ocean mouthed pearly syllables along Chicago's
      Lakeshore
& reverberating in Pittsburgh's National Banks—Dance with the golden
      Trident of Fame in Hollywood
Lift the Inspired Lyre to Strike the Ears of hotels in Los Angeles? . . .
I know your present mind, old heart, I'll satisfy that as you wish
Unspoken, I know your work & nature beyond the wildest daydream
Y'ever had naked in hot sunshine summer noon ecstatic far from mankind
or downy-bearded in your animal bed embraced with glad phantom heroes
in midnight reverie down below Orion's belt, right hand clasped in the heat
      of Creaturehood,
I saw your hard revelry with bodiless immortal companions," the messen-
      ger cajoled,
laying his mournful sweet visage on the silenced Sage's shoulder, drawing
      his right arm down his nippled thin-ribbed chest.
He shook & trembled chill, for the low moon paled over green ocean
      waves
and cold bright sun-fire passed upward whitening the long horizon—

The cloud-glory'd orange Orb arc'd living in blue still space, then lifting
    its bulk aflame
circled slowly over the breathing earth, while tiny oil tankers moved thru
    dawn
floating across the widespread ocean's far edge silently going from world to
    world . . .

The boy looked in his elder's eyes, which gazed in his while bare branches
    on the hillside stood trembling in sky
blue dawn light. Honey bees woke under heaven inland and sought the
    lilac, Honeysuckle, rose,
pale dew dript from day-lily leaf to leaf, green lamps went out in windows
    on Minneapolis avenues,
Lovers rose to work in subways, buses ground down empty streets in early
    light, the country
robin lit from the maple leaf whistling, cat scratched the farmhouse door
bulls groaned in barns, the aluminum pail clanked on cement by wooden
    stools in steaming flop
& stainless-steel mouths sucked milk from millions of cows into shining
    vats,
Black nannygoats whinnied nubian complaints to the stinking spotted dog
whose clump'd hair hung from his belly tangled with thistle, Church
    organs sang,
Radios Chattered the nasal weather from barn to barn, the last snow patch
    slipped from the tarpaper roof of the tractor lean-to,
Ice melted in the willow bog, stars vanished from the sky over gravestones
    stained with water melt,
The White House shined near pillared Courts on electric-lit avenues wide
    roaring with cars . . .

The naked messenger returned his thought. "I came for Love, old bard,
    tho you mistook
my youth for Innocence; I came for love, Old Prophet, and I brought you
    Prophecy,
Though you knew all; I came from Beauty, I came to Beauty, and I brought
    more beauty . . .

You read my youthful Beauty, tender lip and merry eye or Changeling
    glance
and love you think this silken muscular body, red hair even-parted curling
    round my skull—
Sir I do love you, but hate this earth and myself in it and the ignorance

creeping in this house! Sir I do love your beard which you know is
    Beautiful to me,
as beardless my tender-muscled abdomen to you: But my Beauty you love
    most
is that of the aethereal Changeling of Poesy, the same I love in you . . .
Naked! Naked! rise with me take all your Secrets in the air, the Sun's at
    height, the morning's ope'd blue sky,
Grandfather Clocks bong noon in oriental Carpet living-rooms in the
    Capital!
Close the stone door behind you, close this tomb lest gulls that swim the
    sea air
pluck the blind eyes of this lion out of its straw-brained head! Come out
    horrid Corpse!
But memorize the rune before we go, it'll encompass our lov'd wanderings!
As Dante had his Virgil & as Blake his own Miltonic Fiend, I your Cherub
    & Punk Idol
'll be Companion of th' Aethereal Ways till we discover our Secret
    Eidolon . . ."

"I knew this Rune once long ago, cold Demon inspired kid, bright boy—
thank you for discovering it me again, 'twas meant for you to read in
    Dreams
and find at your own bare foot one day. I hardly visioned to be here when
    you came
naked maddened with delight into my room, demanding I respect your lips
    & loins.
Listen now, my turn to tell the story of a day when I was young as you . . .
I gathered icy diamonds in the salt sea, plucked the blue eye of the whale
    for wisdom.
Green emeralds I found in the growing grass and on tree boughs in their
    Springtime buds,
For thirty years enriched with witty penury I gathered Amber from the
    generous laurel
and Rubies rolled out of my heart. I threw away the Pearl, back to the sea
To keep God out of trouble under his blue wet blanket, and be done
with clammy envy and his watery blisses and grasping waves . . .
Beloved Stranger, Naked Beauty, terrible Eidolon O my youth I never
    dreamt that you would come."

Washington, January 22, 1977, 3 A.M.–11:30 A.M.

III

Epilogue

THE ARGUMENT: Last words spoken by the bard to the boy on a train between Washington and N.Y.

"Some day when we surrender to each other and become One friend,
we'll walk back to this hermitage, returned from America
thru Cities and Bars and Smoking Factories & State Capitols
Universities, Crowds, Parks and Highways, returned from glass-glittering
 shrines
& diamond skyscrapers whose windows gleam sunset wealth Golden &
 Purple,
White & Red & Blue as Clouds that reflect Smog thru Western
 heavens . . .
Now we go from our Chambered Cranium forth thru Strangeness:
Careful to respect our Heart, mindful of Beauty's slow working Calm
 Machine,
Cigarette Vending Contraption or neon yellow Sun its face to your face—
All faces different, all forms present a Face to look into with Care:
The College boy his ignorant snub nose is a button whereon Sexual
 mercies
Press their lusty thumbs & wake his studious energy. The grey hair'd dirty
Professor of history's sought thru ages to find that Country where Love's
 face is King,
While the Care on his face is King of Centuries. And thoughts in his mind
 are
Presidents elected by fresh nerves every seven years to pass new laws of
 Consciousness.
Each Maple waits our gaze erecting tricky branches in the air we breathe.
Nothing is stupid but thought, & all thought we think's our own . . .
Plebeian Prince of the Suburb, I return to my eastern office pleased with
 our work
accident of our causes & Eidolons, Planned Careful in your Dreams & in
 my daylight Frenzies: failed Projections!
Our icy wills resolved in watery black ink's translucent tears,
Love's vapors are dissolved on seaboard's clear noon open to the Sun
shining thru railroad windows on new-revealed faces, our own inner
 forms!"

January 23, 1977

Punk Rock Your My Big Crybaby

I'll tell my deaf mother on you! Fall on the floor
and eat your grandmother's diapers! Drums,
Whatta lotta Noise you want a Revolution?
Wanna Apocalypse? Blow up in Dynamite Sound?
I can't get excited, Louder! Viciouser!
Fuck me in the ass! Suck me! Come in my ears!
I want those pink Abdominal bellybuttons!
Promise you'll murder me in the gutter with Orgasms!
I'll buy a ticket to your nightclub, I wanna get busted!
50 years old I wanna Go! with whips & chains & leather!
Spank me! Kiss me in the eye! Suck me all over
from Mabuhay Gardens to CBGB's coast to coast
Skull to toe Gimme yr electric guitar naked,
Punk President, eat up the FBI w/ yr big mouth.

Mabuhay Gardens, May 1977

X
PLUTONIAN
ODE
(1977–1980)

'La science, la nouvelle noblesse! Le progrès. Le monde marche!
Pourquoi ne tournerait-il pas?'

To LUCIEN CARR

for friendship
all these years

Love Replied

Love came up to me
& got down on his knee
& said I am here to serve
you what you deserve
All that you wish
as on a gold dish
eyes tongue and heart
your most private part.

Why do you eat
my behind & my feet
Why do you kiss
my belly like this
Why do you go down
& suck my cock crown
when I bare you the best
that is inside my breast

I lay there reproved
aching my prick moved
But Love kissed my ear
& said nothing to fear
Put your head on my breast
There let your skull rest
Yes hug my breast, this
is my heart you can kiss

Then Love put his face
in my tenderest place
where throbbed my breast sweet
with red hot heart's heat
There, love is our bed
There, love lay your head
There you'll never regret
all the love you can get.

From the hair to the toes
neck & knees in repose

Take the heart that I give
Give heart that you live
Forget my sweet cock
my buttock like a rock
Come up from my thighs
Hear my heart's own straight sighs

I myself am not queer
Tho I hold your heart dear
Tho I lie with you naked
tho my own heart has ached
breast to breast with your bare
body,   yes tho I dare
hug & kiss you all night
This is straight hearts' delight.

So bring your head up
from my loins or the cup
of my knees and behind
where you touch your lips blind
Put your lips to my heart
That is my public part
Hold me close and receive
All the love I can give

Boulder, June 18, 1977, 5 A.M.

Manhattan May Day Midnight

I walked out on the lamp shadowed concrete at midnight May Day passing
    a dark'd barfront,
police found corpses under the floor last year, call-girls & Cadillacs lurked
    there on First Avenue
around the block from my apartment, I'd come downstairs for tonight's
    newspapers—
refrigerator repair shop's window grate padlocked, fluorescent blue
light on a pile of newspapers, pages shifting in the chill Spring wind
'round battered cans & plastic refuse bags leaned together at the pavement
    edge—
Wind wind and old news sailed thru the air, old *Times* whirled above the
    garbage.
At the Corner of 11th under dim Street-light in a hole in the ground
a man wrapped in work-Cloth and wool Cap pulled down his bullet skull
stood & bent with a rod & flashlight turning round in his pit halfway sunk
    in earth
Peering down at his feet, up to his chest in the asphalt by a granite Curb
where his work mate poked a flexible tube in a tiny hole, a youth in gloves
who answered my question "Smell of gas—Someone must've reported
    in"—
Yes the body stink of City bowels, rotting tubes six feet under
Could explode any minute sparked by Con Ed's breathing Puttering truck
I noticed parked, as I passed by hurriedly Thinking Ancient Rome, Ur
Were they like this, the same shadowy surveyors & passers-by
scribing records of decaying pipes & Garbage piles on Marble, Cuneiform,
ordinary midnight citizen out on the street looking for Empire News,
rumor, gossip, workmen police in uniform, walking silent sunk in thought
under windows of sleepers coupled with Monster squids & Other-Planet
    eyeballs in their sheets
in the same night six thousand years old where Cities rise & fall & turn to
    dream?

                     May 1, 1978, 6 A.M.

Nagasaki Days: *Everybody's Fantasy*

I walked outside & the bomb'd
    dropped lots of plutonium
    all over the Lower East Side
There weren't any buildings left just
    iron skeletons
groceries burned, potholes open to
    stinking sewer waters

There were people starving and crawling
    across the desert
the Martian UFOs with blue
    Light destroyer rays
passed over and dried up all the
    waters

Charred Amazon palmtrees for
    hundreds of miles on both sides
    of the river

August 10, 1978

Plutonian Ode

I
1 What new element before us unborn in nature? Is there a new thing
       under the Sun?
    At last inquisitive Whitman a modern epic, detonative, Scientific
       theme
    First penned unmindful by Doctor Seaborg with poisonous hand,
       named for Death's planet through the sea beyond Uranus
    whose chthonic ore fathers this magma-teared Lord of Hades, Sire of
       avenging Furies, billionaire Hell-King worshipped once
5 with black sheep throats cut, priest's face averted from underground
       mysteries in a single temple at Eleusis,
    Spring-green Persephone nuptialed to his inevitable Shade, Demeter
       mother of asphodel weeping dew,
    her daughter stored in salty caverns under white snow, black hail, gray
       winter rain or Polar ice, immemorable seasons before
    Fish flew in Heaven, before a Ram died by the starry bush, before the
       Bull stamped sky and earth
    or Twins inscribed their memories in cuneiform clay or Crab'd flood
10 washed memory from the skull, or Lion sniffed the lilac breeze in
       Eden—
    Before the Great Year began turning its twelve signs, ere constella-
       tions wheeled for twenty-four thousand sunny years
    slowly round their axis in Sagittarius, one hundred sixty-seven thou-
       sand times returning to this night

    Radioactive Nemesis were you there at the beginning black Dumb
       tongueless unsmelling blast of Disillusion?
    I manifest your Baptismal Word after four billion years
15 I guess your birthday in Earthling Night, I salute your dreadful
       presence lasting majestic as the Gods,
    Sabaot, Jehova, Astapheus, Adonaeus, Elohim, Iao, Ialdabaoth, Aeon
       from Aeon born ignorant in an Abyss of Light,
    Sophia's reflections glittering thoughtful galaxies, whirlpools of star-
       spume silver-thin as hairs of Einstein!
    Father Whitman I celebrate a matter that renders Self oblivion!
    Grand Subject that annihilates inky hands & pages' prayers, old
       orators' inspired Immortalities,

20   I begin your chant, openmouthed exhaling into spacious sky over
          silent mills at Hanford, Savannah River, Rocky Flats, Pantex,
          Burlington, Albuquerque
    I yell thru Washington, South Carolina, Colorado, Texas, Iowa, New
          Mexico,
    where nuclear reactors create a new Thing under the Sun, where
          Rockwell war-plants fabricate this death stuff trigger in nitro-
          gen baths,
    Hanger-Silas Mason assembles the terrified weapon secret by ten
          thousands, & where Manzano Mountain boasts to store
    its dreadful decay through two hundred forty millennia while our
          Galaxy spirals around its nebulous core.
25   I enter your secret places with my mind, I speak with your presence, I
          roar your Lion Roar with mortal mouth.
    One microgram inspired to one lung, ten pounds of heavy metal dust
          adrift slow motion over gray Alps
    the breadth of the planet, how long before your radiance speeds blight
          and death to sentient beings?
    Enter my body or not I carol my spirit inside you, Unapproachable
          Weight,
    O heavy heavy Element awakened I vocalize your consciousness to six
          worlds
30   I chant your absolute Vanity. Yeah monster of Anger birthed in fear O
          most
    Ignorant matter ever created unnatural to Earth! Delusion of metal
          empires!
    Destroyer of lying Scientists! Devourer of covetous Generals, Incin-
          erator of Armies & Melter of Wars!
    Judgment of judgments, Divine Wind over vengeful nations, Mo-
          lester of Presidents, Death-Scandal of Capital politics! Ah
          civilizations stupidly industrious!
    Canker-Hex on multitudes learned or illiterate! Manufactured Spec-
          tre of human reason! O solidified imago of practitioners in
          Black Arts

35   I dare your Reality, I challenge your very being! I publish your cause
         and effect!
      I turn the Wheel of Mind on your three hundred tons! Your name
         enters mankind's ear! I embody your ultimate powers!
      My oratory advances on your vaunted Mystery! This breath dispels
         your braggart fears! I sing your form at last
      behind your concrete & iron walls inside your fortress of rubber &
         translucent silicon shields in filtered cabinets and baths of
         lathe oil,
      My voice resounds through robot glove boxes & ingot cans and
         echoes in electric vaults inert of atmosphere,
40   I enter with spirit out loud into your fuel rod drums underground on
         soundless thrones and beds of lead
      O density! This weightless anthem trumpets transcendent through
         hidden chambers and breaks through iron doors into the
         Infernal Room!
      Over your dreadful vibration this measured harmony floats audible,
         these jubilant tones are honey and milk and wine-sweet water
      Poured on the stone block floor, these syllables are barley groats I
         scatter on the Reactor's core,
      I call your name with hollow vowels, I psalm your Fate close by, my
         breath near deathless ever at your side
45   to Spell your destiny, I set this verse prophetic on your mausoleum
         walls to seal you up Eternally with Diamond Truth! O
         doomed Plutonium.

II

The Bard surveys Plutonian history from midnight lit with Mercury
Vapor streetlamps till in dawn's early light

he contemplates a tranquil politic spaced out between Nations'
thought-forms proliferating bureaucratic

& horrific arm'd, Satanic industries projected sudden with Five Hun-
dred Billion Dollar Strength

around the world same time this text is set in Boulder, Colorado
before front range of Rocky Mountains

50   twelve miles north of Rocky Flats Nuclear Facility in United States on
North America, Western Hemisphere

of planet Earth six months and fourteen days around our Solar System
in a Spiral Galaxy

the local year after Dominion of the last God nineteen hundred
seventy eight

Completed as yellow hazed dawn clouds brighten East, Denver city
white below

Blue sky transparent rising empty deep & spacious to a morning star
high over the balcony

55   above some autos sat with wheels to curb downhill from Flatiron's
jagged pine ridge,

sunlit mountain meadows sloped to rust-red sandstone cliffs above
brick townhouse roofs

as sparrows waked whistling through Marine Street's summer green
leafed trees.

III

This ode to you O Poets and Orators to come, you father Whitman as
    I join your side, you Congress and American people,
you present meditators, spiritual friends & teachers, you O Master of
    the Diamond Arts,
60 Take this wheel of syllables in hand, these vowels and consonants to
    breath's end
take this inhalation of black poison to your heart, breathe out this
    blessing from your breast on our creation
forests cities oceans deserts rocky flats and mountains in the Ten
    Directions pacify with this exhalation,
enrich this Plutonian Ode to explode its empty thunder through
    earthen thought-worlds
Magnetize this howl with heartless compassion, destroy this moun-
    tain of Plutonium with ordinary mind and body speech,
65 thus empower this Mind-guard spirit gone out, gone out, gone be-
    yond, gone beyond me, Wake space, so Ah!

July 14, 1978

Old Pond

The old pond—a frog jumps in, kerplunk!
Hard road! I walked till both feet stunk—
Ma!Ma! Whatcha doing down on that bed?
Pa!Pa! what hole you hide your head?

Left home   got work down town today
Sold coke,   got busted looking gay
Day dream, I acted like a clunk
Th'old pond—a frog jumps in, kerplunk!

Got hitched, I bought a frying pan
Fried eggs, my wife eats like a man
Won't cook, her oatmeal tastes like funk
Th'old pond—a frog jumps in, kerplunk!

Eat shit   exactly what she said
Drink wine, it goes right down my head
Fucked up, they all yelled I was drunk
Th'old pond—a frog jumps in, kerplunk!

Saw God at six o'clock tonight
Flop house, I think I'll start a fight
Head ache like both my eyeballs shrunk
Th'old pond—a frog jumps in, kerplunk!

Hot dog! I love my mustard hot
Hey Rube! I think I just got shot
Drop dead   She said you want some junk?
Th'old pond—a frog jumps in, kerplunk!

Oh ho   your dirty needle stinks
No no I don't shoot up with finks
Speed greed I stood there with the punk
Th'old pond—a frog jumps in, kerplunk!

Yeh yeh   gimme a breath of fresh air
Guess who   I am well you don't care
No name   call up the mocking Monk
Th'old pond—a frog jumps in, kerplunk!

No echo, make a lot of noise
Come home   you owe it to the boys
Can't hear   you scream your fish's sunk
Th'old pond—a frog jumps in, kerplunk!

Just folks, we bought a motor car
No gas   I guess we crossed the bar
I swear we started for Podunk
Th'old pond—a frog jumps in, kerplunk!

I got his banjo on my knee
I played it like an old Sweetie
I sang plunk-a-plunk-a-plunk plunk plunk plunk
Th'old pond—a frog jumps in, kerplunk!

One hand   I gave myself the clap
Unborn, but still I took the rap
Big deal, I fell out of my bunk
Th'old pond—a frog jumps in, kerplunk!

Hey hey! I ride down the blue sky
Sit down with worms until I die
Fare well! Hūṃ Hūṃ Hūṃ Hūṃ Hūṃ Hūṃ!
Th'old pond—a frog jumps in, kerplunk!

Red barn   rise wet in morning dew
Cockadoo   dle do oink oink moo moo
Buzz buzz—flyswatter in the kitchen, thwunk!
Th'old pond—a frog jumps in, kerplunk!

August 22, 1978

Spring Fashions

Full moon over the shopping mall—
    in a display window's silent light
the naked mannequin observes her fingernails

Boulder, 1979

Ruhr-Gebiet

Too much industry
too much eats
too much beer
too much cigarettes

Too much philosophy
too many thought forms
not enough rooms—
not enough trees

Too much Police
too much computers
too much hi fi
too much Pork

Too much coffee
too much smoking
under gray slate roofs
Too much obedience

Too many bellies
Too many business suits
Too much paperwork
too many magazines

Too much industry
No fish in the Rhine
Lorelei poisoned
Too much embarrassment

Too many fatigued
workers on the train
Ghost Jews scream
on the streetcorner

Too much old murder
too much white torture
Too much one Stammheim
too many happy Nazis

Too many crazy students
Not enough farms
not enough Appletrees
Not enough nut trees

Too much money
Too many poor
Turks without vote
"Guests" do the work

Too much metal
Too much fat
Too many jokes
not enough meditation

Too much anger
Too much sugar
Too many smokestacks
Not enough snow

Too many radioactive
plutonium wastebarrels
Take the Rhine gold
Build a big tomb

A gold walled grave
to bury this deadly nuclear slag
all the Banks' gold
Shining impenetrable

All the German gold
will save the Nation
Build a gold house
to bury the Devil

Heidelberg, December 15, 1979

Love Forgiven

Straight and slen - der Youth - ful ten - der
Love shows the way And ne - ver says nay
Light and gen - tle Heart - ed men - tal Tones sing and
play Gui - tar in bright day Voi - cing al - ways
Me - lo - dies, please Sing sad and say What - ev - er you may
Right - eous hon - est Heart's for give - ness Drives woes a -
way Gives Love to cold clay

Straight and slender
Youthful tender
Love shows the way
And never says nay

Light & gentle-
Hearted mental
Tones sing & play
Guitar in bright day

Voicing always
Melodies, please
Sing sad, & say
Whatever you may

Righteous honest
Heart's forgiveness
Drives woes away,
Gives Love to cold clay

Tübingen, December 16, 1979

Homework

Homage Kenneth Koch

If I were doing my Laundry I'd wash my dirty Iran

I'd throw in my United States, and pour on the Ivory Soap, scrub up Africa,
    put all the birds and elephants back in the jungle,

I'd wash the Amazon river and clean the oily Carib & Gulf of Mexico,

Rub that smog off the North Pole, wipe up all the pipelines in Alaska,

Rub a dub dub for Rocky Flats and Los Alamos, Flush that sparkly Cesium
    out of Love Canal

Rinse down the Acid Rain over the Parthenon & Sphinx, Drain Sludge out
    of the Mediterranean basin & make it azure again,

Put some blueing back into the sky over the Rhine, bleach the little Clouds
    so snow return white as snow,

Cleanse the Hudson Thames & Neckar, Drain the Suds out of Lake Erie

Then I'd throw big Asia in one giant Load & wash out the blood & Agent
    Orange,

Dump the whole mess of Russia and China in the wringer, squeeze out the
    tattletail Gray of U.S. Central American police state,

& put the planet in the drier & let it sit 20 minutes or an Aeon till it came
    out clean.

Boulder, April 26, 1980

Lower East Side *(After Reznikoff)*

That round faced woman, she owns the street with her three big dogs,
screeches at me, waddling with her shopping bag across Avenue B
Grabbing my crotch, "Why don't you talk to me?"
baring her teeth in a smile, voice loud like a taxi horn,
"Big Jerk . . . you think you're famous?"—reminds me of my mother.

April 29, 1980

τεθνάκην δ' ὀλίγω 'πιδεύης φαίνομ' ἀλαία

Red cheeked boyfriends tenderly kiss me sweet mouthed
under Boulder coverlets winter springtime
hug me naked laughing & telling girl friends
         gossip till autumn

Aging love escapes with his Childish body
Monday one man visited sleeping big cocked
older mustached crooked-mouthed not the same teen-
         ager I sucked off

This kid comes on Thursdays with happy hard ons
long nights talking heart to heart reading verses
fucking hours he comes in me happy but I
         can't get it in him

Cherub, thin-legged Southern boy once slept over
singing blues and drinking till he got horny
Wednesday night he gave me his ass I screwed him
         good luck he was drunk

Blond curl'd clear eyed gardener passing thru town
teaching digging earth in the ancient One Straw
method lay back stomach bare that night blew me
         I blew him and came

Winter dance Naropa a barefoot wild kid
jumped up grabbed me laughed at me took my hand and
ran out saying   Meet you at midnight your house
         Woke me up naked

Midnight crawled in bed with me breathed in my ear
kissed my eyelids   mouth on his cock it was soft
"Doesn't do nothing for me," turned on belly
         Came in behind him

Future youth I never may touch any more
Hark these Sapphics lipped by my hollow spirit
everlasting tenderness breathed in these vowels
         sighing for love still

Song your cadence formed while on May night's full moon
yellow onions tulips in fresh rain pale grass
iris pea pods radishes grew as this verse
          blossomed in dawn light

Measure forever his face eighteen years old
green eyes blond hair muscular gold soft skin whose
god like boy's voice mocked me once three decades past
          Come here and screw me

Breast struck   scared to look in his eyes   blood pulsing
my ears   mouth dry   tongue never moved ribs shook a
trembling fire ran down from my heart to my thighs
          Love-sick to this day

Heavy limbed I sat in a chair and watched him
sleep naked all night afraid to kiss his mouth
tender dying waited for sun rise years a-
          go in Manhattan

Boulder, May 17–June 1, 1980

τεθνάκην δ' ὀλίγω 'πιδεύης φαίνομ' ἀλαία   **325**

Fourth Floor, Dawn,
Up All Night Writing Letters

Pigeons shake their wings on the copper church roof
out my window across the street, a bird perched on the cross
surveys the city's blue-gray clouds. Larry Rivers
'll come at 10 A.M. and take my picture. I'm taking
your picture, pigeons. I'm writing you down, Dawn.
I'm immortalizing your exhaust, Avenue A bus.
O Thought, now you'll have to think the same thing forever!

New York, June 7, 1980, 6:48 A.M.

Birdbrain!

Birdbrain runs the World!

Birdbrain is the ultimate product of Capitalism

Birdbrain chief bureaucrat of Russia, yawning

Birdbrain ran FBI 30 years appointed by F. D. Roosevelt and never chased
Cosa Nostra!

Birdbrain apportions wheat to be burned, keep prices up on the world market!

Birdbrain lends money to Developing Nation police-states thru the International Monetary Fund!

Birdbrain never gets laid on his own he depends on his office to pimp for him

Birdbrain offers brain transplants in Switzerland

Birdbrain wakes up in middle of night and arranges his sheets

I am Birdbrain!

I rule Russia Yugoslavia England Poland Argentina United States El Salvador

Birdbrain multiplies in China!

Birdbrain inhabits Stalin's corpse inside the Kremlin wall

Birdbrain dictates petrochemical agriculture in Afric desert regions!

Birdbrain lowers North California's water table sucking it up for Orange
County Agribusiness Banks

Birdbrain clubs baby harp seals and wears their coats to Paris

Birdbrain runs the Pentagon his brother runs the CIA, Fatass Bucks!

Birdbrain writes and edits *Time Newsweek Wall Street Journal Pravda
Izvestia*

Birdbrain is Pope, Premier, President, Commissar, Chairman, Senator!

Birdbrain voted Reagan President of the United States!

Birdbrain prepares Wonder Bread with refined white flour!

Birdbrain sold slaves, sugar, tobacco, alcohol

Birdbrain conquered the New World and murdered mushroom god
Xochopili on Popocatepetl!

Birdbrain was President when a thousand mysterious students were machinegunned at Tlatelulco

Birdbrain sent 20,000,000 intellectuals and Jews to Siberia, 15,000,000
never got back to the Stray Dog Café

Birdbrain wore a mustache & ran Germany on Amphetamines the last year
of World War II

Birdbrain conceived the Final Solution to the Jewish Problem in Europe

Birdbrain carried it out in Gas Chambers

Birdbrain borrowed Lucky Luciano the Mafia from jail to secure Sicily for
U.S. Birdbrain against the Reds

Birdbrain manufactured guns in the Holy Land and sold them to white
    goyim in South Africa
Birdbrain supplied helicopters to Central America generals, kill a lot of
    restless Indians, encourage a favorable business climate
Birdbrain began a war of terror against Israeli Jews
Birdbrain sent out Zionist planes to shoot Palestinian huts outside Beirut
Birdbrain outlawed Opiates on the world market
Birdbrain formed the Black Market in Opium
Birdbrain's father shot skag in hallways of the lower East Side
Birdbrain organized Operation Condor to spray poison fumes on the
    marijuana fields of Sonora
Birdbrain got sick in Harvard Square from smoking Mexican grass
Birdbrain arrived in Europe to Conquer cockroaches with Propaganda
Birdbrain became a great International Poet and went around the world
    praising the Glories of Birdbrain
I declare Birdbrain to be victor in the Poetry Contest
He built the World Trade Center on New York Harbor waters without
    regard where the toilets emptied—
Birdbrain began chopping down the Amazon Rainforest to build a wood-
    pulp factory on the river bank
Birdbrain in Iraq attacked Birdbrain in Iran
Birdbrain in Belfast threw bombs at his mother's ass
Birdbrain wrote *Das Kapital*! authored the *Bible*! penned *The Wealth of
    Nations*!
Birdbrain's humanity, he built the Rainbow Room on top of Rockefeller
    Center so we could dance
He invented the Theory of Relativity so Rockwell Corporation could
    make Neutron Bombs at Rocky Flats in Colorado
Birdbrain's going to see how long he can go without coming
Birdbrain thinks his dong will grow big that way
Birdbrain sees a new Spy in the Market Platz in Dubrovnik outside the
    Eyeglass Hotel—
Birdbrain wants to suck your cock in Europe, he takes life very seriously,
    brokenhearted you won't cooperate—
Birdbrain goes to heavy duty Communist Countries so he can get KGB
    girlfriends while the sky thunders—
Birdbrain realized he was Buddha by meditating
Birdbrain's afraid he's going to blow up the planet so he wrote this poem to
    be immortal—

Hotel Subrovka, Dubrovnik, October 14, 1980, 4:30 A.M.

"Defending the Faith"

Stopping on the bus from Novi Pazar in the rain
I took a leak by Maglić Castle walls
and talked with the dogs on Ivar River Bank
They showed me their teeth & barked a long long time.

October 20, 1980

Capitol Air

I don't like the government where I live
I don't like dictatorship of the Rich
I don't like bureaucrats telling me what to eat
I don't like Police dogs sniffing round my feet

I don't like Communist Censorship of my books
I don't like Marxists complaining about my looks
I don't like Castro insulting members of my sex
Leftists insisting we got the mystic Fix

I don't like Capitalists selling me gasoline Coke
Multinationals burning Amazon trees to smoke
Big Corporation takeover media mind
I don't like the Top-bananas robbing Guatemala banks blind

I don't like K.G.B. Gulag concentration camps
I don't like the Maoists' Cambodian Death Dance
15 Million were killed by Stalin Secretary of Terror
He has killed our old Red Revolution for ever

I don't like Anarchists screaming Love Is Free
I don't like the C.I.A. they killed John Kennedy
Paranoiac tanks sit in Prague and Hungary
But I don't like counterrevolution paid for by the C.I.A.

Tyranny in Turkey or Korea Nineteen Eighty
I don't like Right Wing Death Squad Democracy
Police State Iran Nicaragua yesterday
Laissez-faire please Government keep your secret police offa me

I don't like Nationalist Supremacy White or Black
I don't like Narcs & Mafia marketing Smack
The General bullying Congress in his tweed vest
The President building up his Armies in the East & West

I don't like Argentine police Jail torture Truths
Government Terrorist takeover Salvador news
I don't like Zionists acting Nazi Storm Troop
Palestine Liberation cooking Israel into Moslem soup

I don't like the Crown's Official Secrets Act
You can get away with murder in the Government that's a fact
Security cops teargassing radical kids
In Switzerland or Czechoslovakia God Forbids

In America it's Attica in Russia it's Lubianka Wall
In China if you disappear you wouldn't know yourself at all
Arise Arise you citizens of the world use your lungs
Talk back to the Tyrants all they're afraid of is your tongues

Two hundred Billion dollars inflates World War
In United States every year They're asking for more
Russia's got as much in tanks and laser planes
Give or take Fifty Billion we can blow out everybody's brains

School's broke down 'cause History changes every night
Half the Free World nations are Dictatorships of the Right
The only place socialism worked was in Gdansk, Bud
The Communist world's stuck together with prisoners' blood

The Generals say they know something worth fighting for
They never say what till they start an unjust war
Iranian hostage Media Hysteria sucked
The Shah ran away with 9 Billion Iranian bucks

Kermit Roosevelt and his U.S. dollars overthrew Mossadegh
They wanted his oil then they got Ayatollah's dreck
They put in the Shah and they trained his police the Savak
All Iran was our hostage quarter-century That's right Jack

Bishop Romero wrote President Carter to stop
Sending guns to El Salvador's Junta so he got shot
Ambassador White blew the whistle on the White House lies
Reagan called him home cause he looked in the dead nuns' eyes

Half the voters didn't vote they knew it was too late
Newspaper headlines called it a big Mandate
Some people voted for Reagan eyes open wide
3 out of 4 didn't vote for him That's a Landslide

Truth may be hard to find but Falsehood's easy
Read between the lines our Imperialism is sleazy
But if you think the People's State is your Heart's Desire
Jump right back in the frying pan from the fire

The System the System in Russia & China the same
Criticize the System in Budapest lose your name
Coca Cola Pepsi Cola in Russia & China come true
Khrushchev yelled in Hollywood "We will bury You"

America and Russia want to bomb themselves Okay
Everybody dead on both sides   Everybody pray
All except the Generals in caves where they can hide
And fuck each other in the ass waiting for the next free ride

No hope Communism no hope Capitalism Yeah
Everybody's lying on both sides Nyeah nyeah nyeah
The bloody iron curtain of American Military Power
Is a mirror image of Russia's red Babel-Tower

Jesus Christ was spotless but was Crucified by the Mob
Law & Order Herod's hired soldiers did the job
Flowerpower's fine but innocence has got no Protection
The man who shot John Lennon had a Hero-worshipper's connection

The moral of this song is that the world is in a horrible place
Scientific Industry devours the human race
Police in every country armed with Tear Gas & TV
Secret Masters everywhere bureaucratize for you & me

Terrorists and police together build a lowerclass Rage
Propaganda murder manipulates the upperclass Stage
Can't tell the difference 'tween a turkey & a provocateur
If you're feeling confused the Government's in there for sure

Aware Aware wherever you are   No Fear
Trust your heart Don't ride your Paranoia dear
Breathe together with an ordinary mind
Armed with Humor Feed & Help Enlighten   Woe Mankind

Frankfurt–New York, December 15, 1980

XI
WHITE
SHROUD
(1980–1985)

'Old lovers yet may have
All that Time denied—
Grave is heaped on grave,
That they may be satisfied—'

To EDITH GINSBERG

Those Two

That tree said
    I don't like that white car under me,
                it smells gasoline
That other tree next to it said
    O you're always complaining
            you're a neurotic
        you can see by the way you're bent over.

July 6, 1981, 8 P.M.

Homage Vajracarya

Now that Samurai bow & arrow, Sumi brush, teacup
& Emperor's fan are balanced in the hand
—What about a glass of water?
Holding my cock to pee, the Atlantic gushes out.
Sitting to eat, the Sun & the Moon fill my plate.

July 8, 1981

Why I Meditate

I sit because the Dadaists screamed on Mirror Street
I sit because the Surrealists ate angry pillows
I sit because the Imagists breathed calmly in Rutherford and Manhattan
I sit because 2400 years
I sit in America because Buddha saw a Corpse in Lumbini
I sit because the Yippies whooped up Chicago's teargas skies once
I sit because No because
I sit because I was unable to trace the Unborn back to the womb
I sit because it's easy
I sit because I get angry if I don't
I sit because they told me to
I sit because I read about it in the Funny Papers
I sit because I had a vision also dropped LSD
I sit because I don't know what else to do like Peter Orlovsky
I sit because after Lunacharsky got fired & Stalin gave Zhdanov a special
        tennis court I became a rootless cosmopolitan
I sit inside the shell of the old Me
I sit for Jean-Arthur Rimbaud's Christmas on Earth
I sit for world revolution

July 19, 1981

Love Comes

I lay down to rest
weary at best
of party life
& dancing nights
Alone, Prepared
all I dared
bed & oil
bath, small toil
to clean my feet
place my slippers neat.

Alone, despair—
lighthearted, bare-
bottom trudged about,
listening the shout
of students down below
rock rolling fast and slow
shaking ash for show,
or love, or joy
hairless girl and boy
goldenhaired goy.

The door creaked loud
far from the crowd
Upstairs he trod
Eros or some god
come to visit,
Washed in the bath
calm as death
patient took a shit
approached me clean
naked serene

I sat on his thighs
looked in his eyes
I touched his hair
Bare body there
head to foot
big man root

I kissed his chest
Came down from above
I took in his rod
he pushed and shoved
That felt best

My behind in his groin
his big boyish loin
stuck all the way in
That's how we began
Both knees on the bed
his head to my head
he shoved in again
I loved him then

I pushed back deep
Soon he wanted to sleep
He wanted to rest
my back to his chest
My rear went down
I rolled it around
He pushed to the bottom
Now I've got 'em
He took control
made the bed roll

I relaxed my inside
loosed the ring in my hide
Surrendered in time
whole body and mind
and heart at the sheet
He continued to beat
his meat in my meat,
held me around
my chest love-bound
sighed without sound

My breast relaxed
my belly a sack
my sphincter loosed
to his hard deep thrust
I clenched my gut tight
in full moon light

thru curtained window
for an hour or so
thin clouds in the sky
I watched pass by
sigh after sigh

He fucked me in the East
he fucked me in the West
he fucked me South
my cock in his mouth
he fucked me North
No sperm shot forth

He continued to love
I spread my knees
pushed apart by his
so that he could move
in and out at ease,
Knelt on the bed
pillow against my head
I wanted release

Tho' it hurt not much
a punishment such
as I asked to feel
back arched for the real
solid prick of control
a youth 19 years old
gave with deep grace,
body fair, curly gold
hair, angelic face

I'd waited a week
the promise he'd keep
if I trusted the truth
of his love in his youth
and I do love him—
tall body, pale skin
Hot heart within
open blue eyes—
a hard cock never lies.

July 4–October 11, 1981

Airplane Blues

why   there's   the   blues   Ma - jes-tic- al

jail - house   our   Joy's   in   the   Cage

Hearts   full   of   hat - red   will   out - last   my   old

age

I drove out to the airport
                    on a blue sunny day
Smog brown over Denver
                    Horizon dung gray
Look down on Missouri
                    vast river bend south
Dakota sky brilliant
                    Cigarette in my mouth

I've had many lovers
                    over half century
I have a new boyfriend
                    Nineteen years, he loves me
But I can't get it up
                    too timid and shy
Growing old in my heaven
                    Singing blues in the sky

Nothing here to complain of
                    White clouds in the sun
Peace in my heart
                    Empty sky Everyone

But earth I look down on
                    Turns round misery
Green dollars fat
                    with the war industry

Mankind's great delusions
                    Scrape sky with red rage
Build bombs out of Atoms
                    to blast out the words on this page
Majestical jailhouse
                    our Joy's in the Cage
Hearts full of hatred
                    will outlast my old age

My mother has perished
                    my father's long dead
I have a sweet brother
                    healed the pain in his head
I'm going to the Apple
                    to eat with my friends
While the radio chatters
                    what the President intends

Down there Mississippi
                    Minneapolis near
Farms and green comforts
                    of the Northern Hemisphere
While Earth's hundred millions
                    Chew miserable clay
Old African kingdoms
                    Starve this century

I'm alone in the sky
                    where there's nothing to lose
The Sun's not eternal
                    That's why there's the blues
Majestical jailhouse
                    our Joy's in the Cage
Hearts full of hatred
                    will outlast my old age

Turn round in the sunset
          over Manhattan isle
Newark was my birthplace
          under the wing for a while
Green gastanks of Kearny
          Smog brown in the sky
Seven million black men and white
          live here and die

Come down over Harlem
          red buildings stand still
Dusk light gleams their windows
          wheels bound on the landfill
Sky streaked with jet streams
          black clouds in the west
In the Lower East Side
          I'll go take my rest.

October 30, 1981

Do the Meditation Rock

Tune: *I fought the Dharma, and the Dharma won*

If you want to learn	how to meditate
I'll tell you now	'cause it's never too late
I'll tell you how	'cause I can't wait
it's just that great	that it's never too late
If you are an old	fraud like me
or a lama who lives	in Eternity
The first thing you do	when you meditate
is keep your spine	your backbone straight
Sit yourself down	on a pillow on the ground
or sit in a chair	if the ground isn't there

    Do the meditation   *Do the meditation*
    Learn a little Patience and Generosity

Follow your breath out	open your eyes
and sit there steady	& sit there wise
Follow your breath right	outta your nose
follow it out	as far as it goes
Follow your breath	but don't hang on
to the thought of yr death	in old Saigon
Follow your breath	when thought forms rise
whatever you think	it's a big surprise

    Do the meditation   *Do the meditation*
    Learn a little Patience and Generosity
    Generosity   Generosity   Generosity & Generosity

All you got to do	is to imitate
you're sitting meditating	and you're never too late
when thoughts catch up	but your breath goes on
forget what you thought	about Uncle Don
Laurel Hardy Uncle Don	Charlie Chaplin Uncle Don
you don't have to drop	your nuclear bomb
If you see a vision come	say Hello Goodbye
play it dumb	with an empty eye
if you want a holocaust	you can recall your mind
it just went past	with the Western wind

    Do the meditation   *Do the meditation*
    Learn a little Patience   *& Generosity*

If you see Apocalypse   in a long red car
or a flying saucer   sit where you are
If you feel a little bliss   don't worry about that
give your wife a kiss   when your tire goes flat
If you can't think straight   & you don't know who to call
it's never too late   to do nothing at all
Do the meditation   follow your breath
so your body & mind   get together for a rest
   Do the meditation   *Do the meditation*
   Learn a little Patience   *and Generosity*

If you sit for an hour   or a minute every day
you can tell the Superpower   to sit the same way
you can tell the Superpower   to watch and wait
& to stop & meditate   'cause it's never too late
   Do the meditation   *Do the meditation*
   Get yourself together   *lots of Energy*
   & Generosity   Generosity   Generosity & Generosity!

St. Mark's Place, Xmas 1981

"What You Up To?"

"Oh just hanging around
    picking my nose . . ."
I replied, embarrassed
    in Naropa's corridor,
the Sanskrit professor'd saluted me
as Americans are wont to do—
What must he think my genius,
    a large red blob on my
    index finger tip—
But I suffer from Bell's palsy
my lower eyelid slightly paralyzed
no longer conducts tears thru
    my nostril
thus my nose corridors dry up
    & crack, for five years
whenever I lift the handkerchief
    from my face
a spot of red stains the pure
    cotton & shames me.
When I walk with bent spine & cane
    will my nose be caked with
blood black & ulcerous? tears
    running down my cheeks
a bony pinkie picking at the
    scarlet scab that got thick
overnight, I forgot to grease my
    wrinkled snout the nite
    of my eightieth birthday

and dreamed all the red
    mountain of mucus accumulated
    round me
Himalaya of suffering gelatinous
    slop my lifetime since 1976
when the right side my face
    drooped dead muscles
'cause an O.D. on Doctor's Antibiotic
    inflamed my seventh cranial nerve inside
    its cheekbone

& left me dry-nosed with crooked
    smile & sneaky finger
Probing the irritation in the
    middle of my face
walking daydreaming in the school hall—
That White boy in a two-piece suit
    Hotel Astor bar on Times Square
I took home one night in 1946
    he fucked me naked in the ass
till I smelled brown excrement
    staining his cock
& tried to get up from bed to go to the
    toilet a minute
but he held me down & kept pumping
    at me, serious & said
"No I don't want to stop I like it dirty
    like this."

April 30, 1982

Maturity

Young I drank beer & vomited green bile
Older drank wine vomited blood red
Now I vomit air

July 1982

136 Syllables at Rocky Mountain Dharma Center

Tail turned to red sunset on a juniper crown a lone magpie cawks.

Mad at Oryoki in the shrine-room—Thistles blossomed late afternoon.

Put on my shirt and took it off in the sun walking the path to lunch.

A dandelion seed floats above the marsh grass with the mosquitos.

At 4 A.M. the two middleaged men sleeping together hold hands.

In the half-light of dawn a few birds warble under the Pleiades.

Sky reddens behind fir trees, larks twitter, sparrows cheep cheep cheep
    cheep cheep.

July 1983

Caught shoplifting ran out the department store at sunrise and woke up.

August 1983

Arguments

I'm sick of arguments
"You threw the butter in the pan"
"I did not you let it melt on the stove"
"You invaded Turkey and killed all the Armenians!"
"I did not! You invaded China got them addicted to Opium!"
"You built a bigger H Bomb than I did"
"You used poison gas in Indochina"
"Your agent orange defoliated ¼ the landmass   It isn't fair"
"You sprayed Paraquat"
"You smoke pot"
"You're under arrest"
"I declare war!"
Why don't we turn off the loudspeakers?

September 5, 1983

White Shroud

I am summoned from my bed
To the Great City of the Dead
Where I have no house or home
But in dreams may sometime roam
Looking for my ancient room
A feeling in my heart of doom,
Where Grandmother aged lies
In her couch of later days
And my mother saner than I
Laughs and cries She's still alive.

I found myself again in the Great Eastern Metropolis,
wandering under Elevated Transport's iron struts—
many-windowed apartments walled the crowded Bronx road-way
under old theater roofs, masses of poor women shopping
in black shawls past candy store news stands, children skipped beside
grandfathers bent tottering on their canes. I'd descended
to this same street from blackened subways Sundays long ago,
tea and lox with my aunt and dentist cousin when I was ten.
The living pacifist David Dellinger walked at my right side,
he'd driven from Vermont to visit Catholic Worker
Tivoli Farm, we rode up North Manhattan in his car,
relieved the U.S. wars were over in the newspaper,
Television's frenzied dance of dots & shadows calmed—Now
older than our shouts and banners, we explored brick avenues
we lived in to find new residences, rent loft offices
or roomy apartments, retire our eyes & ears & thoughts.
Surprised, I passed the open Chamber where my Russian Jewish
Grandmother lay in her bed and sighed eating a little Chicken
soup or borscht, potato latkes, crumbs on her blankets, talking
Yiddish, complaining solitude abandoned in Old Folks House.
I realized I could find a place to sleep in the neighborhood, what
relief, the family together again, first time in decades!—
Now vigorous Middle aged I climbed hillside streets in West Bronx
looking for my own hot-water furnished flat to settle in,
close to visit my grandmother, read Sunday newspapers
in vast glassy Cafeterias, smoke over pencils & paper,
poetry desk, happy with books father'd left in the attic,
peaceful encyclopedia and a radio in the kitchen.

An old black janitor swept the gutter, street dogs sniffed red hydrants,
nurses pushed baby carriages past silent house fronts.
Anxious I be settled with money in my own place before
nightfall, I wandered tenement embankments overlooking
the pillared subway trestles by the bridge crossing Bronx River.
How like Paris or Budapest suburbs, far from Centrum
Left Bank junky doorstep tragedy intellectual fights
in restaurant bars, where a spry old lady carried her
Century Universal View camera to record Works
Progress Administration newspaper metropolis
double-decker buses in September sun near Broadway El,
skyscraper roofs upreared ten thousand office windows shining
electric-lit above tiny taxis street lamp'd in Mid-town
avenues' late-afternoon darkness the day before Christmas,
Herald Square crowds thronged past traffic lights July noon to lunch
Shop under Macy's department store awnings for dry goods
pause with satchels at Frankfurter counters wearing stylish straw
hats of the decade, mankind thriving in their solitudes in shoes.
But I'd strayed too long amused in the picture cavalcade,
Where was I living? I remembered looking for a house
& eating in apartment kitchens, bookshelf decades ago, Aunt
Rose's illness, an appendix operation, teeth braces,
one afternoon fitting eyeglasses first time, combing wet hair
back on my skull, young awkward looking in the high school mirror
photograph. The Dead look for a home, but here I was still alive.
      I walked past a niche between buildings with tin canopy
shelter from cold rain warmed by hot exhaust from subway gratings,
beneath which engines throbbed with pleasant quiet drone.
A shopping-bag lady lived in the side alley on a mattress,
her wooden bed above the pavement, many blankets and sheets,
Pots, pans, and plates beside her, fan, electric stove by the wall.
She looked desolate, white haired, but strong enough to cook and stare.
Passersby ignored her buildingside hovel many years,
a few businessmen stopped to speak, or give her bread or yogurt.
Sometimes she disappeared into state hospital back wards,
but now'd returned to her homely alleyway, sharp eyed, old
Cranky hair, half paralyzed, complaining angry as I passed.
I was horrified a little, who'd take care of such a woman,
familiar, half-neglected on her street except she'd weathered
many snows stubborn alone in her motheaten rabbit-fur hat.
She had tooth troubles, teeth too old, ground down like horse molars—
she opened her mouth to display her gorge—how can she live

with that, how eat I thought, mushroom-like gray-white horseshoe of
incisors she chomped with, hard flat flowers ranged around her gums.
Then I recognized she was my mother, Naomi, habiting
this old city-edge corner, older than I knew her before
her life disappeared. What are you doing here? I asked, amazed
she recognized me still, astounded to see her sitting up
on her own, chin raised to greet me mocking "I'm living alone,
you all abandoned me, I'm a great woman, I came here
by myself, I wanted to live, now I'm too old to take care
of myself, I don't care, what are you doing here?" I
was looking for a house, I thought, she has one, in poor
Bronx, needs someone to help her shop and cook, needs her children now,
I'm her younger son, walked past her alleyway by accident,
but here she is survived, sleeping at night awake on that
wooden platform. Has she an extra room? I noticed her cave
adjoined an apartment door, unpainted basement storeroom
facing her shelter in the building side. I could live here,
worst comes to worst, best place I'll find, near my mother in
our mortal life. My years of haunting continental city streets,
apartment dreams, old rooms I used to live in, still paid rent for,
key didn't work, locks changed, immigrant families occupied
my familiar hallway lodgings—I'd wandered downhill homeless
avenues, money lost, or'd come back to the flat—But couldn't
recognize my house in London, Paris, Bronx, by Columbia
library, downtown 8th Avenue near Chelsea Subway—
Those years unsettled—were over now, here I could live
forever, here have a home, with Naomi, at long last,
at long long last, my search was ended in this pleasant way,
time to care for her before death, long way to go yet,
lots of trouble her cantankerous habits, shameful blankets
near the street, tooth pots, dirty pans, half paralyzed irritable,
she needed my middle aged strength and worldly money knowledge,
housekeeping art. I can cook and write books for a living,
she'll not have to beg her medicine food, a new set of teeth
for company, won't yell at the world, I can afford a telephone,
after twenty-five years we could call up Aunt Edie in California,
I'll have a place to stay. "Best of all," I told Naomi
"Now don't get mad, you realize your old enemy Grandma's
still alive! She lives a couple blocks down hill, I just saw her,
like you!" My breast rejoiced, all my troubles over, she was
content, too old to care or yell her grudge, only complaining
her bad teeth. What long-sought peace!

　　　　　　　　　　Then glad of life I woke
in Boulder before dawn, my second story bedroom windows
Bluff Street facing East over town rooftops, I returned
from the Land of the Dead to living Poesy, and wrote
this tale of long lost joy, to have seen my mother again!
And when the ink ran out of my pen, and rosy violet
illumined city treetop skies above the Flatiron Front Range,
I went downstairs to the shady living room, where Peter Orlovsky
sat with long hair lit by television glow to watch
the sunrise weather news, I kissed him & filled my pen and wept.

October 5, 1983, 6:35 A.M.

Written in My Dream by W. C. Williams

"As Is
you're bearing

a common
Truth

Commonly known
as desire

No need
to dress

it up
as beauty

No need
to distort

what's not
standard

to be
understandable.

Pick your
nose

eyes ears
tongue

sex and
brain

to show
the populace

Take your
chances

on
your accuracy

Listen to
yourself

talk to
yourself

and others
will also

gladly
relieved

of the burden—
their own

thought
and grief.

What began
as desire

will end
wiser."

Baoding, November 23, 1984

Reading Bai Juyi

I

I'm a traveler in a strange country
China and I've been to many cities
Now I'm back in Shanghai, days
under warm covers in a room with electric heat—
a rare commodity in this country—
hundreds of millions shiver in the north
students rise at dawn and run around the soccerfield
Workmen sing songs in the dark to keep themselves warm
while I sleep late, smoke too much cough,
turn over in bed on my right side
pull the heavy quilt over my nose and go back
to visit the dead my father, mother and immortal
friends in dreams. Supper's served me,
I can go out and banquet, but prefer
this week to stay in my room, recovering
a cough. I don't have to sell persimmons on the streetcurb
in Baoding like the lady with white bandanna'd head
Don't have to push my boat oars around a rocky corner
in the Yangtze gorges, or pole my way downstream
from Yichang through yellow industrial scum, or carry water
buckets on a bamboo pole over my shoulder
to a cabbage field near Wuxi—I'm famous,
my poems have done some men good
and a few women ill, perhaps the good
outweighs the bad, I'll never know.
Still I feel guilty I haven't done more;
True I praised the dharma from nation to nation
But my own practice has been amateur, seedy
—even I dream how bad a student I am—
My teacher's tried to help me, but I seem
to be lazy and have taken advantage of money
and clothes my work's brought me, today
I'll stay in bed again & read old Chinese poets—
I don't believe in an afterworld of god or even
another life separate from this incarnation
Still I worry I'll be punished for my carelessness
after I'm dead—my poems scattered and my name

forgotten and myself reborn a foolish workman
freezing and breaking rocks on a roadside in Hebei.

Shanghai, December 5, 1984, 10 A.M.

V   *China Bronchitis*

I sat up in bed and pondered what I'd learned
while I lay sick almost a month:
That monks who could convert Waste to Treasure
were no longer to be found among the millions
in the province of Hebei. That *The Secret of the Golden Lotus*
has been replaced by the Literature of the Scar, nor's hardly
anybody heard of the *Meditation Cushion of the Flesh*
That smoking Chinese or American cigarettes makes me cough;
Old men had got white haired and bald before
my beard showed the signs of its fifty-eight snows.
That of Three Gorges on the Yangtze the last one downstream
is a hairpin turn between thousand-foot-high rock mountain gates.
I learned that the Great Leap Forward caused millions
of families to starve, that the Anti-Rightist Campaign
against bourgeois "Stinkers" sent revolutionary poets
to shovel shit in Xinjiang Province a decade before
the Cultural Revolution drove countless millions of readers
to cold huts and starvation in the countryside Northwest.
That sensitive poetry girls in Shanghai dream
of aged stars from Los Angeles movies. That down the alley
from the stone bridge at Suzhou where Jiang Ji spent
a sleepless night wakened by the bell of Cold Mountain Temple,
water lapping against his boat a thousand years ago,
a teahouse stands with two-stringed violin and flutes
and wooden stage. That the gold in the Sun setting
at West Lake Hangzhou is manufactured from black Soft Coal.
That roast red-skinned juicy entire dogs with eyes
bulging from their foreheads hang in the market at Canton
That So-Chan meditation's frowned on and martial health
Qi-Gong's approved by Marxist theoreticians. That men in
deep-blue suits might be kind enough to file a report
to your Unit on gossip they've heard about your secret loves.
That "Hang yu hang yu!" song is heard when workmen labor
yodeling on bamboo scaffolds over the street outside all night.
That most people have thought "We're just little men,
what can we count" since the time of Qin Shi Huang.

VI

Tho the body's heavy meat's sustained
on our impalpable breath, materialists
argue that Means of Production cause History:
once in power, materialists argue what
the right material is, quarrel with each other,
jail each other and exile tens of millions
of people with 10,000 thoughts apiece.
They're worse than Daoists who quibbled about immortality.
Their saving grace this year's that all the peasants are fed.

VII   Transformation of Bai's *"A Night in Xingyang"*

I grew up in Paterson New Jersey and was
just a virginal kid when I left
forty years ago. Now I'm around the world,
but I did go back recently to visit my stepmother.
Then I was 16 years old, now I'm fifty eight—
All the fears I had in those days—I can still see myself
daydreaming reading N.Y. Times on the Chinese rug on the living room
floor on Graham avenue. My childhood houses are torn down,
none of my old family lives here any more,
mother under the ground in Long Island, father underground
near the border of Newark where he was born.
A highway cuts thru the Fair Street lot where I remember our earliest
apartment, & a little girl's first kiss. New buildings rise on that street,
all the old stores along Broadway have disappeared.
Only the Great Falls and the Passaic river flow
noisy with mist then quietly along the brick factory sides
as they did before.

10:15 P.M.

XII
COSMOPOLITAN GREETINGS
(1986–1992)

"I'm going to try speaking some reckless words,
and I want you to try to listen recklessly."

To STEVEN TAYLOR

If music be the food of love, play on.

Sphincter

I hope my good old asshole holds out
60 years it's been mostly OK
Tho in Bolivia a fissure operation
      survived the *altiplano* hospital—
a little blood, no polyps, occasionally
      a small hemorrhoid
active, eager, receptive to phallus
      coke bottle, candle, carrot
      banana & fingers—
Now AIDS makes it shy, but still
      eager to serve—
out with the dumps, in with the condom'd
      orgasmic friend—
still rubbery muscular,
      unashamed wide open for joy
But another 20 years who knows,
      old folks got troubles everywhere—
necks, prostates, stomachs, joints—
      I hope the old hole stays young
      till death, relax

March 15, 1986, 1:00 P.M.

Cosmopolitan Greetings

To Struga Festival Golden Wreath Laureates
& International Bards 1986

Stand up against governments, against God.

Stay irresponsible.

Say only what we know & imagine.

Absolutes are coercion.

Change is absolute.

Ordinary mind includes eternal perceptions.

Observe what's vivid.

Notice what you notice.

Catch yourself thinking.

Vividness is self-selecting.

If we don't show anyone, we're free to write anything.

Remember the future.

Advise only yourself.

Don't drink yourself to death.

Two molecules clanking against each other require an observer to become
scientific data.

The measuring instrument determines the appearance of the phenomenal
world after Einstein.

The universe is subjective.

Walt Whitman celebrated Person.

We are observer, measuring instrument, eye, subject, Person.

Universe is Person.

Inside skull vast as outside skull.

Mind is outer space.

"Each on his bed spoke to himself alone, making no sound."

"First thought, best thought."

Mind is shapely, Art is shapely.

Maximum information, minimum number of syllables.

Syntax condensed, sound is solid.

Intense fragments of spoken idiom, best.

Consonants around vowels make sense.

Savor vowels, appreciate consonants.

Subject is known by what she sees.

Others can measure their vision by what we see.

Candor ends paranoia.

Kral Majales
June 25, 1986
Boulder, Colorado

Personals Ad

"I will send a picture too
if you will send me one of you"
—R. Creeley

Poet professor in autumn years
seeks helpmate companion protector friend
young lover w/empty compassionate soul
exuberant spirit, straightforward handsome
athletic physique & boundless mind, courageous
warrior who may also like women & girls, no problem,
to share bed meditation apartment Lower East Side,
help inspire mankind conquer world anger & guilt,
empowered by Whitman Blake Rimbaud Ma Rainey & Vivaldi,
familiar respecting Art's primordial majesty, priapic carefree
playful harmless slave or master, mortally tender passing swift time,
photographer, musician, painter, poet, yuppie or scholar—
Find me here in New York alone with the Alone
going to lady psychiatrist who says Make time in your life
for someone you can call darling, honey, who holds you dear
can get excited & lay his head on your heart in peace.

October 8, 1987

Proclamation

For Carlos Edmondo de Ory

I am the King of the Universe
I am the Messiah with a new dispensation
Excuse me I stepped on a nail.
A mistake
Perhaps I am not the Capitalist of Heaven.
Perhaps I'm a gate keeper snoring
      beside the Pearl Columns—
No this isn't true, I really am God himself.
Not at all human. Don't associate me
      w/that Crowd.
In any case you can believe every word
      I say.

October 31, 1987
Gas Station, N.Y.

May Days 1988

I

As I cross my kitchen floor the thought of Death returns,
day after day, as I wake & drink lemon juice & hot water,
brush my teeth & blow my nose, stand at toilet a yellow stream
issuing from my body, look out curtained windows, across the street
Mary Help of Christians R.C. Church, how many years
empty the garbage pail, carry black plastic bags to the sidewalk,
before I boil the last soft egg,
day after day glance my altar sitting pillow a sidelong look & sigh,
pass bookcases' Greek lyrics & volumes of Military Industrial Secrecy?
How many mornings out the window Springtime's grey clouds drift over a
    wooden owl
on the Rectory roof, pigeons flutter off the street lamp to an iron fence, I
    return to kitchen
oatmeal cooking in an iron pot, sit in a wooden chair, choose a soupspoon,
    dreaming out the window eat my gruel
as ailanthus trees bud & grow thick green, like seaweed in rainy Atlantis,
lose leaves after snowfall, sit bare-branched in January's rusty winds?
Snap photographs focus'd on the clothesline, courtyard chimneypots a
    block away?
How many years lie alone in bed and stroke my cock
or read the Times on a pillow midnite, answer telephone talk, my Step-
    mother
or Joe in Washington, wait for a knock on the door it's portly Peter sober
    hesitant
inquiring supper, rarely visiting, rueful a life gone by—you got the
    monthly rent?
armfuls of mid-morn mail arriving with despairing Secretaries—
rise and tuck my shirt in, turn the doorlock key, go down hallway stairs,
enter New York City, Christine's Polish restaurant around East 12th Street
    corner on 1st Avenue
taxi uptown to art museums or visit Dr. Brown, chest x-rays, smoking
    cough or flu
Turn on the News from Palestine, Listen to Leadbelly's tape lament, *Black
    Girl, Jim Crow, Irene*—and
Sunday Puerto Ricans climb concrete steps week after week to church.

II

Sox in the laundry, snap on the kitchen light midnite icebox
raid, sun-dried tomatoes, soft swiss cheese & ham, Pineapple juice,
low rent control $260 per mo, clear sanded gymseal'd floors, white walls,
Blake's *Tyger* on the bedroom bookcase, cabs rattling on dark asphalt
        below,
Silence, a solitary house, Charles Fourier on bedside table waiting inspec-
        tion, switch light off—
Pajamas in drawer for sleep, 80 volumes behind the headboard for
        browsing—
Irving Howe's Yiddish Poetry, Atilla József, Sashibusan Das Gupta's *Ob-
        scure Religious Cults*, Céline, *De Vulgari Eloquentia*—
What riches for old age? What cozy naps and long nights' dreams? Brows-
        ing in Persepolis and Lhasa!
What more ask existence? Except time, more time, ripe time & calm
& Warless time to contemplate collapsing years, tho body teeth brain
        elbow ache,
a crooked creak at backbone bottom, dry nostrils, mottled ankle
& smart tongue, how many years to talk, snap photos, sing in theaters
improvise in classroom street church radio, far from Congress?
How many more years eyes closed 9 A.M. wake worrying
the ulcer in my cheek is't cancer? Should I have charged Burroughs'
        biographer for photos
reprinted from 40 years ago? Should I rise & meditate
or sleep in daylight recuperate flu? phone ringing half an hour ago
What's on the Answer Machine? Give back Advances to Harper's?
Who promised deadlines for this photo book? Wasn't I up 2 A.M. revising
        Poems?
Spontaneous verse?!? Take a plane to Greenland, visit Dublin?
PEN Club meet May 17, decision Israeli Censorship Arabic Press?
Call C—— O—— Yiddish translator poetess Zionist yenta?
Write concentration camp expert moralist Elie Wiesel, what's his word
"Arabs shd throw words not stones?"—that quote accurate from the
        Times?
Should I get up right now, crosslegged scribbling Journals
with motor roar in street downstairs, stolen autos doctor'd at the curb
or pull the covers over achy bones? How many years awake or sleepy
How many mornings to be or not to be?
How many morning Mays to come, birds chirp insistent on six-story roofs?
buds rise in backyard cities? Forsythia yellow by brick walls & rusty
        bedsprings near the fence?

III

How many Sundays wake and lie immobile eyes closed remembering
    Death,

7 A.M. Spring Sunlight out the window the noise a Nuyorican drunkard on
    the corner

reminds me of Peter, Naomi, my nephew Alan, am I mad myself, have
    always been so

waking in N.Y. 61st year to realize childless I am a motherless freak

like so many millions, worlds from Paterson Los Angeles to Amazon

Humans & Whales screaming in despair from Empire State Building top
    to Arctic Ocean bottom—?

May 1–3, 1988

Return of Kral Majales

This silver anniversary much hair's gone from my head and I am the King
  of May
And tho I am King of May my howls & proclamations present are banned
  by FCC on America's electric airwaves 6 A.M. to midnight
So King of May I return through Heaven flying to reclaim my paper crown
And I am King of May with high blood pressure, diabetes, gout, Bell's
  palsy, kidneystones & calm eyeglasses
And wear the foolish crown of no ignorance no wisdom anymore no fear
  no hope in capitalist striped tie & Communist dungarees
No laughing matter the loss of the planet next hundred years
And I am the King of May returned with a diamond big as the universe an
  empty mind
And I am the King of May lacklove bouzerant in Springtime with a feeble
  practice of meditation
And I am King of May Distinguished Brooklyn English Professor singing
All gone all gone all overgone all gone sky-high now old mind so Ah!

April 25, 1990

Hum Bom!

I
Whom bomb?
We bomb'd them!
Whom bomb?
We bomb'd them!
Whom bomb?
We bomb'd them!
Whom bomb?
We bomb'd them!

Whom bomb?
We bomb you!
Whom bomb?
We bomb you!
Whom bomb?
You bomb you!
Whom bomb?
You bomb you!

What do we do?
Who do we bomb?
What do we do?
Who do we bomb?
What do we do?
Who do we bomb?
What do we do!
Who do we bomb?

What do we do?
You bomb! You bomb them!
What do we do?
You bomb! You bomb them!
What do we do?
We bomb! We bomb you!
What do we do?
You bomb! You bomb you!

May 1971

II

For Don Cherry

Whydja bomb?
We didn't wanna bomb!
Whydja bomb?
We didn't wanna bomb!
Whydja bomb?
You didn't wanna bomb!
Whydja bomb?
You didn't wanna bomb!

Who said bomb?
Who said we hadda bomb?
Who said bomb?
Who said we hadda bomb?
Who said bomb?
Who said you hadda bomb?
Who said bomb?
Who said you hadda bomb?

Who wantsa bomb?
We don't wanna bomb!
Who wantsa bomb?
We don't wanna bomb!
Who wantsa bomb?
We don't wanna bomb!
We don't wanna
        we don't wanna
                we don't wanna bomb!

Who wanteda bomb?
Somebody musta wanteda bomb!
Who wanteda bomb?
Somebody musta wanteda bomb!
Who wanteda bomb?
Somebody musta wanteda bomb!
Who wanteda bomb?
Somebody musta wanteda bomb!

They wanteda bomb!
They neededa bomb!

They wanteda bomb!
They neededa bomb!
They wanteda bomb!
They neededa bomb!
They wanteda bomb!
They neededa bomb!

They thought they hadda bomb!
They thought they hadda bomb!
They thought they hadda bomb!
They thought they hadda bomb!

III
Armageddon did the job
Gog & Magog Gog & Magog
Armageddon did the job
Gog & Magog Gog & Magog

Babylon & Ur got bombed
Gog & Magog Gog & Magog
Babylon & Ur got bombed
Gog & Magog Gog & Magog

Armageddon for the mob
Gog & Magog Gog & Magog
Armageddon for the mob
Gog & Magog Gog & Magog

Gog & Magog Gog & Magog
Gog Magog Gog Magog
Gog & Magog Gog & Magog
Gog Magog Gog Magog

Gog Magog Gog Magog
Gog Magog Gog Magog
Gog Magog Gog Magog
Gog Magog Gog Magog

Ginsberg says Gog & Magog
Armageddon did the job.

February–June 1991

After the Big Parade

Millions of people cheering and waving flags for joy in Manhattan
Yesterday've returned to their jobs and arthritis now Tuesday—
What made them want so much passion at last, such mutual delight—
Will they ever regain these hours of confetti'd ecstasy again?
Have they forgotten the Corridors of Death that gave such victory?
Will another hundred thousand desert deaths across the world be
                          cause for the next rejoicing?

June 11, 1991, 2:30 P.M.

Yiddishe Kopf

I'm Jewish because love my family matzoh ball soup.
I'm Jewish because my fathers mothers uncles grandmothers said "Jewish,"
    all the way back to Vitebsk & Kaminetz-Podolska via Lvov.
Jewish because reading Dostoyevsky at 13 I write poems at restaurant
    tables Lower East Side, perfect delicatessen intellectual.
Jewish because violent Zionists make my blood boil, Progressive indigna-
    tion.
Jewish because Buddhist, my anger's transparent hot air, I shrug my shoul-
    ders.
Jewish because monotheist Jews Catholics Moslems're intolerable
    intolerant—
Blake sd. "6000 years of sleep" since antique Nobodaddy Adonai's mind
    trap—Oy! such Meshuggeneh absolutes—
Senior Citizen Jewish paid my dues got half-fare card buses subways,
    discount movies—
Can't imagine how these young people make a life, make a living.
How can they stand it, going out in the world with only $10 and a
    hydrogen bomb?

October 1991

After Lalon

I

It's true I got caught in
               the world
When I was young Blake
              tipped me off
Other teachers followed:
Better prepare for Death
Don't get entangled with
              possessions
That was when I was young,
          I was warned
Now I'm a Senior Citizen
and stuck with a million
              books
a million thoughts a million
            dollars a million
                   loves
How'll I ever leave my body?
Allen Ginsberg says, I'm
          really up shits creek

II

I sat at the foot of a
           Lover
  and he told me everything
Fuck off, 23 skidoo,
         watch your ass,
         watch your step
exercise, meditate, think
        of your temper—
Now I'm an old man and
        I won't live another
20 years maybe not another
        20 weeks,
maybe the next second I'll
       be carried off to
             rebirth

the worm farm, maybe it's
        already happened—
How should I know, says
        Allen Ginsberg
Maybe I've been dreaming
        all along—

III

It's 2 A.M. and I got to
        get up early
and taxi 20 miles to satisfy
        my ambition—
How'd I get into this fix,
this workaholic show-
        biz meditation market?
If I had a soul I sold it
        for pretty words
If I had a body I used
        it up spurting my essence
If I had a mind it got
        covered with Love—
If I had a spirit I forgot
        when I was breathing
If I had speech it was
        all a boast
If I had desire it went
        out my anus
If I had ambitions to
        be liberated
how'd I get into this
        wrinkled person?
With pretty words, Love essences,
        breathing boasts, anal
        longings, famous crimes?
What a mess I am, Allen Ginsberg.

IV

Sleepless I stay up &
        think about my Death
—certainly it's nearer

than when I was ten
                years old
and wondered how big the
                universe was—
If I dont get some rest I'll die faster
If I sleep I'll lose my
                chance for salvation—
asleep or awake, Allen
        Ginsberg's in bed
            in the middle of the night.

V

4 A.M.

Then they came for me,
        I hid in the toilet stall
They broke down the toilet door
        It fell in on an innocent boy
Ach the wooden door fell
        in on an innocent kid!
I stood on the bowl & listened,
        I hid my shadow,
they shackled the other and
        dragged him away
in my place— How long can
        I get away with this?
Pretty soon they'll discover
        I'm not there
They'll come for me again, where
        can I hide my body?
Am I myself or some one else
        or nobody at all?
Then what's this heavy flesh this
        weak heart leaky kidney?
Who's been doing time
        for 65 years
in this corpse? Who else went
        into ecstasy besides me?
Now it's all over soon,
        what good was all that come?
Will it come true? Will
        it really come true?

VI

I had my chance and lost it,
many chances & didn't
    take them seriously enuf.
Oh yes I was impressed, almost
    went mad with fear
I'd lose the immortal chance,
    One lost it.
Allen Ginsberg warns you
    dont follow my path
    to extinction.

March 31, 1992

Put Down Your Cigarette Rag (Dont Smoke)

smoke dont smoke dont smoke dont smoke dont smoke

Dont smoke dont smoke dont smoke
Dont smoke
It's a nine billion dollar
Capitalist Communist joke
    Dont smoke dont smoke dont smoke dont smoke
                    Dont smoke

Smoking makes you cough,
You cant sing straight
You gargle on saliva
& vomit on your plate
    Dont smoke dont smoke dont smoke dont smoke,
        Dont smoke smoke smoke smoke

You smoke in bed
You smoke on the hill
Smoke till yr dead
You smoke in Hell
    Dont smoke dont smoke in living Hell Dope Dope
        Dont smoke dont smoke dont smoke

You puff your fag
You suck your butt
You choke & gag
Teeth full of crud
    Smoke smoke smoke smoke Dont dont dont
        Dont Dont Dope Dope Dope Dont Smoke Dont Dope

Pay your two bucks
        for a deathly pack
Trust your bad luck
        & smoke in the sack
    Dont Smoke Dont Smoke Nicotine Nicotine No
    No dont smoke the official Dope Smoke Dope Dope

Four Billion dollars in Green
'swat Madison Avenue gets
t' advertise nicotine
& hook you radical brats
  Dont Smoke Dont Smoke Dont Smoke
    Nope Nope Dope Dope Hoax Hoax Hoax Hoax
  Dopey Dope Dopey Dope Dope Dope dope dope

Black magic pushes dope
Sexy chicks in cars
America loses hope
& smokes and drinks in bars
  Dont smoke dont smoke dont smoke,
  dont smoke dont dont dont dont
  choke choke choke choke kaf kaf
  Kaf Kaf Choke Choke
  Choke Choke Dope Dope

Communism's flopped
Let's help the Soviet millions
Sell 'em our Coffin-Nails
& make a couple billions
  Big Bucks Big Bucks bucks bucks
    bucks bucks smoke smoke smoke smoke
      smoke Bucks smoke bucks Dope bucks big
      Dope Bucks Dig Big Dope Bucks Big Dope
        Bucks dont smoke big dope bucks
        Dig big Pig dope bucks

Nine billion bucks a year
a Southern Industry
Buys Senator Jesse Fear who pushes Tobacco subsidy
In the Senate Foreign Relations Committee
  Dope smokes dope smokes dont smoke dont smoke
    Cloak cloak cloak room cloak & dagger
    smoke room cloak room dope cloak
    cloak room dope cloak room dope dont smoke

Nine billion bucks for dope
approved by Time & Life
America loses hope

The President smokes Tobacco votes
    Dont Smoke dont smoke dont smoke dont smoke
        Dont smoke nope nope nope nope

30 thousand die of coke or
    Illegal speed each year
430 thousand cigarette deaths
    That's the drug to fear
        In USA Dont smoke Dont smoke Dont smoke

Get Hooked on Cigarettes
Go Fight the War on Drugs
Smoke any other Weed
Get bust by Government Thugs
    Dont smoke dont smoke the official dope

If you will get in bed
& give your girlfriend head
then you wont want a fag
Nor evermore a drag
    Dont Smoke dont smoke Hope Hope Hope Hope
        O Please Dont Smoke Dont Smoke
        O Please O Please O Please
        I'm calling on my knees

Twenty-four hours in bed
& give your boyfriend head
Put something in your mouth
Like skin not cigarette filth
    Suck tit suck tit suck cock suck cock
        suck clit suck prick suck it
        but dont smoke nicotine dont smoke
        dont smoke nicotine nicotine it's
        too obscene dont smoke dont smoke
        nicotine suck cock suck prick suck tit
        suck clit suck it But dont smoke shit nope
        nope nope nope Dope Dope Dope Dope
            the official dope Dont Smoke

Make believe yer sick
Stay in bed and lick

yr cigarette habit greed
One day's all you need
      In deed in deed in deed in deed smoke weed
        smoke weed Put something green
        in between but don't smoke smoke dont smoke
        hope hope hope hope Nicotine dont
        smoke the official dope
        Dope Dope Dope Dope Dont Smoke
Smoke weed indeed   smoke grass yass yass
smoke pot but not nicotine no no
indeed it's too obscene
              put something green
in between your lips get   hip not square
listen to my wail   don't dare smoke coffin nails
ugh ugh ugh ugh the government Drug
official habit for Mr. Babbitt
Dont smoke the official dope
dope dope dope dope don't smoke
        Dont Smoke Dont Smoke.

1971; May 20, 1996

The Charnel Ground

> . . . rugged and raw situations, and having accepted them as part
> of your home ground, then some spark of sympathy or compas-
> sion could take place. You are not in a hurry to leave such a place
> immediately. You would like to face the facts, realities of that
> particular world. . . .
>
> CHÖGYAM TRUNGPA, RINPOCHE

Upstairs Jenny crashed her car & became a living corpse, Jake sold grass,
    the white-bearded potbelly leprechaun silent climbed their stair-
    case
Ex-janitor John from Poland averted his eyes, cheeks flushed with vodka,
    wine who knew what
as he left his groundfloor flat, refusing to speak to the inhabitant of Apt. 24
who'd put his boyfriend in Bellevue, calling police, while the artistic
    Buddhist composer
on sixth floor lay spaced out feet swollen with water, dying slowly of AIDS
    over a year—
The Chinese teacher cleaned & cooked in Apt. 23 for the homosexual poet
    who pined for his gymnast
thighs & buttocks— Downstairs th' old hippie flower girl fell drunk over
    the banister, smashed her jaw—
her son despite moderate fame cheated of rocknroll money, twenty thou-
    sand people in stadiums
cheering his tattooed skinhead murderous Hare Krishna vegetarian drum
    lyrics—
Mary born in the building rested on her cane, heavy-legged with heart
    failure on the second landing, no more able
to vacation in Caracas & Dublin— The Russian landlady's husband from
    concentration camp disappeared again—nobody mentioned he'd
    died—
tenants took over her building for hot water, she couldn't add rent & pay
    taxes, wore a long coat hot days
alone & thin on the street carrying groceries to her crooked apartment
    silent—
One poet highschool teacher fell dead mysterious heart dysrhythmia,
    konked over
in his mother's Brooklyn apartment, his first baby girl a year old, wife
    stoical a few days—
their growling noisy little dog had to go, the baby cried—

Meanwhile the upstairs apartment meth head shot cocaine & yowled up
and down
East 12th Street, kicked out of Christine's Eatery till police cornered him,
'top a hot iron steamhole
near Stuyvesant Town Avenue A telephone booth calling his deaf
mother—sirens speed the way to Bellevue—
past whispering grass crack salesman jittering in circles on East 10th
Street's
southwest corner where art yuppies come out of the overpriced Japanese
Sushi Bar—& they poured salt into potato soup heart failure vats
at KK's Polish restaurant
—Garbage piled up, nonbiodegradable plastic bags emptied by diabetic
sidewalk homeless
looking for returnable bottles recycled dolls radios half-eaten ham-
burgers—thrown-away Danish—
On 13th Street the notary public sat in his dingy storefront, driver's lessons
& tax returns prepared on old metal desks—
Sunnysides crisped in butter, fries & sugary donuts passed over the lun-
cheonette counter next door—
The Hispanic lady yelled at the rude African-American behind the Post
Office window
"I waited all week my welfare check you sent me notice I was here yester-
day
I want to see the supervisor bitch dont insult me refusing to look in—"
Closed eyes of Puerto Rican wino lips cracked skin red stretched out
on the pavement, naphtha backdoor open for the Korean family dry
cleaners at the 14th Street corner—
Con Ed workmen drilled all year to bust electric pipes 6 feet deep in brown
dirt
so cars bottlenecked wait minutes to pass the M14 bus stopped midroad,
heavy dressed senior citizens step down in red rubble
with Reduced Fare Program cards got from grey city Aging Department
offices downtown up the second flight by elevators don't work—
News comes on the radio, they bomb Baghdad and the Garden of Eden
again?
A million starve in Sudan, mountains of eats stacked on docks, local gangs
& U.N.'s trembling bureaucrat officers sweat near the equator
arguing over
wheat piles shoved by bulldozers—Swedish doctors ran out of medicine—
The Pakistan taxi driver
says Salman Rushdie must die, insulting the Prophet in fictions—
"No that wasn't my opinion, just a character talking like in a poem no
judgment"—

"Not till the sun rejects you do I," so give you a quarter by the Catholic
     church 14th St. you stand half drunk
waving a plastic glass, flush-faced, live with your mother a wounded look
     on your lips, eyes squinting,
receding lower jaw sometimes you dry out in Bellevue, most days cadging
     dollars for sweet wine
by the corner where Plump Blindman shifts from foot to foot showing his
     white cane, rattling coins in a white paper cup some weeks
where girding the subway entrance construction sawhorses painted orange
guard steps underground— And across the street the NYCE bank ma-
     chine cubicle door sign reads
Not in Operation as taxis bump on potholes asphalt mounded at the cross-
     road when red lights change green
& I'm on my way uptown to get a CAT scan liver biopsy, visit the cardiolo-
     gist,
account for high blood pressure, kidneystones, diabetes, misty eyes &
     dysesthesia—
feeling lack in feet soles, inside ankles, small of back, phallus head, anus—
Old age sickness death again come round in the wink of an eye—
High school youth the inside skin of my thighs was silken smooth tho
     nobody touched me there back then—
Across town the velvet poet takes Darvon N, Valium nightly, sleeps all day
     kicking methadone
between brick walls sixth floor in a room cluttered with collages & gold dot
     paper scraps covered
with words: "The whole point seems to be the idea of giving away the
     giver."

                                                          August 19, 1992

Autumn Leaves

At 66 just learning how to take care of my body
Wake cheerful 8 A.M. & write in a notebook
rising from bed side naked leaving a naked boy asleep by the wall
mix miso mushroom leeks & winter squash breakfast,
Check bloodsugar, clean teeth exactly, brush, toothpick, floss, mouthwash
oil my feet, put on white shirt white pants white sox
sit solitary by the sink
a moment before brushing my hair, happy not yet
to be a corpse.

September 13, 1992, 9:50 A.M.

American Sentences

Tompkins Square Lower East Side N.Y.

Four skin heads stand in the streetlight rain chatting under an umbrella.

1987

*　*　*

Bearded robots drink from Uranium coffee cups on Saturn's ring.

May 1990

*　*　*

On Hearing the Muezzin Cry Allah Akbar While Visiting the Pythian Oracle at Didyma Toward the End of the Second Millennium

At sunset Apollo's columns echo with the bawl of the One God.

*　*　*

The weary Ambassador waits relatives late at the supper table.

*　*　*

To be sucking your thumb in Rome by the Tiber among fallen leaves . . .

June 1990

*　*　*

12AM Answering Mail

Rainy night on Union Square, full moon. Want more poems? Wait till I'm dead.

August 8, 1990, 3:30 AM

*　*　*

Approaching Seoul by Bus in Heavy Rain

Get used to your body, forget you were born, suddenly you got to get out!

August 1990

*　*　*

Put on my tie in a taxi, short of breath, rushing to meditate.

Nov 1991
N.Y.

*   *   *

Taxi ghosts at dusk pass Monoprix in Paris 20 years ago.

*   *   *

Two blocks from his hotel in a taxi the fat Lama punched out his mugger.

*   *   *

I can still see Neal's 23 year old corpse when I come in my hand.

January 1992
Amsterdam

*   *   *

He stands at the church steps a long time looking down at new white
sneakers—
Determined, goes in the door quickly to make his Sunday confession.

September 21, 1992

*   *   *

The midget albino entered the hairy limousine to pipi.

September 25, 1992
Modesto

XIII
NEW POEMS
(1992–)

C'mon Pigs of Western Civilization
Eat More Grease

Eat Eat more marbled Sirloin more Pork'n
       gravy!
Lard up the dressing, fry chicken in
       boiling oil
Carry it dribbling to gray climes, snowed with
       salt,
Little lambs covered with mint roast in racks
       surrounded by roast potatoes wet with
       buttersauce,
Buttered veal medallions in creamy saliva,
       buttered beef, by glistening mountains
       of french fries
Stroganoffs in white hot sour cream, chops
       soaked in olive oil,
surrounded by olives, salty feta cheese, followed
       by Roquefort & Bleu & Stilton
       thirsty
for wine, beer Cocacola Fanta Champagne
       Pepsi retsina arak whiskey
       vodka
Agh! Watch out heart attack, pop more
       angina pills
order a plate of Bratwurst, fried frankfurters,
couple billion Wimpys', MacDonald burgers
       to the moon & burp!
Salt on those fries! Boil onions
       & breaded mushrooms even zucchini
       in deep hot Crisco pans—Hot Dog!
Forget greenbeans, everyday a few carrots,
       a mini big spoonful of salty rice'll
       do, make the plate pretty;
throw in some vinegar pickles, briney sauerkraut
       check yr. cholesterol, swallow a pill
and order a sugar Cream donut, pack 2 under
       the size 44 belt

Pass out in the vomitorium come back cough
        up strands of sandwich still chewing
        pastrami at Katz's delicatessen
Back to central Europe & gobble Kielbasa
        in Lódź
swallow salami in Munich with beer, Liverwurst
on pumpernickel in Berlin, greasy cheese in
        a 3 star Hotel near Syntagma, on white
        bread thick-buttered
Set an example for developing nations, salt,
        sugar, animal fat, coffee tobacco Schnapps
Drop dead faster! make room for
        Chinese guestworkers with alien soybean
        curds green cabbage & rice!
Africans Latins with rice beans & calabash can
        stay thin & crowd in apartments for working
        class foodfreaks—

Not like western cuisine rich in protein
        cancer heart attack hypertension sweat
        bloated liver & spleen megaly
Diabetes & stroke —monuments to carnivorous
        civilizations
presently murdering Belfast
        Bosnia Cypress Ngorno Karabach Georgia
mailing love letter bombs in
        Vienna or setting houses afire
        in East Germany — have another coffee,
        here's a cigar.
And this is a plate of black forest chocolate cake,
        you deserve it.

Athens, December 19, 1993

New Stanzas for *Amazing Grace*

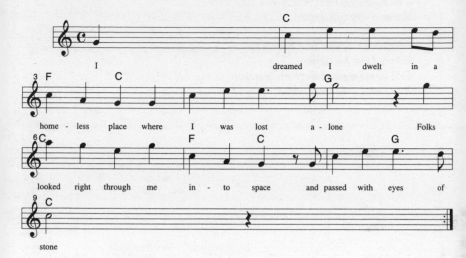

I dreamed I dwelled in a homeless place
Where I was lost alone
Folk looked right through me into space
And passed with eyes of stone

O homeless hand on many a street
Accept this change from me
A friendly smile or word is sweet
As fearless charity

Woe workingman who hears the cry
And cannot spare a dime
Nor look into a homeless eye
Afraid to give the time

So rich or poor no gold to talk
A smile on your face
The homeless ones where you may walk
Receive amazing grace

I dreamed I dwelled in a homeless place
Where I was lost alone
Folk looked right through me into space
And passed with eyes of stone

April 2, 1994

The Ballad of the Skeletons

Said the Presidential Skeleton
I won't sign the bill
Said the Speaker skeleton
Yes you will

Said the Representative Skeleton
I object
Said the Supreme Court skeleton
Whaddya expect

Said the Military skeleton
Buy Star Bombs
Said the Upperclass Skeleton
Starve unmarried moms

Said the Yahoo Skeleton
Stop dirty art
Said the Right Wing skeleton
Forget about yr heart

Said the Gnostic Skeleton
The Human Form's divine
Said the Moral Majority skeleton
No it's not it's mine

Said the Buddha Skeleton
Compassion is wealth
Said the Corporate skeleton
It's bad for your health

Said the Old Christ skeleton
Care for the Poor
Said the Son of God skeleton
AIDS needs cure

Said the Homophobe skeleton
Gay folk suck
Said the Heritage Policy skeleton
Blacks're outa luck

Said the Macho skeleton
Women in their place
Said the Fundamentalist skeleton
Increase human race

Said the Right-to-Life skeleton
Foetus has a soul
Said Pro Choice skeleton
Shove it up your hole

Said the Downsized skeleton
Robots got my job
Said the Tough-on-Crime skeleton
Tear gas the mob

Said the Governor skeleton
Cut school lunch
Said the Mayor skeleton
Eat the budget crunch

Said the Neo Conservative skeleton
Homeless off the street!
Said the Free Market skeleton
Use 'em up for meat

Said the Think Tank skeleton
Free Market's the way
Said the Savings & Loan skeleton
Make the State pay

Said the Chrysler skeleton
Pay for you & me
Said the Nuke Power skeleton
& me & me & me

Said the Ecologic skeleton
Keep Skies blue
Said the Multinational skeleton
What's it worth to you?

Said the NAFTA skeleton
Get rich, Free Trade,
Said the Maquiladora skeleton
Sweat shops, low paid

Said the rich GATT skeleton
One world, high tech
Said the Underclass skeleton
Get it in the neck

Said the World Bank skeleton
Cut down your trees
Said the I.M.F. skeleton
Buy American cheese

Said the Underdeveloped skeleton
We want rice
Said Developed Nations' skeleton
Sell your bones for dice

Said the Ayatollah skeleton
Die writer die
Said Joe Stalin's skeleton
That's no lie

Said the Middle Kingdom skeleton
We swallowed Tibet
Said the Dalai Lama skeleton
Indigestion's whatcha get

Said the World Chorus skeleton
That's their fate
Said the U.S.A. skeleton
Gotta save Kuwait

Said the Petrochemical skeleton
Roar Bombers roar!
Said the Psychedelic skeleton
Smoke a dinosaur

Said Nancy's skeleton
Just say No
Said the Rasta skeleton
Blow Nancy Blow

Said Demagogue skeleton
Don't smoke Pot
Said Alcoholic skeleton
Let your liver rot

Said the Junkie skeleton
Can't we get a fix?
Said the Big Brother skeleton
Jail the dirty pricks

Said the Mirror skeleton
Hey good looking
Said the Electric Chair skeleton
Hey what's cooking?

Said the Talkshow skeleton
Fuck you in the face
Said the Family Values skeleton
My family values mace

Said the NY Times skeleton
That's not fit to print
Said the CIA skeleton
Cantcha take a hint?

Said the Network skeleton
Believe my lies
Said the Advertising skeleton
Don't get wise!

Said the Media skeleton
Believe you me
Said the Couch-potato skeleton
What me worry?

Said the TV skeleton
Eat sound bites
Said the Newscast skeleton
That's all Goodnight

February 12–16, 1995

NOTES

II
THE GREEN AUTOMOBILE
(1953–1954)

The Green Automobile

page

26 NEAL: Neal Cassady, to whom the poem is dedicated.

Neal Cassady (1925–1968) in his first suit, bought secondhand in Chinatown, 1946, the day before his return to Denver on Greyhound bus.

Siesta in Xbalba

33 UXMAL . . . : Proper names mentioned in the first part of the poem are those of ruined cities. Xbalba, translatable as Morning Star in Region Obscure, or Hope, and pronounced Chivalvá, is the area in Chiapas between the Tabasco border and the Usumacinta River at the edge of the Petén rain forest; the boundary of lower Mexico and Guatemala today is

thereabouts. The locale was considered a Purgatory, or Limbo (the legend is vague), in the (Old) Mayan Empire. To the large tree at the crest of what is now called Mount Don Juan, at the foot of which this poem was written, ancient craftsmen came to complete work left unfinished at their death.

On Burroughs' Work

42 Written on receiving early "routines" from Burroughs in Tangier, including *Dr. Benway in the Operating Room* and *The Talking Asshole*.

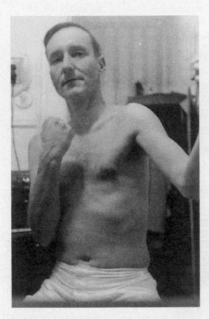

W. S. Burroughs, 206 East 7th Street, N.Y.C., Fall 1953, at time assembling "Yage Letters" and visioning Interzone Market Naked Lunch. Photo by A.G.

HOWL, BEFORE & AFTER:
SAN FRANCISCO BAY AREA
(1955–1956)

Malest Cornifici Tuo Catullo

page
47 MALEST, CORNIFICI, TUO CATULLO: Catullus #38, probably addressed
to the erotic "new poet" friend of Catullus, a verse note beginning "I'm
ill, Cornificus, your Catullus is ill," asking for a little friendly word, and
ending *"Maestius lacrimis Simonideis"*—"Sad as the tears of old Si-
monides." Ginsberg to Kerouac, on meeting Peter Orlovsky.

Peter Orlovsky by Robert LaVigne, 1954, San Francisco. Au-
thor met Orlovsky immediately after viewing this painting, 1403
Gough Street.

48 HUNCKE: Herbert E. Huncke, American prose writer, b. Chicago 1915. Friend and early contact for Kerouac, Burroughs and the author in explorations circa 1945 around Times Square, where he hung out at center of the hustling world in early stages of his opiate addictions. He served as connection to midtown's floating population for Dr. Alfred Kinsey's interviews with that population segment in his celebrated surveys of human sexuality. Huncke introduced Burroughs and others to the slang, information and ritual of the emergent "hip" or "beat" subculture. See the author's preface to Huncke's book of sketches and stories, *The Evening Sun Turned Crimson* (Cherry Valley, N.Y.: Cherry Valley Editions, 1980): "Huncke's figure appears in Clellon Holmes's novel *Go*, there is an excellent early portrait in Kerouac's first bildungsroman *The Town and the City*, fugitive glimpses of Huncke as Gotham morphinist appear in William Lee's *Junkie*, Burroughs' dry first classic of prose. He walked on the snowbank docks with shoes full of blood into the middle of *Howl*, and is glimpsed in short sketches by Herb Gold, Carl Solomon and Irving Rosenthal scattered through subsequent decades. . . . Kerouac always maintained that he was a great story teller."

Herbert Huncke, 1984. Photo by A.G.

Jack Kerouac on Avenue A, Manhattan, 1953, at time of *The Subterraneans*. Photo by A.G.

Howl

49 PARADISE ALLEY: A slum courtyard N.Y. Lower East Side, site of Kerouac's *Subterraneans*, 1958.

54 ELI ELI LAMMA LAMMA SABACTHANI: "My God, my God, why have you forsaken me?" Christ's last words from the cross ("Eli, Eli, lama sabachthani": Matthew 27:46).

54 MOLOCH: Or Molech, the Canaanite fire god, whose worship was marked by parents burning their children as propitiatory sacrifice. "And thou shalt not let any of thy seed pass through the fire to Molech" (Leviticus 18:21). See paperback *Annotated Howl*, fully annotated by author, edited by Barry Miles (New York: HarperPerennial, 1995) for exhaustive footnotes.

Sir Francis Drake Hotel tower, Powell and Sutter streets, San Francisco, seen from Nob Hill, original motif of Moloch section of "Howl," Part II. Photo 1959 by Harry Redl. (See n. p. 409.)

A Supermarket in California

59 GARCÍA LORCA

Not for one moment, old beautiful Walt Whitman,
have I failed to see your beard full of butterflies
nor your corduroy shoulders worn down by the moon . . .
Not for one moment, virile beauty
who in mountains of coal, posters and railroads,
dreamed of being a river and sleeping like a river
with whatever comrade would lay on your breast
the little pain of an ignorant leopard.
—FEDERICO GARCÍA LORCA
"Oda a Walt Whitman" (adapted by Allen Ginsberg)

62 WOBBLIES: International Workers of the World, strong on Northwest coast, some Anarchist-Buddhist-Populist tinge, primarily lumber and mining workers, pre-World War I activist precursors to organized American labor unions. For "I dreamed I saw Joe Hill last night . . ." see *Little Red Song Book*.

63 TOM MOONEY: (1882–1942) Labor leader accused of bomb-throwing, 1919 San Francisco Preparedness Day Parade; imprisoned still protesting innocence till pardoned 1939 by Governor Earl Warren; cause célèbre in left-wing populist circles worldwide.

63 SACCO & VANZETTI: Nicola Sacco and Bartolomeo Vanzetti, Italian-American anarchists convicted of robbery and murder, executed in Massachusetts, 1927, after international protest. Vanzetti's last speech to the court: "I found myself compelled to fight back from my eyes the tears, and quanch my heart trobling to my throat to not weep before him. But Sacco's name will live in the hearts of the people when your name, your laws, institutions and your false god are but a dim rememoring of a cursed past in which man was wolf to the man." And a letter to his son, April 1927: "If it had not been for this thing I might have live out my life talking at street corners to scorning men. I might have die unmarked, unknown, a failure. Now we are not a failure. This is our career and our triumph. Never in our full life could we hope to do such work for tolerance, for justice, for man's understanding of man, as now we do by accident. . . . Our words—our lives—our pains: nothing. The taking of our lives—lives of a good shoemaker and a poor fish peddler—all! That last moment, belongs to us—that agony is our triumph."

63 SCOTTSBORO BOYS: Nine black youths arrested 1931 by mob in Paint Rock, Alabama, jailed in Scottsboro, set up and sentenced to death for alleged train rape of two white girls, despite popular belief in their innocence. Their cause focused international attention on Southern U.S. legal injustice and racial discrimination. Supreme Court reversed convictions twice, setting landmark precedents for adequate counsel representation and fair race-balanced juries.

63 SCOTT NEARING: (1883–1983) Sociology professor bounced from Academe for anti-World War I views, Socialist congressional candidate 1919, staunch pro-Soviet historian and autobiographer. In old age, Nearing evolved into "new age" counterculture role model with publication of *Living the Good Life* (pioneering, building, organic gardening, cooperation and vegetarian living on a self-subsistent Vermont homestead; working plans for a twenty-year project), 1954; and *The Maple Sugar Book* (account of the art and history of sugaring; practical details for modern sugar-making; remarks on pioneering as a way of living in the twentieth century), 1950; both coauthored with Helen Nearing (reprint ed., New York: Schocken Books, 1970, 1971).

63 MOTHER BLOOR: Ella Reeve Bloor (1862–1951) Communist leader, writer, traveling union strike organizer and speechmaker.

63 EWIG-WEIBLICHE: (German) Eternal feminine.

63 ISRAEL AMTER: (1881–1954) A leading American Communist, Yiddish part of movement, traveling orator, ran for N.Y. governor 1930s.

IV
REALITY SANDWICHES: EUROPE! EUROPE!
(1957–1959)

To Aunt Rose

page

84 *THE ATTIC OF THE PAST* and *EVERLASTING MINUTE:* Books of lyric poetry by the author's father, Louis Ginsberg (1896–1976). *The Everlasting Minute* was published 1937 by Horace Liveright, N.Y. Certain poems were anthologized in various editions of Louis Untermeyer's standard anthology *Modern American and British Poetry*. See *Collected Poems*, Louis Ginsberg, ed. Michael Fournier (Orono, Maine: Northern Lights, 1992).

V
KADDISH AND RELATED POEMS
(1959–1960)

Kaddish

page

93 FIRST POISONOUS TOMATOES OF AMERICA: Russian immigrants to U.S. at turn of the century had not seen tomatoes; some believed them poisonous.

95 YPSL: Young People's Socialist League.

97 GRAF ZEPPELIN: Refers to giant hydrogen-inflated German airship *Hindenburg*, destroyed in flames with 36 deaths while mooring at Lakehurst, N.J., May 6, 1937, arrived on its first transatlantic crossing.

98 PARCAE: The Three Fates: goddess Clotho, spinning thread of life; Lachesis, holding and fixing length; and Atropos, whose shears cut thread's end.

98 THE GREEN TABLE: German Jooss Ballet's 1930s classic, wherein warmonger capitalists in black tie and tails pirouette round long green table at diplomatic conference, arranging mobilization, combat, arms profit, refugee fate and division of spoils, with Death figure dancing in foreground throughout eight-scene parable WWI.

99 DEBS: Eugene Victor Debs (1855–1926) Rail union organizer, founder IWW, "one big union," Socialist presidential candidate 1900–1920, ran from Atlanta penitentiary during ten-year sentence under so-called Espionage Act for speech denouncing U.S. entry into WWI; received nearly 1 million votes 1920.

99 ALTGELD: John P. Altgeld (1847–1902) First Democratic governor of Illinois (1892–1896) since Civil War. Pardoned surviving anarchists of 1886 Haymarket Riots, initiated prison reform, protected laboring women and reformed child labor laws, opposed use of fed troops to suppress RR strikes, incorruptible, rich entering governorship, which he left penniless. See Vachel Lindsay's poem "The Eagle That Is Forgotten": "Sleep softly . . . eagle forgotten . . . under the stone. Time has its way with you there, and clay has its own. / 'We have buried him now,' thought his foes, and in secret rejoiced . . . / Sleep on, O brave hearted, O wise man, that kindled the flame—/ To live in mankind is far more than to live in a name . . ."—Vachel Lindsay, *Collected Poems* (New York: Macmillan, 1925).

99 LITTLE BLUE BOOKS: Tiny blue-covered booklets, first mass-market paperbacks in U.S., freethinking content, distributed from immigrant socialist town Girard, southeast Kansas, by E. Haldeman-Julius (1889–1951), whose mission was to educate the masses by offering great literature

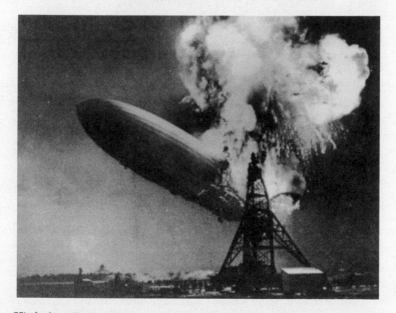

Hindenburg Explosion. (See n. p. 412.) The Bettmann Archive, Inc.

Naomi, Allen, and Louis Ginsberg, New York World's Fair, June 15, 1940.

at cheapest price, including all Shakespeare, much Oscar Wilde, Tom
Paine, Clarence Darrow, Upton Sinclair, the agnostic orator Robert
Ingersoll, and Mark Twain. For publishing *The FBI—The Basis of an
American Police State, The Alarming Methods of J. Edgar Hoover,* by Clifton
Bennett, 1948, Haldeman-Julius was hounded by FBI; withdrew *The
Black International,* by Joseph McCabe, 20-pamphlet series exposing rela-
tion between Roman Catholic Church and fascist Axis.

100 ZHDANOV: Andrei Aleksandrovich Zhdanov (1896–1948) Bolshevik
Central Committee Secy., Politburo member, etc., later noted for

"anticosmopolitan" chauvinistic pronouncements, 1946, as Stalin's literary and cultural affairs chief. "Doctors' Plot" accusations that ten Jewish Kremlin physicians were responsible for the death of Zhdanov and other high military figures signaled a purging of the Party in the year preceding Stalin's death in 1953.

101 METRAZOL: Used with insulin for shock treatment in common but now abandoned mental therapy experiments.

101 STENKA RAZIN: Russian song, name of folk-heroic Cossack river pirate, tortured and killed in Moscow in 1671.

103 WORKMEN'S CIRCLE: Newark-area Jewish immigrants' Socialist community service organization.

103 DR. LOURIA: Leon Louria, Naomi's boyfriend, "Dr. Isaac" of "Kaddish," had served as consulting physician for National maritime Union until purged as left-winger in Senator Joe McCarthy era, early 1950s.

104 YISBORACH ... B'RICH HU: Heart of Kaddish prayer for the dead; for translation see lines 1–2, "Hymmnn" section of *Kaddish*.

105 BUBA: (Yiddish) Grandmother.

106 SHEMA Y'ISRAEL: (Hebrew) Rejoice, O Israel!

106 SRUL AVRUM: (Hebrew) Israel Abraham, equivalent to Irwin Allen, names on the author's birth certificate.

107 CAMP NICHT-GEDEIGET: (Yiddish) Camp "No Worry," near Monroe, N.Y., summer settlement used by left-wing families, 1930s.

The End

115 *The End* records visions experienced after drinking Ayajuasca (Yage or Soga de Muerte, *Banisteriopsis caapi*), a vine infusion used by Amazon *curanderos* as spiritual potion, for medicine and sacred vision. See author's *The Yage Letters*, w/ William S. Burroughs (San Francisco: City Lights Books, 1963). The message is: Widen the area of consciousness.

115 YIN: Feminine principle, receptivity or emptiness, in Chinese Taoist apposition to Yang, active masculine form.

VI
PLANET NEWS: TO EUROPE AND ASIA
(1961–1963)

Television Was a Baby Crawling Toward That Deathchamber

page
119 ENKIDU: Friend-servant of Gilgamesh, for whose shade's sake Gilgamesh visited the dusts of Deathworld.

119 BARDO THODOL: Experience of gap between death and rebirth; see *The Tibetan Book of the Dead: The Great Liberation Through Hearing in the Bardo*, trans. Francesca Fremantle, commentary by Chögyam Trungpa (Boulder: Shambhala, 1975).

123 ANGELICA BALABANOFF: (1876–1965) Kiev-born aristocrat, first Secretary of Third Communist International 1919, quit disillusioned 1923 with Lenin's & Trotsky's use of "unscrupulous calumny" for centralization of power, went her own way, radical, poet. Earlier as Benito Mussolini's mistress she sheltered and introduced him to Socialist ideology, co-edited Rome socialist daily *Avanti*; later broke with him, was betrayed and confined, when he formed Italian Fascist Party. See *My Life as a Rebel* (New York: Harper & Brothers, 1938; reprint, Indiana University Press, 1978). Author met her briefly at pacifist gathering, Brooklyn, 1945.

124 DEVAS: Hindu or Buddhist gods, attendant psychological spirits.

124 RAY BREMSER: American poet (b. 1934) See *The New American Poetry*, ed. Donald M. Allen (New York: Grove Press, 1960). Much praised by Kerouac and Bob Dylan for his celebrated word-syncopation, as in *Blowing Mouth* (Cherry Valley Editions, 1978).

Describe: The Rain on Dasaswamedh Ghat

128 KALI MA: Benares beggar lady with a holy name; see her photograph, *Indian Journals* (San Francisco: City Lights Books, 1970).

128 JAI RAM: "Victory to Ram" (aspect of Vishnu the Preserver).

129 JAI SHANKAR: Shankar or Shiva, patron lord of Benares.

129 BAUL: Mystical sect of wandering, patchwork-clothed Vaishnav singers, some devoted to Krishna, in North Bengal. See *Obscure Religious Cults*, Sashi Bhusan Das Gupta (Calcutta: Firma K. L. Makhopadhyay, 1959). "The elephant is caught in the spider web, and the ant bursts out laughing." Influenced Tagore songs.

Patna–Benares Express

130 MAIDAN: Area that contains a horse track and polo field in Bankipore, sector of Patna city.

130 PATNA: Capital, Bihar state on right bank of Ganges, 125 miles from Benares.

The Change: Kyoto–Tokyo Express

132 ". . . CONVOLUTED . . .": See "The Clouds," part IV, in William Carlos Williams, *The Collected Later Poems* (New York: New Directions, 1963), p. 128.

VII
KING OF MAY: AMERICA TO EUROPE
(1963–1965)

Today

page
142 SWAMI SHIVANANDA: (1887–1962) "Your own heart is the guru." Spoken to author, Rishikesh, 1962. See dedication, Ginsberg, *Indian Journals*.

145 BENJAMIN PÉRET & RENÉ CREVEL: Péret—French surrealist poet (1899–1959); Crevel—French dada dandy poet suicide (1900–1935).

145 FAINLIGHT: Harry Fainlight, young British poet active N.Y. underground film literary circles early 1960s. Participated Albert Hall, London, Poetry Incarnation, 1965. Died 1982.

145 ED: Edward Sanders (b. 1939) American poet, classicist, and musician, leader of Fugs rock group, editor *Fuck You/A Magazine of the Arts*.

Kral Majales

147 KRAL MAJALES: May King. Traditional May festival, suspended after German occupation prior to WWII. Previous years' student disturbances persuaded Czech government to restore May King and Queen crowning ceremony in 1965, the occasion of massive public park demonstration by festive Prague populace. Nominated by Polytechnic students, author was elected May King by 100,000 citizens; ministers of culture and education objected. A week later, detained incommunicado, his Prague notebook confiscated, author was deported by plane to London, poem scribed en route.

147 KABIR: (1450?–1518) Illiterate Benares mystic poet-singer, weaver, disciple of Saint Ramanand, comparable to Blake: "If I heard love in exchange for the head in market is being sold,/I shall lose no time in entering the bargain and instantly sever my head, and offer it." (*Sufis, Mystics and Yogis of India*, trans. Bankey Behari [Bombay: Bharatiya Vidya Bhaven, 1962], p. 224.) See Kabir poems also translated by Tagore, Bly, Linda Hess.

147 BOUZERANT: (Czech slang) Homosexual.

147 AND I WAS SENT FROM HAVANA: Author was deported from Cuba, February 1965 for private criticism of speech at Havana University in which Fidel Castro denounced homosexuals and ordered purge of theater school. Detained in hotel room, held incommunicado from Casa de las Americas, which hosted the month-long Interamerican Poetry contest he'd been invited to help judge, author was expelled by plane to Prague.

147 JOSEPH K: See Kafka, *The Trial*.

148 BUNHILL FIELDS: Chief nonconformist burial ground of Old London. Site where Blake's bones are buried, adjacent to gravestones of Daniel Defoe, John Wesley and Isaac Watts.

148 HAMPSTEAD HEATH: "The great old piece of uncultivated common land and woods whose ancient oaks were protected by Royal Charter in North London, haunt of painter John Constable and poet John Keats, who wrote 'Ode to a Nightingale' in a house which still stands at the heath's edge in Hampstead."—Tom Pickard.

The author setting forth from hotel with throne and crown on flatbed truck to Prague Culture-Park for May King election; May 1, 1965. Note students formal-dressed for May Day holiday. Fellow in bowler hat, Karel Kovanda, was Czech Republic Ambassador to UN *circa* 1994.

Guru

149 Poem occasioned by a nap at dusk on the site of Druid mysteries, the grassy crest of London's Primrose Hill, overlooking London's towery skyline.

Who Be Kind To

150 HARRY: Harry Fainlight (see "Today" note, p. 417).
152 MONK IN THE 5 SPOT: Thelonious Monk (1918–1982) Genius of spare precise "out" piano harmony and innovator of "bop" rhythm, long denied by drug bureaucracy the necessary police "cabaret card" permit to work in N.Y., returned early 1960s to play many months at Bowery's Five Spot, jazz club.

VIII
THE FALL OF AMERICA
(1965–1971)

Thru the Vortex West Coast to East
(1965–1966)

Wichita Vortex Sutra

page
160 PRAJNAPARAMITA SUTRA: Highest Perfect Wisdom Sutra, central to Zen and Tibetan Buddhist practice. It includes the phrase "Form is emptiness, emptiness is form," and mantra "Gate Gate Paragate Parasamgate Bodhi Svaha."
161 CARDINAL VIETNAM: See 1990s biographies for posthumous accounts of homosexual activities of New York's Cardinal Spellman (Nicholas van Hoffman, *Citizen Cohn* [New York: Doubleday, 1988], pp. 280–81) & F.B.I. Director J. Edgar Hoover (Anthony Summers, *Official and Confidential: The Secret Life of J. Edgar Hoover* [New York: G. P. Putnam's Sons, 1993], pp. 253–58).

Wichita Vortex Sutra Part II

161 AIKEN REPUBLICAN: George D. Aiken (1892–1984) Vermont senator from 1940 through Vietnam War, author, *Pioneering with Wildflowers*, 1933, other nature books. Interviewed by newsmen on *Face the Nation* broadcast through Midwest heard by author (through Volkswagen radio) February 20, 1966, on Kansas roads. Senator Aiken pronounced the

entire Indochina war involvement "a bad guess" by policymakers who had predicted 1962 that "8,000 American troops could handle the situation." Defense Secretary McNamara contended that U.S. was defending South Vietnam from invasion by North Vietnam. "China Lobby" ideologues saw Chinese expansionist plot behind Hanoi and urged nuclear bombing of China.

Senator Aiken argued that the quarter-million South Vietnamese Viet Cong guerrilla army outweighed Hanoi's troops in confounding the U.S. technologic army then massing toward half-million men. That month, Senator Strom Thurmond backed nuclear arms to win the war.

Later, General Curtis LeMay urged America to "bomb North Vietnam back to the Stone Age." Carpet bombing of north did take place, and Mekong jungle cover was saturated with Agent Orange.

In mid-'70s chaos after American withdrawal, North Vietnam dismantled and bypassed what was left of the same South Vietnamese Provisional Revolutionary Government (P.R.G. or Viet Cong) political infrastructure U.S. had rejected 1966. Traditional hostilities were renewed between Vietnam and China at disputed border areas. By then, U.S. was allied with China. Doves & hawks both lost the war, always "a bad guess."

162 MCNAMARA: Robert S. McNamara (b. 1916) Defense secretary under President LBJ during 1960s Vietnam War, brought managerial sophistication to Pentagon mechanized warfare, though privately doubted its purpose. By 1995 in his book *In Retrospect: The Tragedy and Lessons of Vietnam*, this Vietnam warrior's public pronouncements came into alignment with antiwar views formulated in "Wichita Vortex Sutra," 1966, & expressed by majority of public by 1968: that the Vietnam War always had been a mistake based on mis-perception, stereotyped language, erroneous information, & mis-diplomacy.

162 MANDATE FOR CHANGE: "It was generally conceded that had an election been held, Ho Chi Minh would have been elected Premier." (pp. 337–38) "I have never talked or corresponded with a person knowledgeable in Indochinese affairs who did not agree that had elections been held as of the time of the fighting, possibly 80 percent of the population would have voted for the Communist Ho Chi Minh as their leader...." (p. 372) Dwight D. Eisenhower, *Mandate for Change* (New York: Doubleday, 1963).

162 STENNIS: John C. Stennis (1901–1995) U.S. senator, Mississippi, Armed Services Committee man and "hawk," urged nuclear war for Indochina, 1966.

162 AUNT BETTY: Highway billboard advertising bread.

163 RUSK SAYS TOUGHNESS . . . VIETNAM WAR BRINGS PROSPERITY: Literal headlines, Midwest newspapers February 1966.

163 BEATRICE: Nebraska town, Route 77.

164 HUTCHINSON . . . EL DORADO: Kansas towns en route between Lincoln, Nebraska, & Wichita.

164 ABILENE: Dwight D. Eisenhower's hometown, site of his Presidential Library.

164 NATION "OF THE FABLED DAMNED": See concluding paragraphs of Whitman's *Democratic Vistas* for prophetic warning against America's hawkish materialism.

166 CLARK: Joseph S. Clark (1901–1990) U.S. senator, Pennsylvania, described Vietnam War at the time as "open-ended"—i.e., could go on forever, including war with China.

166 MORSE: Wayne Morse (1900–1974) U.S. senator, Oregon, outstanding legislative "dove" in active opposition to America's undeclared war in Vietnam.

166 OR SMOKING CIGARETTES / AND WATCHING CAPTAIN KANGAROO: Pop song of the day referring to children's TV program.

167 UNITED FRUIT: United Fruit Company's law firm, Sullivan and Cromwell, had employed State Secretary John Foster Dulles, whose brother, Allen, heading CIA, coordinated the 1954 then-covert overthrow of Jacobo Arbenz, elected president of Guatemala. The event is notorious throughout Latin America as a mid-twentieth-century example of "banana republic" repression by North American imperium. By 1980, the U.S.-trained Guatemalan military had reportedly genocided 10 percent of jungle Indian population as part of "pacification" program to "create a favorable business climate."

167 OAKLAND ARMY TERMINAL: California students had passed leaflets and picketed this Pacific war transshipment center. Gary Snyder & Zen companions had sat meditating at its gates.

168 MILLIONAIRE PRESSURE: Refers to a Mr. Love from Wichita, second biggest backer of cold-war-conspiracy-obsessed John Birch Society.

168 TELEPHONE VOICES: When Peter Orlovsky and author came to read poetry, Philosophy Department hosts at Wichita's Kansas State University received many crank phone complaints.

168 AGING WHITE HAIRED GENERAL: Lewis B. Hershey (1893–1977) Selective Service director since Truman appointment 1948, time of first U.S. peacetime draft.

169 REPUBLICAN RIVER: Runs from Kansas City to Junction City.

170 OLD HEROES OF LOVE: Neal Cassady, born in Independence, Mo.

170 MCCLURE: Michael McClure, American Romantic bard and playwright (b. 1932), Marysville, Kansas. See *The New American Poetry*, Donald M. Allen, ed. (New York: Grove Press, 1960), for McClure's part as key biological philosopher-poet in 1950s "San Francisco Renaissance" and subsequent "generational" culture.

170 OLD MAN'S STILL ALIVE: Ex-President Harry S Truman.

170 SHAMBU BHARTI BABA: A Naga (naked) saddhu the author often met at

Benares's Manikarnika Ghat cremation ground. See photographs, *Indian Journals*.

170 KHAKI BABA: North Bengali (Birbhum area) 19th-century saint who, dressed in khaki loincloth, is pictured sometimes sitting surrounded by dog friends and protectors.

170 DEHORAHAVA BABA: A yogi author met at Ganges River across from Benares, 1963.

171 SATYANANDA: Calcutta swami encountered by author 1962, had twin-thumbed hands, and said, "Be a sweet poet of the Lord."

171 KALI PADA GUHA ROY: Tantric acharya or guru visited by author in Benares, 1963.

171 SHIVANANDA: Swami, teacher to Satchitananda, visited by author, Peter Orlovsky, Gary Snyder and Joanne Kyger, Rishikesh, 1962: "Your own heart is your Guru."

171 SRIMATA KRISHNAJI: Contemporary Brindaban lady saint, translator of poet Kabir, advised author thus.

171 BRINDABAN: Holy town near Delhi where Krishna spent childhood in play as cow herder.

Birbhum yogi, likely Khaki Baba. Photographer unknown.

171 CHAITANYA: 16th-century North Bengali saint, founder of Hare Krishna Mahamantra lineage, pictured dancing, singing.

171 DURGA-MA: Mother Durga, aspect of shiva's consort Parvati emphasized in Bengali Hindu mythology, 10-armed goddess of war fields, who consumes evil through violence.

171 TATHAGATA: (Sanskrit) Buddha characterized as "He who has passed through," or "that which passed." ("Thus come," and also "Thus gone": "Thus come [One].")

171 DEVAS: Indian gods, seen as aspects of human or divine being.

171 MANTRA: Sacred verbal spell or prayer composed of elemental sound "seed" syllables, used in meditative concentration practice. Literally, "mind protection" speech.

172 "KENNEDY URGES CONG GET CHAIR" . . . : February 14, 1966, news headlined Senator Robert Kennedy's proposal that U.S. offer Viet Cong share of power in South Vietnam. This was major break with administration war policy.

172 CONTINUED FROM PAGE ONE: In February 14, 1966, *Wichita Eagle.*

172 BONG SON: 100 Viet Cong soldiers were killed close to Bong Son and were reported struck by many bullets before falling.

173 LA DRANG: Vietnamese battlefield mentioned in news reports third week February 1966.

173 BURNS: Tiny Kansas town near Wichita.

174 KELLOGG: Main drag in Wichita.

174 HYDRAULIC: Street name.

174 NEWSPAPER LANGUAGE FACTORY: *Wichita Eagle-Beacon* office.

174 HOTEL EATON: On Douglas Street, near local Vortex Gallery patronized by Charles Plymell and Kansas artists.

174 CARRY NATION: "(b. Garrard Co., 1846; d. Leavenworth, Kans., 1911), temperance agitator. An ignorant, unbalanced, and contentious woman of vast energies, afflicted with an hereditary paranoia, she was subjected to early hardships that fused all her great physical and emotional powers into a flaming enmity toward liquor and its corrupt purveyors. From her first saloon-smashing ventures at Medicine Lodge, Kans., she carried her campaign to Wichita (1900), where her distinctive weapon, the hatchet, was first used, and then on to many of the principal American cities. Arrested thirty times for 'disturbing the peace,' she paid fines from sales of souvenir hatchets, lecture tours, and stage appearances. Her autobiography was published, 1904."—*Concise Dictionary of American Biography* (New York: Scribner's, 1964), p. 721.

175 NIGGERTOWN: Area of Wichita between Hydraulic and 17th streets.

Kansas City to Saint Louis

176 KENNEY . . . MORPHY: Friends of William S. Burroughs in 1930s St. Louis.

176 W.S.B.: William Seward Burroughs.

177 CRANE: See Hart Crane's address to Whitman, *The Bridge*, end of Cape Hatteras section.

Uptown

179 MADAME GRADY: Panna Grady, patron of letters, friend of poets Charles Olson, John Wieners and William Burroughs, once lived at Dakota Apartments, Central Park West, N.Y., and held literary salon there.

Zigzag Back Thru These States
(1966–1967)

Iron Horse

184 FULBRIGHT: Senator James William Fulbright (1905–1995) Head of Senate Foreign Relations Committee 1959–1974, made eloquent public attack on President Johnson's expansion of the Vietnam War.
184 XOCHIMILCO: Ancient floating gardens, Mexico City, where Kerouac, Orlovsky and the author met a party of Mexican ballet boys in a sightseeing boat. See Kerouac's *Desolation Angels*, Book Two, Part One, section 20.
185 FIJIJIAPAN: town close to Guadalajara, Mexico, notable for its candy.
185–86 KEDERNATH & BADRINATH & GANGOTRI: Northwest India Hindu pilgrimage sites on the way to Kailash, Shiva's sacred Tibetan border mountain abode, source of Ganges.
186 MANASAROVAR: Iced lake on Kailash.
186 SRI RAMANA MAHARSHI: 20th-century South Indian ascetic saint, instructed meditation practice, "Who Am I?" Quotations are from his book *Maha Yoga*.

Sri Ramana Maharshi. Photographer unknown.

City Midnight Junk Strains

189 FRANK O'HARA: (1926–1966) Gay central figure in N.Y. literary a:
1950s till his death; MoMA exhibitions department curator, inspii
whole generation of N.Y. "Personism" poets; died struck by beach bu
dark midnight accident Fire Island. See "The Day Lady Died," in
Collected Poems (New York: Knopf, 1972).

189 KLINE: Franz Kline (1910–1962) American abstract expressionist
oneer painter, on whose work Frank O'Hara wrote monograph, died
heart attack.

190 EDWIN DENBY: (1903–1983) China-born, influential dance critic, poe
friend of younger writers of "New York School," 1960s–1980s; fre
quented N.Y.C. Ballet and St. Mark's Poetry Project. (*Collected Poem,*
published by Full Court Press, New York, 1975.)

Wales Visitation

195 VISITACIONE: Ancient bardic visiting round in Wales.

195 LLANTHONY VALLEY: Pastoral vale, Welsh Black Mountains.

197 CAPEL-Y-FFN: Ancient ruined chapel at green bottom of Llanthony Val-
ley. Eric Gill, type-font designer and craftsman, dwelt there 1920s with
arts commune.

197 LORD HEREFORD'S KNOB: Mountain walling north side Llanthony Val-
ley.

197 (LSD): First draft main body of poem was written in fifth hour LSD-
inspired afternoon.

Elegies for Neal Cassady
(1968)

Elegy for Neal Cassady

199 SHABDA: (Sanskrit) Sound or vibration, a path of yoga.

199 GREAT YEAR: 24,000-year cycle of the sun, which rises for 2,000 years
each through 12 zodiacal constellations, as it wobbles almost impercepti-
bly on its sidereal axis; presently entering Age of Aquarius.

200 HEJIRA: Mohammed's flight from Mecca, A.D. 622; Kesey's bus trip, A.D.
1964, Neal Cassady at driver's wheel.

200 LOWELL: Massachusetts Merrimack River redbrick mill town where Jack
Kerouac was raised, site of many novels.

Ecologues of These States
(1969–1971)

Memory Gardens

206 MEMORY GARDENS: Cemetery near Albany Airport glimpsed on way to
Jack Kerouac's funeral in Lowell, Mass. Poem was written on that trip.

Milarepa Taste

208 MILAREPA: "Cotton-clad" Himalayan yogi poet, early father of Kagyu lineage, Tibetan Buddhist hero, author *The Hundred Thousand Songs of Milarepa*, trans. Garma C. C. Chang, 2 vols. (New Hyde Park, N.Y.: University Books, 1962).

September on Jessore Road

211 JESSORE ROAD: At time of author's visit, millions of Hindu refugees from East Pakistan communal strife crowded starving in floods on this main road between Bangladesh and Calcutta.

214 SUNIL POET: Calcutta poet Sunil Ganguly (Ganghopadhyay), with whom author traveled Jessore Road, in company with American Buddhist student and poet John Giorno.

IX
MIND BREATHS ALL OVER THE PLACE
(1972–1977)

Sad Dust Glories
(1972–1974)

Mind Breaths

258 AH: Calligraphy by Chögyam Trungpa, Rinpoche, 1978. Symbol of Tibetan Buddhist Kagyu order; one syllable summary of Prajnaparamita Sutra; mantra for purification of speech, and appreciation of space; related to Samatha meditation practice, mindfulness of outbreath; a vocalization of the outbreath.

259 SANGHA: (Sanskrit) Community of Buddhist practitioners.

259 KITKITDIZZE: Wintun Indian name for tarweed, bear clover or mountain misery, dark green shrub varying 3–15 inches in height, tarry touch and smell, belonging to rose family. Typical ground cover, western slope Sierra ponderosa pine forest. Poet Gary Snyder's Sierra household is named Kitkitdizze, after this common plant, *Chamaebatia foliolosa*.

260 BO TREE: The ancient pipal, *Ficus religiosa*, or sacred fig tree, in Bodh Gaya, India, under which Buddha meditated till enlightened.

Jaweh and Allah Battle

267 SNAKE COCK AND PIG EAT EACH OTHER'S TAILS: Symbols of anger, vanity and ignorance at center axle of Time Wheel Mandala.

267 CALLER OF THE GREAT CALL: According to Barbelo-Ophitic myth of Garden of Eden, the snake (as caller of the Great Call) was Sophia's

messenger to waken awareness in Adam and Eve. Sabaot, archon of their acon, was but seven-acon-times-removed reflection of Sophia's first thought. See Hans Jonas, *Gnostic Religion* (Boston: Beacon Press, 1963). Refer also to "Plutonian Ode," note to verse 16, *Sabaot*.

267 STERN GANG IRGUN: Terrorist groups under British mandate, fought for Zionist cause.

267–68 AL FATAH BLACK SEPTEMBER: Terrorist groups after Israeli sovereignty, fought for Palestinian cause.

268 MEYER LANSKY: U.S. organized-crime chief reported to've supplied guns to Zionist terrorist/freedom fighters. Retired to Israel for years, was deported back to U.S. after public scandal, 1972, and arrested for income tax evasion.

268 MY FATHER HAD A COFFEE SHOP IN JERUSALEM: See poem "Write It Down, Allen Said," in *Clean Asshole Poems & Smiling Vegetable Songs*, Peter Orlovsky (San Francisco: City Lights Pocket Poet Series #37, 1978), pp. 118–20.

268 COMMENTARY: American highbrow crypto-Zionist right-wing ideological journal edited by ambitious early prose critic of Kerouac's poetic prose, later hawkish proponent of military hard-line hardware equated as alternative discipline for supposed loose 1960s national morals including public acknowledgment of gaiety.

268 PALESTINE REVIEW: Pro-Palestinian journal.

269 SHEMA YISROEL ADONOI ELUHENU: End of Hebrew chant: "Rejoice, O Israel, the Lord is one, the Lord is God."

269 LA ILAH . . . : Sufi chant: "There is no god but Allah."

269 HU: Sufi mantric out-breath.

269 SHALOM! SHANTIH! SALAAM!: Hebrew, Sanskrit, Arabic for "Peace!"

Ego Confessions *(1974–1977)*

Ego Confession

274 GYALWA KARMAPA: 16th lama head of Milarepa lineage, Kagyu order of Tibetan Buddhism.

274 WEATHERMEN GOT NO MOSCOW GOLD: Timothy Leary, held incommunicado for years, early 1970s, by Feds, refused to testify falsely that Weathermen were directed by Moscow finance. FBI heads were later convicted of illegal wiretapping since no evidence that antiwar protesters were agents of foreign powers could be found.

274 VAJRASATTVA: Central image of Nyingma old-school Tibetan meditation practice, blue-bodied, with diamond lightning bolt (vajra) form held in right hand at breast, bell (ghanta) of empty (open) space held at left hip. Dharmakaya Buddha.

274 OVERTHREW THE CIA WITH A SILENT THOUGHT: Refers to 1970 Georgetown dinner bet between author and then CIA chief Richard

Helms: whether or not Central Intelligence Agency had working relationship with opium traffickers at "secret" CIA base, Long Cheng, Laos. Author offered his vajra, if misinformed, and requested CIA Director Helms to practice meditation an hour a day for life if his denial proved incorrect. The wager was accepted, a bet either party might profit from by losing. Note also:

The New York Times
3 rue Scribe
75 Paris 9c

April 11, 1978

Dear Allen,

I fear I owe you an apology. I have been reading a succession of pieces about CIA involvement in the dope trade in Southeast Asia and I remember when you first suggested I look into this I thought you were full of beans. Indeed you were right and I acknowledge the fact plus sending my best personal wishes.

C. L. Sulzberger

Gospel Noble Truths

288 YOU GOT TO SUFFER: First stanza refers to Buddhist doctrine of three "marks" or characteristics of existence: (1) suffering, (2) change, (3) Anatma (no permanent selfhood). Stanzas 1–3 refer to the Four Noble Truths of Buddhist philosophy: (1) Existence contains suffering; (2) Suffering is caused by ignorance; (3) Ignorance can be changed by practice of detachment, wisdom and compassion (4) and by following an eightfold path as paraphrased in song lines 13–20: (1) right views, (2) right aspiration, (3) right speech, (4) right activity, (5) right labor, (6) right energy, (7) right mindfulness, (8) right meditation. There follows brief instruction for sitting and review of six sense fields.

Contest of Bards

296 ETERNAL RUNE CUT IN STONE: Rune (Old Norse), character of Old Teutonic or Scandinavian alphabets; magical cipher.
300 EIDOLON: Platonic Image. See Whitman's poem "Eidolons."

Punk Rock Your My Big Crybaby

302 MABUHAY GARDENS TO CBGB'S: Punk rock/new wave youth clubs, on San Francisco's North Beach and New York's Bowery.

X
PLUTONIAN ODE
(1977–1980)

Plutonian Ode

Allen Ginsberg, Peter Orlovsky and friends of Rocky Flats Truth Force, meditating on R.R. Tracks outside Rockwell Corporation Nuclear Facility's Plutonium bomb trigger factory, Colorado, halting trainload of waste fissile materials on the day Plutonian Ode was completed, July 14, 1978. Photo by Steve Groer, *Rocky Mountain News*.

311 THREE HUNDRED TONS: 300 tons of Plutonium, estimate circa 1978 of the amount produced for American bombs.

311 I SING YOUR FORM: "The Reactor hath hid himself thro envy. I behold him. But you cannot behold him till he be revealed in his System."— Blake, *Jerusalem*, Chap. II, Plate 43, lines 9–10.

311 HONEY . . . WATER: Traditional libation to Hades poured at Temple of Eleusis, and by Odysseus at the Necromanteion at Acheron.

311 DIAMOND TRUTH: Reference to Buddhist doctrine of Sunyatā, i.e., existence as simultaneously void and solid, empty and real, all-penetrating egoless (empty void) nature symbolized by adamantine Vajra or Diamond Sceptre.

312 FIVE HUNDRED BILLION DOLLAR: Estimated world military budget; 116 billion, U.S. share, October 1978.

313 TAKE THIS INHALATION . . . THOUGHT-WORLDS: Four characteristics of Buddha-nature activity: to pacify, enrich, magnetize & destroy.

313 GONE OUT . . . AH!: Americanese approximation and paraphrase of

Sanskrit Prajnaparamita (Highest Perfect Wisdom) Mantra: Gate Gate Paragate Parasamgate Bodhi Svaha.

Ruhr-Gebiet

318 STAMMHEIM: Isolation prison where "terrorist" Baader-Meinhof gang members (originally armed by police double agents) were subject to continuous interrogation under 24-hour glare lighting.

319 "GUESTS" DO THE WORK: *Gastarbeiter,* "guest workers" of post–WWII West Germany: Turks, Italians, Slavs imported for heavy labor or menial work.

Lower East Side

323 LOWER EAST SIDE: After Charles Reznikoff.

Birdbrain!

327 XOCHOPILI: Formerly referred to as "God of Flowers" in tourist guidebooks. Vegetable forms incised on his celebrated statue in Mexico City's Archaeological Museum have been identified by Harvard Botanical Museum director Richard E. Schultes as peyote, morning glory, amanita mushroom, tobacco, etc. Evidence of Xochopili culture was obliterated during Spanish conquest.

327 RAN GERMANY ON AMPHETAMINES: Among other books, *Inside the Third Reich,* memoirs of Albert Speer (New York: Macmillan, 1970), gives evidence on Hitler's rug-chewing speed addiction.

XI
WHITE SHROUD
(1980–1985)

Homage Vajracarya

page
337 Ven. Chögyam Trungpa, Vajracarya's Shambhala Arts included mind training with Archery (Kyudo), Calligraphy, Tea Ceremony, etc.

Why I Meditate

338 MIRROR STREET: Dadaist original Cabaret Voltaire was on Zürich's Spiegelgasse Strasse.

338 RUTHERFORD: William Carlos Williams. Manhattan: Charles Reznikoff.

XII
COSMOPOLITAN GREETINGS
(1986–1992)

Part-opening epigraph

366 Dedication: Response to Macedonian request for message to Struga Evenings of Poetry festival, on receiving 1986 Golden Laurel Wreath prize.

366 MOLECULES CLANKING AGAINST EACH OTHER: See "Winter Night," *Atilla József's Selected Poems and Texts*, trans. John Bátki (Iowa City: International Writing Program, University of Iowa, 1976).

367 FIRST THOUGHT, BEST THOUGHT: Chögyam Trungpa (Boston: Shambhala Press, 1984).

367 MIND IS SHAPELY, ART IS SHAPELY: "If the mind is shapely, the art will be shapely," from Jack Kerouac and Allen Ginsberg, conversation 1958, Cherry Plains, N.Y.

May Days 1988

372 ARABS SHD THROW WORDS NOT STONES: Elie Wiesel, quoted in *New York Post*, sometime 1988.

Return of Kral Majales

374 See "Kral Majales," p. 147 and notes.

374 BANNED BY FCC: Sen. Jesse Helms & Heritage Foundation's October 1988 law directed Federal Communications Commission to enforce 24-hour ban on "indecent" language over all airwaves, declared unconstitutional by subsequent court decisions. At poem's writing, ban extended 6:00 A.M. to midnight. Court decisions 1993–1996 froze ban as of 6:00 A.M. to 10:00 P.M., leaving as "safe harbor" late evening to 6:00 A.M. Daytime broadcast for students (& adults) reading the author's "questionable" poems in school anthologies is now forbidden by law.

374 ALL GONE ALL GONE . . . : version of *Prajnaparamita*, Highest Perfect Wisdom, 17-syllable Sanskrit mantra: "Gate Gate Paragate Parasamgate Bodhi Svaha."

Hum Bom!

375 Part I and shorter version of Part II were published in *Collected Poems 1947–1980*. Additional verses added 1991–1995.

After Lalon

379 Lalon Shah (1774–1890), Bengali Baul singer, devotional forerunner of Rabindranath Tagore. See *Songs of Lalon Shah*, trans. Abu Rushd (Dhaka: Bangla Academy Press, 1991).

Put Down Your Cigarette Rag (Dont Smoke)

383 Originally published in *First Blues* (New York: Full Court Press, 1975). Here updated statistics, additional stanzas.

The Charnel Ground

388 Epigraph and final quotation, "The whole point seems to be the idea of giving away the giver," taken from lectures on *The Sadhana of Mahamudra*, by Ven. Chögyam Trungpa, Rinpoche, Karma Dzong, December 1973, privately printed.

American Sentences

392 *On Hearing the Muezzin Cry Allah Akbar While Visiting the Pythian Oracle at Didyma Toward the End of the Second Millennium*
Didyma, Asia Minor's shore site where Magna Mater and Pythian oracle were displaced by Judeo-Christian-Islamic Father God. In response to imperial Roman request for prophecy circa 4th century A.D., the oracle's last utterance declared the gods had departed, Apollo no longer dwelled among the temple's pillars.

12 AM Answering Mail

392 Answering office mail late night, response to request from little magazine.

Approaching Seoul by Bus in Heavenly Rain

392 Bus over steep mountains from Kangnung to Seoul one rainy night was delayed along precipice by a mile of ambulance lights marking crash of bus I'd missed, scheduled an hour earlier.
393 Monoprix, familiar department store, onetime right bank of Seine across from Place St. Michel.

XIII
NEW POEMS
(1992–   )

The New Amazing Grace

page
397 Composed at the request of Ed Sanders for his production of *The New Amazing Grace* performed November 20, 1994 at the Poetry Project in St. Mark's Church in the Bouwerie.

Index of Proper Names

Index of Titles, First Lines, and Original Book Sources

Poem titles appear in *italics*. Books in which the poem originally appear are abbreviated as follows:

CG	*Cosmopolitan Greetings*	Kaddish	*Kaddish*
EM	*Empty Mirror*	MB	*Mind Breaths*
Fall	*The Fall of America*	Mss.	Unpublished Manuscript
GW	*The Gates of Wrath*	PN	*Planet News*
Howl	*Howl*	PO	*Plutonian Ode*
IH	*Iron Horse*	RS	*Reality Sandwiches*
J	*Journals: Early Fifties*	SHD	*Straight Hearts' Delight*
	Early Sixties	WS	*White Shroud*

A Crazy Spiritual (EM), 17
A drunken night in my house with a, 48
A faithful youth, 17
After Lalon (CG), 379
After the Big Parade (CG), 378
Airplane Blues (WS), 342
All afternoon cutting bramble blackberries, 58
a lot of mouths and cocks, 255
America (Howl), 62
America I've given you all and now I'm nothing, 62
American Sentences (CG), 392
. . . And ninety-nine soldiers piled on the train at Amarillo, 180
And the Communists have nothing to offer but fat cheeks, 147
Arguments (WS), 352
As I cross my kitchen floor the thought of Death returns, 371
"As Is. . .," 357
A Strange New Cottage in Berkeley (Howl), 58
A Supermarket in California (Howl), 59
At 66 just learning how to take care of my body, 391
Aunt Rose—now—might I see you, 83
. . . Autumn again, you wouldn't know in the city, 192
Autumn Gold: New England Fall (Fall), 192
Autumn Leaves (CG), 391
A Western Ballad (GW), 6
Ayers Rock/Uluru Song (MB), 241

Because this world is on the wing and what cometh no man can know, 113

Be kind to your self, it is only one, 150
Birdbrain! (PO), 327
Birdbrain runs the World!, 327
Black Magicians, 131
Blues is like a hardon comes right in your mouth, 271
. . . Blue Starfish, 236
Born in this world, 289
Broken Bone Blues, 252
Broken Bone Bone Bone, 252
Bus Ride Ballad Road to Suva, 237

Capitol Air (PO), 330
City Midnight Junk Strains (PN), 189
C'mon Pigs of Western Civilization Eat More Grease, 397
Come all you Jewish boy friends, 229
Come Back Christmas: Blues Stanza, 232
Contest of Bards (MB), 296
Cool black night thru the redwoods, 157
Cosmopolitan Greetings (CG), 366
covered with yellow leaves, 206

Death to Van Gogh's Ear! (Kaddish), 71
"Defending the Faith" (PO), 329
Delicate eyes that blinked blue Rockies all ash, 205
Describe: The Rain on Dasaswamedh Ghat (PN), 128
Don't Grow Old (MB), 292
"Don't Grow Old" (PO), 292
Dont smoke dont smoke dont smoke, 383
Dope Fiend Blues, 278
Do the Meditation Rock (WS), 346

Contemporary ... Provocative ... Outrageous ...
Prophetic ... Groundbreaking ... Funny ... Disturbing ...
Different ... Moving ... Revolutionary ... Inspiring ...
Subversive ... Life-changing ...

What makes a modern classic?

At Penguin Classics our mission has always been to make the best
books ever written available to everyone. And that also means
constantly redefining and refreshing exactly what makes a 'classic'.
That's where Modern Classics come in. Since 1961 they have been an
organic, ever-growing and ever-evolving list of books from the last
hundred (or so) years that we believe will continue to be read over and
over again.

They could be books that have inspired political dissent, such as
Animal Farm. Some, like *Lolita* or *A Clockwork Orange*, may have
caused shock and outrage. Many have led to great films, from *In Cold
Blood* to *One Flew Over the Cuckoo's Nest*. They have broken down
barriers – whether social, sexual, or, in the case of *Ulysses*, the
boundaries of language itself. And they might – like *Goldfinger* or
Scoop – just be pure classic escapism. Whatever the reason, Penguin
Modern Classics continue to inspire, entertain and enlighten millions
of readers everywhere.

'No publisher has had more influence on reading habits than Penguin'
Independent

'Penguins provided a crash course in world literature'
Guardian

The best books ever written

PENGUIN CLASSICS

SINCE 1946

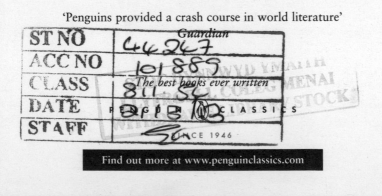

Find out more at www.penguinclassics.com